Praise for # WAY TOO BIG TO FAIL

How Government and
Private Industry Can Build a
Fail-Safe Mortgage System

"This is an important study that broadens our understanding of problems at the core of the mortgage finance industry. Bill Frey provides an excellent analysis of incentive conflicts arising from mortgage securitization and discusses their effects on the resolution of the current crisis. Remarkably, the book not only contains a critical analysis of the past and current government policies, but also provides a set of interesting ideas on how to reform the mortgage finance industry going forward. I strongly recommend it to policymakers, analysts, and researchers."

Tomasz Piskorski, *Associate Professor of Finance and Economics*
Columbia Business School

"*Way Too Big to Fail* is a crisp, well-written and fascinating analysis of policymakers missing the forest for the trees and unnecessarily prolonging the financial crisis. Written by an astute observer and participant in the financial market, the book offers an insider's perspective of the causes and consequences of the failure of the securitization market.

The book paints top policymakers as the modern Captain Smiths of the financial Titanic, and shows how the textbook lessons they learned about the Great Depression worked against them in commanding the modern ship of finance. By pursuing policies rescuing individual banks deemed "systemically important," these policymakers actually accelerated the decline of the securitization market at the heart of the modern financial system.

The author also offers prescriptions to right the ship. I don't agree with all of his proposed solutions, but all deserve consideration. Most importantly, the author shows that policymakers can't come to a rational solution without first understanding the true causes of the problem."

John Berlau, *Director of the Center for Investors and Entrepreneurs*
Competitive Enterprise Institute

"Unlike the other books written on the credit crisis, Mr. Frey was there, witnessing first-hand the unseemly creations of Wall Street and acting to protect clients from massive losses. Using his in-depth knowledge of the mortgage securitization and servicing areas, Mr. Frey offers sound thoughts on ways to correct the underlying problems. Way too Big to Fail is a must read for anyone interested in the prospective health of our economy and in turn, our country."

Sean J. Egan, *Managing Director*
Egan-Jones Ratings Co.

WAY TOO BIG TO FAIL

How Government and Private Industry Can Build a Fail-Safe Mortgage System

By William A. Frey

Edited by Isaac M. Gradman

Table of Contents

Foreword

It was essentially by chance that my career path led me directly into the heart of the mortgage crisis and ultimately across the path of Bill Frey. In 2007, after graduating from New York University School of Law and fresh off of a two-year U.S. District Court clerkship in the Southern District of Florida, I went to work for the Howard Rice law firm in San Francisco to get a taste of real commercial litigation. It turned out that my first major client was Walnut Creek-based PMI Mortgage Insurance Co., the second largest mortgage insurer in the country, which was discovering a disturbingly high number of delinquencies in its insured portfolios. I must admit that the prospect of becoming an instant expert in mortgage backed securities and the contracts establishing them seemed daunting at first. Up to then, my only background in securitization was having read Michael Lewis's *Liars Poker* many years before, which provided an interesting but surface-level overview of the origins and principles behind this financial innovation.

However, I soon immersed myself in this material, captivated by the immediacy and the far-reaching implications of mortgage crisis developments. Over the next three years, I participated in numerous mortgage-related lawsuits and investigations, beginning with the representation of PMI in a suit against originator WMC Mortgage Corp. (and its parent, GE Money Bank) alleging misrepresentations relating to a $1 billion pool of subprime mortgages—one of the first suits of this kind. Partly for the benefit of our clients and partly out of my own curiosity, I began following all of the mortgage crisis-related lawsuits, rulings, and regulatory actions that were cropping up, seemingly every day. If I had not seen them with my own eyes in the course of conducting investigations for our mortgage clients, I would have barely believed the revelations emerging in news reports and court cases around the country regarding the improprieties that were taking place in mortgage lending in the years leading up to the mortgage crisis.

Soon after the PMI case against WMC was settled, I was asked to give a presentation to the other attorneys at Howard Rice regarding the case and our work on PMI's behalf. I realized that, in order for the audience to have any frame of reference regarding the work we had done, it was necessary to give them a primer on mortgage securitization. By walking the participants through the life cycle of a mortgage loan and by breaking down this complex subject into a layperson's terms, I found that the audience not only was able to understand the legal issues at stake, but was also fascinated by what had happened. The success of this presentation led to the idea of launching a law blog—one that educated readers about the critical legal developments in the fallout from the mortgage crisis in a simple and straightforward manner.

With that goal in mind, I launched *The Subprime Shakeout* law blog (www.subprimeshakeout.com) in the summer of 2008. Since I had been only recently a relative novice in this area, I felt that I was particularly well suited to bring others up to speed. Yet I soon realized that laypeople were not the only ones with little understanding of the causes and ramifications of the mortgage crisis. Indeed, the political representatives, financial professionals, lawyers, and investors that should have had much greater knowledge of this crisis than the average reader often seemed to have serious misconceptions and fallacies in their views on this topic. In particular, I wondered why elected representatives were foisting losses onto institutional investors and why these investors—who held valuable contractual rights similar to the mortgage insurers—were not stepping up and enforcing their claims with the same tenacity as the mortgage insurers for whom I worked. Soon, my approach shifted from one of explaining developments to my readers to one of advocating for institutional investors to do more to protect the assets of the average citizens whose money they managed.

In October 2008, when I was writing extensively about the settlement struck by dozens of state Attorneys General with Countrywide/Bank of America over predatory lending practices, I noticed that a broker-dealer from Greenwich, Connecticut had filed one of the first investor actions seeking to enforce mortgage trust contracts. The case, *Greenwich Financial Services v. Countrywide, et al.*, was filed in New York State Court and asked the court to declare that Countrywide re-purchase the loans it had agreed to modify as part of the AG settlement, as per the investors' trust agreements. As I would learn over the next few days, the moving force behind this lawsuit was Bill Frey, a self-styled "advocate for investors' contractual rights" who had been vocal in his opposition to loan modifications since March of 2008, and who maintained that he was on a crusade to protect the rights of all investors who purchased Triple A-rated bonds. As a result of this vocal opposition, Frey had received pressure from Washington legislators, including in the form of a letter signed by, among others, Barney Frank (D-MA), Maxine Waters (D-CA), and Luis V. Gutierrez (D.-IL), to back off of his position. This letter is included as appendix II.

As I read more about Frey, including his letter to Ben Bernanke and Hank Paulson (appendix I) and his response to the letter from Barney Frank and others (appendix III), I became increasingly curious about his background and his interests in the mortgage crisis. He seemed to be quite knowledgeable about securitization and had well-thought-out suggestions for what needed to be done to protect investors' interests and the future of housing finance. Yet he was also a polarizing figure, having been vilified in the congressional letter as a "threat to [Congress's] efforts to respond to the current economic crisis," (appendix II) and having witnessed a protest of three to four hundred homeowners on his front lawn for allegedly being a "predator" who contributed to the loss of their homes.

I decided to delve deeper into the question of who this controversial character really was. In the process, I came across an article in the *Wall Street Journal* that quoted Frey as saying that his lawsuit against Countrywide was just "an opening salvo," and that he planned to file other lawsuits on behalf of investors.[1] The article also revealed that Frey had acquired the mortgage bonds at issue for the express purpose of bringing this lawsuit on behalf of an investor that wanted to remain anonymous. This only piqued my curiosity further.

In February 2009, I posted an article on *The Subprime Shakeout* entitled, "Greenwich CEO William Frey Primed to Become the Lorax For Investors Without a Voice?"[2] Therein, I suggested that Frey viewed himself as the eponymous Dr. Seuss character from the timeless masterpiece, *The Lorax*, who spoke for the speechless trees being threatened by greedy businessmen; except in this case, Frey was speaking for mortgage bondholders who had no voice in the Countrywide settlement. After noting that Frey was actually the spokesperson for a wealthy investor who wanted to remain in the shadows—and that Frey and this investor would likely turn a profit on these bonds if they were successful—I challenged the notion that Frey was driven by some higher moral calling. Instead, I suggested that Frey was driven by the same quest for profits that drove Countrywide to churn out billions of dollars of defective loans in the first place, ending the article with this quote from the book's antagonist: "Business is business, and business must grow."

Just a few days later, my phone rang. It was Bill Frey. He explained that he had been reading my blog and that he appreciated that I had put a substantial amount of original thought and research into understanding the issues behind the Countrywide lawsuit. He thought that I showed comprehension well beyond most journalists in this space but wanted to get something straight—though it was true that his motives were not 100 percent altruistic, he felt that it was possible to "do well by doing good." He explained that he held a strong belief that preserving bondholder contract rights was critical if we ever wanted to see the housing market recover and provide affordable housing for ordinary Americans. He also explained that while he had spent 25 years in securitization and knew every nook and cranny of the business, he had never put together a subprime deal because he was skeptical about the collateral. Since he owned his own firm and got paid based on the long term health of the business rather than a bonus cycle, he had been willing to forego the income stream from subprime business to avoid damaging his investors. Indeed, he had only decided to get involved in the Countrywide matter when his mother asked him how much of her pension fund was invested in mortgage backed securities, and what he was going to do about it. Thus, while he had to pay the legal bills involved in taking Countrywide to court, he had an interest in seeing these issues resolved that extended well beyond this deal.

This was but the first of many exciting and enlightening conversations that I would have with Bill. At first, we simply discussed current events and exchanged ideas. I would frequently bounce concepts off of him when trying to analyze newsworthy events and formulate articles. Out of all the people with whom I spoke regarding mortgage crisis legal issues—and there were many—Bill had the most consistently logical and practical approach. He had crucial expertise that enabled him to predict whether and why government programs or proposed legal actions would or would not work; and most of the time, he was right.

Along the way, I learned that Bill had gone to Russia in 2004 to build securitizations in a new way—one that contained the proper incentives for success—and that these deals had been wildly successful during a time when U.S. securitizations (and other Russian mortgage deals) were toppling like dominos. I realized that Bill, who had had to think through these same issues five years earlier, might be the only person in America who could solve the mortgage problems crippling our economy.

In June 2010, Bill invited me out to his house in Connecticut. I decided that I would go out there with an idea: to write a book together that discussed this country's mortgage problems, how they had come about, and how to fix them. As far as I could tell, though many books had been published that pointed fingers at the causes or villains behind this crisis, few offered a cogent plan for rebuilding this critical piece of the U.S. and global economies. And, as outraged as I was about some of the misconduct perpetuated by banks, borrowers, and politicians in engendering this crisis, I was far more interested in moving forward and working on a solution. I figured that with Bill's experience and my legal and writing skills, we could present some thought-provoking proposals in a way that would be difficult to ignore.

A few weeks later, I found myself sitting on Bill's back porch overlooking his sprawling backyard and listening to Bill decry the conflicts of interest inherent in subprime deals above the summer song of swallows and cicadas. Bill appeared squarely in his element and was getting very animated in discussing the problems with proposed government solutions and why such efforts would irreparably harm investor confidence. Finally, I stopped him and asked, "Have you ever thought about writing a book about these problems and how to fix them?" He gave me a wry smile and said, "Wait right here." When he returned, he was holding the manuscript that would later become this book. As I flipped through the chapter headings that day, I saw that he had already taken a stab at doing exactly what I was proposing, and though it needed some organization and streamlining, all of the major topics were there.

In October 2010, I left the law firm and launched my own mortgage litigation consulting firm, IMG Enterprises. In addition to keeping me immersed in mortgage crisis legal issues, this move provided me with a more flexible schedule, thus allowing me to take a more active role in Bill's book as its editor. It has been a pleasure working with Bill on this project over the past year, and I could not be happier or prouder about the results. The ideas presented herein, many of which have not changed substantially from those that Bill articulated in his public letters back in 2008, remain as logical, as practical, and as necessary as ever. At their core, they are about realigning economic incentives so that millions of Americans can have access to the capital they need to make the dream of homeownership a reality once again. I have tried to present these ideas in the same straightforward manner in which I present the ideas on my blog—with an eye towards allowing readers of varied backgrounds to understand and appreciate the issues at stake. I hope you find, as I do, that this book provides essential insight into the workings of a complex but all-important system and that it presents a comprehensive plan for a better mortgage system in a way that few have attempted, let alone pulled off. Though Bill's ideas may not inspire universal agreement (indeed, Bill rarely does), they should at least begin the conversation that is a long time coming.

Isaac M. Gradman

Petaluma, CA

September 2011

Acknowledgments

The author would like to thank the following people for their comments, encouragement and, most of all, challenges to the ideas in this book. I can assure you that any errors in logic are mine and all of the good ideas belong to the following friends and colleagues: Jon Byron, Vincent Fiorillo, Talcott Franklin, David Gussmann, Rob Fry, Olivia S. Mitchell, Tomasz Piskorski, Sharon Psyhojos, Allison Pyburn, Jody Shenn and Brandt Zembsch.

I would also like to acknowledge the special efforts of David Grais, an attorney and friend who had the initial idea for a short paper on how to fix the mortgage backed securities problem. This is what the "short paper" has become.

I would like to thank Carrie Galehouse Frey, my better half, for being a massive contributor to the ideas in this book and for helping me present complex ideas in ways that can be understood by folks without a background in finance. Her assistance was invaluable in the completion of this book. I am sure that without her patience, encouragement, and assistance this book would have remained a good idea and nothing more.

I would also be remiss if I did not single out Isaac Gradman for his incredible dedication and commitment to this project. In addition to taking a scrambled pile of ideas and making it readable, he is someone who challenged me on every idea and statement. His legal background and experience has proven to be extremely valuable and his absolute commitment to a just cause is commendable and unshakable.

Finally, I would like to thank my three children, Abbie, Trevor, and Zachary, for providing me with the inspiration to remain focused on doing whatever I could to fix the mortgage backed securities problem in a manner that respects contract rights and encourages transparency and honesty. They, and their generation, are the primary beneficiaries of an honest financial system, and it is what my generation owes to them as their birthright.

William A. Frey

Greenwich, CT

September 2011

"You told us to become capitalists, now where is the capital?"
—*Aleksander Semenyaka, General Director, Russia's
Agency for Housing Mortgage Lending*

Prologue

The subprime mortgage crisis of 2007, known as "the mortgage crisis," was a creature of misaligned economic incentives. Its fallout will spread, costs will increase, and resolution will be delayed unless we recognize that many participants lack the incentives to fix the underlying problems. For all the recent talk of banks being "strategically important" to the United States economy or "too big to fail," there has been no recognition of the fact that the mortgage securitization market, valued at over $10 trillion, is nearly as big as all of the United States banks *combined*. If the United States' housing market and broader economy are to rebound, our financial and political leaders must realize that this market is *way too big to fail* and take meaningful steps to rebuild it.

With the consequences of the mortgage crisis still making headlines more than four years after its onset, there can be little doubt that we are facing one of the greatest financial calamities in United States history. The *Daily Telegraph*, Britain's leading newspaper, estimated that the crisis had destroyed an estimated 40 percent of the world's wealth by 2009,[3] well before the true depth of U.S. mortgage problems had come to light. Beyond the decline in property values, the wealth destruction caused by the crisis has taken the form of significantly slower economic growth and anemic stock prices that have shrunk the retirement nest eggs for millions of Americans. In the face of this financial disaster, few mortgage investors have emerged from the shadows to publicly challenge the blatant misconduct of the nation's largest banks. Perhaps more disappointingly, even fewer securitization trustees—the financial institutions charged with protecting investor interests—have lifted a finger to help investors enforce their rights. As we will discuss, remedying the problems with mortgage securitizations issued prior to the crisis is vitally important to restoring investor confidence in the American financial system and ensuring a healthy housing market going forward.

The pages that follow offer a detailed analysis of the problems with, and a comprehensive set of proposed reforms for revitalizing, the mortgage finance system in the United States and beyond. The object of this book is to make the following clear: we, as a nation, must make a critical choice between a future mortgage market that is dominated by the government and one that is powered by the private sector. The mortgage market in the United States today is, in essence, fully supported by the government. However, the recent statements of many of our policymakers indicate that they would like the private sector to re-assume primary responsibility for financing America's homes. If this transition is to take place, we must first understand the composition and motivations of this private sector. But before getting into the substance, I offer a brief description of the experiences that have profoundly shaped my perspective and the proposals I present herein.

A Summary of Recommended MBS Reforms

If you read nothing else in this book, please focus on the following table which summarizes the steps necessary to once again get private sector money flowing into the U.S. mortgage market. While I go into much greater detail in Chapter 10, specific recommendations as to the steps required by government and the private sector are on the following page.

SUMMARY OF PROPOSED REFORMS NECESSARY TO REOPEN THE PUBLIC MORTGAGE SECURITIZATION MARKET

	Must	Should	Can
Governmental Changes	• Ban Short Positions • Require Skin in the Game • Eliminate Subsequent Second Liens • Ban Captive Servicing Arrangements • Make Investor Lists Available • Allow Investor Audits • Ensure Homeowner Responsibility • Avoid Governmental Interference	• Allow Bankruptcy Cramdowns • Avoid Subsidizing Defaults • Eliminate or Redesign Interest Tax Deduction • Make GSEs Unambiguously Either Public or Private	• Minimize Incentives to Refinance • Overhaul Deed Recording System • Overhaul Ratings Agency Selection and Fee Structure
Private (Contractual) Changes	• Ban Trustee Indemnification • Insist on Independent Trustee • Strengthen Investor Standing to Sue • Implement Variable Default Servicing Fees • Have Trust Retain Late Fees	• Eliminate Servicer Advances • Require Uniform Underwriting • Standardize Deal Documents • Minimize Systemic Risk • Redesign Subordination Structure	• Encourage Deal Transparency • Create Independent Custodian • Require a Standby Servicer • Require Servicer Independence

My Introduction to Mortgage Finance

I became involved in the securitization of mortgages in the early 1980s as a newly minted MBA. My interests were twofold: first, the business was new and exciting, and second, it required an aptitude for mathematics. The math component was missing in many of my peers, giving me a competitive advantage. I also found the complexities and structural beauty of securitization—the process of converting raw assets into tradable securities—to be endlessly fascinating, and I still appreciate the beauty of a well-structured transaction.

Over the years, I have had about every position imaginable in the mortgage securitization business. At different times, I wore the hat of banker, trader, researcher, and salesperson for firms such as Morgan Stanley, Smith Barney, and Bear Stearns. In 1995, I left Bear Stearns and started my own firm, Greenwich Financial Services, with a small amount of capital and a conviction that I could attract institutional clients. As luck would have it, every one of the clients with whom I did business at Bear Stearns continued to do business with me after I left. I will be forever grateful to those investors who trusted and believed in me.

As my firm evolved and brought in additional partners, we began to do the structuring work behind mortgage transactions, creating bonds that met the needs of my investors. To me, this process was simple: I went into the markets, purchased mortgages, structured them into Mortgage Backed Securities (MBS), and placed the resulting securities on a "shelf," meaning that I added them to an offering being made by a larger firm. I found this to be a fantastically enjoyable and interesting business.

Building a New MBS Market

In the latter part of the 1990s, I was asked by the accounting firm KPMG if I would like to partner with it on a proposal to become the financial advisor to the Government National Mortgage Association (GNMA or Ginnie Mae). The job was to advise Ginnie

Mae on securitization matters. This task encompassed everything from determining if the government-owned corporation should build a large investment portfolio to providing general updates on events in the MBS market for Ginnie Mae executives at their meetings. KPMG felt that it needed specific mortgage expertise to be a viable competitor for this consulting contract. I agreed to participate, and a short time later, we were awarded the contract.

It was at one of Ginnie Mae's executive meetings that the then-president of Ginnie Mae, George Anderson, asked me if I had ever considered establishing an MBS market in another country. As myopic as this may sound, I was caught completely off guard by that question. I quickly dismissed the request by answering that I had a lifetime of work in the American markets and didn't need to go elsewhere; yet this question planted a seed in my head.

Some months later, a few Canadian clients asked me to talk to them about the possibility of creating a Canadian MBS market similar to that in the United States. This time I was not caught off guard and instead welcomed the opportunity to talk about how the United States had set up its market and how Canada could import the good things from the American securitization market as a foundation for building its own.

The more involved I became in this project, however, the more I realized that there were embedded interests within Canada that did not want a securitization market to be created. I also realized that Canada's banking system was strong and solvent, and thus the benefits of a securitization market would not be as extensive as in a market that lacked such a solvent banking system. My list of criteria for the right country within which to build an MBS market from scratch expanded and, along with it, my desire to be the one to build it.

In 2004, Vladimir Putin, then president of Russia, gave a speech in which he made it clear that Russia needed a mortgage market and that the laws would be amended so that it would be possible to securitize mortgages. At that time, I was crazy enough to believe that I could be the one to go into the old Soviet Union and set up both a mortgage market and an MBS market.

I started one step at a time. On July 29, 2005, my firm completed the first asset-backed securitization in Russia. The collateral was Russian auto loans, and the seller of the collateral was Soyuz Bank. I teamed up with Moscow Narodny Bank, an investment arm of the Russian Central Bank, and we figured out how to create a Russian securitization. Auto loans were selected as the raw materials for this securitization for two reasons. First, when a product is new and has no proven track record, it is easier to sell a shorter-term bond (such as an auto loan) than a longer-term bond (such as a mortgage). Second, a sizeable portfolio of properly underwritten collateral was available at the time and suitable for securitization in short order. When the deal was completed, Moody's rated the senior tranches of these asset-backed securities Baa3 (at the time the sovereign debt ceiling of the Russian Federation). We were able to sell the full offering of securities in the public market, and the transaction performed as promised. This deal was awarded the Eastern Europe, Middle East and Africa (EEMEA) Deal of the Year for 2005 by *International Securitization Report*, a leading structured finance periodical published by Thompson Reuters.

Soon after, I turned my attention to the Russian mortgage market. For this inaugural Russian mortgage transaction, I had to design everything from the lending guidelines that determined who would qualify for a loan to the legal agreements that dictated how those loans would be securitized. To develop a governing trust agreement, known as a Pooling and Servicing Agreement (PSA), my team reviewed existing American PSAs in detail. By studying the shortcomings present in American securitizations (discussed in detail later), we were able to avoid injecting these same flaws into the Russian transaction. Of course, bending to the realities of the marketplace, some risks remained in the Russian MBS that I would have liked to exclude, but sometimes one must be pragmatic to be effective.

On August 10, 2006, we completed the first Russian securitization of mortgage certificates in history, which was also the first Russian securitization structured as a Rule 144A transaction (a rule of the Securities and Exchange Commission [SEC] allowing U.S. private placement with qualified investors). The collateral for this transaction consisted of thirty-year home loans meeting the underwriting guidelines and standards established by my firm. These standards were based on historical underwriting criteria from the Federal National Mortgage Association (FNMA or Fannie Mae) and the Federal Home Loan Mortgage Corporation (FHLMC or Freddie Mac) with adaptations for the realities of the Russian market. The transaction was successful, receiving a rating of Baa2 for its senior securities from Moody's (again, the sovereign debt ceiling of the Russian Federation at the time), and has performed as promised. This deal was awarded the EEMEA Deal of the Year for 2006 by *ISR*. There have been no losses in this transaction and less than 2 percent of the original loans were delinquent as of mid-2011 (as compared to 20 percent to 30 percent in comparable U.S. securitizations). Notwithstanding the tumultuous global credit environment of the last half decade, it turns out that Russians respond rationally to logical economic incentives, as do most people.

One experience made a lasting impression on me at a meeting in Russia with Aleksander Semenyaka from Russia's Agency for Housing Mortgage Lending (AHML), the housing arm of the Russian government. Semenyaka's job was to run the agency and attract enough money to rebuild Russia. While I deeply respected the commitment and dedication with which Semenyaka had pursued this end, I did not envy his task. Russia needed, and still needs, massive inflows of capital to rebuild much of its housing stock before it falls down. This is not an exaggeration: literally tens of thousands of buildings will simply fall down in the coming years if nothing is done to repair or replace them. On the heels of my success in completing securitizations in Russia, Semenyaka wanted to speak to me about a private sale of mortgage notes. In one of my first meetings with AHML, we discussed how we could work together to structure a securitization that would get capital flowing into Russia. It was obvious that Russia could desperately use a well thought-out MBS system. It was equally obvious that AHML had the ability to provide access to a substantial amount of quality collateral.

Our meeting was rather long and plodding, as everything I said had to be translated into Russian, and everything that Semenyaka said was translated back into English. I was therefore stunned at the close of the meeting when Semenyaka turned to me and said, in perfect English, "You told us to become capitalists, now where is the capital?" When I heard his remark, the magnitude of the task in front of me became all too real. I realized that in the United States, we had long been able to take the availability of capital for granted. The challenge in Russia was that there was little capital available. Nevertheless, I am happy to report that my firm completed the largest private sale of mortgages to date in Russia, purchasing the mortgage notes on about seven thousand homes. I am as proud of this and the other Russian securitizations as I am of any accomplishment in my professional career. It is not often that one gets to take part in setting up a system that will house literally millions of people in the coming years.

Over the last five years or so, I have had the honor of continuing to develop the Russian MBS market and investor acceptance of that market. These transactions have not only won acclaim from industry groups and publications, they have funded over ten thousand homes for ordinary Russian citizens. The nascent Russian mortgage system and these transactions have stood the test of time, despite the fact that the Russian real estate market has undergone some of the same problems that the U.S. market has experienced in recent years. The Russian mortgage system is small today, but one must ask, "Why has it held up, while the U.S. mortgage market has been destroyed?"

The answer to this question is threefold.

First, while some Russian mortgage lenders—or in the parlance of the industry, loan originators—did adopt the lax origination and underwriting standards that were made infamous by, and which ultimately destroyed, lenders such as Countrywide and New Century, these few lax Russian originators were not large enough to destroy an entire market, let alone a sizeable financial institution. To the contrary, most of the collateral for the Russian MBS was properly underwritten and is performing well, in large part because Russian loan originators had a stake in the success of the Russian deals, and thus they were motivated to care whether borrowers paid back the loans they received.

Second, I structured the deals so that the other parties that could affect the credit performance of the transaction had contractual and economic incentives to ensure that the transactions went well. That is, I made sure that the economic interests of the parties were properly aligned.

Third, the Russian government did not react to the problems that arose in the Russian housing market by restricting investor rights or investors' ability to foreclose, nor has the Russian government turned the financial problems into an opportunity to vilify any sector, least of all the investment community. As we will discuss, this is a far cry from than the behavior of the United States in that regard.

The primary reason that the Russian government has not touched any of the securitizations or tampered with foreclosure laws during the last few tumultuous years is that it experienced the havoc such actions could wreak during the twentieth century in the Soviet Union. When I first went to Russia in 2004, I was surprised to learn that the Russians were not only more capitalistic than Americans, but that they were also willing to go to great lengths to make sure that Russia was viewed as a place where capital could be invested and treated fairly. It took some time before I believed the statements of Russian officials, but their actions have backed up their words. There have been some mistakes, but the errors of the Russian government have been small relative to the errors of the U.S. government since the onset of the mortgage crisis. Russians now understand that government cannot treat capital and businesspeople as enemies of the state.

Another of my most vivid memories from Russia is of a speech by a senior financial minister, whose words could have been written by a free market economist in the West. At the end of the speech, the official used a phrase that I had heard Russians use several other times when referring to the last several generations of Russia's history: "The Disaster Called the Twentieth Century." This phrase continues to ring in my ears as I watch the handling of the U.S. mortgage crisis. It makes me wonder whether my descendants will be referring to the current period in United States history as the beginning of "The Disaster Called the Twenty-First Century."

I never expected that the lessons I learned in creating the Russian MBS from scratch would become so directly applicable to the market back in my own country. It was already remarkable to have taken a small part in helping Russia recover from the spectacularly misguided economic policies that had brought down the Soviet Union, particularly because I spent some of my childhood under a school desk practicing what to do if a Soviet nuclear bomb exploded. To then turn around and use the knowledge gained in the Russian MBS market to help fix the American mortgage mess? This seemed an irony rivaling that of any O. Henry short story. Unfortunately for the United States and global economies, the true story of the mortgage crisis is far stranger than any work of fiction. I devote the majority of this work to understanding these events and what they mean for the future of housing finance.

My Involvement in the U.S. Mortgage Crisis Cleanup and Public Education

My involvement in the cleanup of the mortgage crisis began as a slow process of talking to clients about the deep problems with the U.S. MBS system and how bad these problems actually were. Many dismissed my views as overly pessimistic, though in retrospect, I was not skeptical enough. Instead, revelations regarding the behavior of the large banks, both leading up to and following the mortgage crisis, have substantiated my cynicism. However, I take no pleasure in having been vindicated, as these revelations have decimated the credibility of the U.S. financial industry, of which I'm a part and to which I've dedicated my professional career.

One of my first attempts to explain these problems came in late 2007, when I addressed a group of African financial ministers in Cape Town at an event sponsored by Standard Bank, a large South African banking concern. During my talk, I told the assembled government and industry officials that the losses from U.S. mortgage underwriting problems would amount to $125–$150 billion if real estate remained flat, but I doubted that real estate would remain flat. There were probably fewer than three people in the audience of two hundred that took me seriously. It would be an understatement to say that the global investment community was in denial about the health of the large U.S. banks and the efficacy of the anticipated U.S. political response to a financial crisis.

In March 2008, I became sufficiently concerned about the mortgage crisis to write a letter to Federal Reserve Chairman Ben Bernanke and Treasury Secretary Henry Paulson. In the wake of the Bear Stearns collapse, I sought to explain to these important policymakers that their advice to banks with respect to MBS was not feasible in view of the legal and contractual constraints governing those securities. Previously, I had believed that Paulson and Bernanke were well-informed individuals seeking to calm the financial markets with their pronouncements. With the Bear Stearns collapse, it dawned on me that there was a dearth of market experience at the highest levels of the government, undermining its ability to deal with the market problems effectively.

I realized that I had a duty to educate policymakers about these important concepts. My goal was not publicity or profit. Rather, I was motivated by a simple recognition that I had a better comprehension of these problems than almost anyone in Washington did. I had devoted my professional life to the securitization market and understood its complexities. I suspected that they were not familiar enough with this market even to ask the right questions.

My letter to Bernanke and Paulson appears in appendix I. When I sent it in March 2008, I felt that I had done my good deed and assumed that little more would come of it. At the least, I felt that I had made some effort to help fix the mortgage problem. I certainly never thought that the letter would get published, nor did I think it likely that anyone would read it. For several months, I was correct.

At around the same time, a foreign bank approached me about helping to correct the U.S. MBS problem. I explained that without a 25 percent ownership interest in a particular transaction, investors lacked the contractual standing to enforce any party's compliance with the PSA. In response, the foreign bank suggested that I aggregate investors into a group large enough to gain that legal standing—a task that I originally thought would be relatively easy. In hindsight, it has been monumental.

In the interim, my MBS-related activities expanded, including working to mitigate losses associated with those products and seeing to it that the contracts underlying those investments were honored. In August 2008, I wrote a letter to the trustees and servicers of transactions in which I had an interest, informing them that a recently enacted government program, Hope for Homeowners (H4H), which sought to deal with the mortgage foreclosure crisis, violated my contracts with servicers. To stem the spike in loan delinquencies and foreclosures, H4H encouraged servicers—the bank entities responsible for interfacing with borrowers and collecting mortgage payments—to engage in loan modifications. These loan modifications, also known as workouts, were designed to keep borrowers paying their loans by measures such as lowering principal balances or interest rates or extending the maturity dates of the loans. The problem with this program was that many of the PSAs governing MBS deals provided that servicers *could not modify loans without investor consent*, which consent could come only through an amendment process that generally required two-thirds of investors to agree.

H4H encouraged modifications without investor approval and without respecting the complexities of, and conflicts of interest inherent in securitization. For example, H4H failed to take into account the fact that many servicers were affiliates of the banks that had originated and sold off the loans at issue. Often, these originating banks still held second lien mortgages on their books that were subordinated to the loans targeted for modification. In fact, the four biggest U.S. banks held approximately $400 billion of second lien loans, or more than 40 percent of the total outstanding in the United States.[4] The promulgation of this government program meant that banks would not have to absorb any of the costs of the disastrous loans that they had originated and sold into the securitization trusts, including credit losses associated with the second lien loans they still held on their books. Instead, those who had provided capital for the mortgages—the investors—would bear the brunt of the irresponsible bank lending that contributed to the mortgage crisis.

This law was an obvious wealth transfer from investors to servicing banks and a flagrant abrogation of trillions of dollars' worth of investors' contractual rights. Accordingly, I informed the banks involved that if they participated in H4H, I would sue them on behalf of the investors—pensioners, savers, and businesses around the world—to recover what was rightfully theirs. It became increasingly clear to me that my experiences in Russia in dealing with investor questions about the Russian government's potential abrogation of contracts would prove relevant to my efforts to protect U.S. investors as well.

In September 2008, Barry Meier, a reporter for *The New York Times*, spoke with me about my firm's business in Russia. During the interview, I mentioned my August 2008 letter to the U.S. trustees and servicers, and he quoted me correctly as saying, "Any investor in mortgage backed securities has the right to insist that their contract be enforced." I told Meier that I had given this letter to a number of other investment firms, which in turn had sent the identical letter to the same servicers and trustees in their own names. The article was published in *The New York Times* in the middle of the business section on October 23, 2008.[5]

The morning the story appeared in the press, my wife and I concluded that I might receive, at the most, a call or two as a result of the article. I drastically underestimated the reaction the story would generate. That morning, my phone exploded with many other reporters wanting to know what I was planning to do. By lunchtime, I had received a public invitation from the U.S. House of Representatives Committee on Financial Services to explain myself (see appendix II). This letter set the stage for me to be publicly excoriated for telling powerful institutions that I would sue them if they violated their contracts with investors.

Given the tone of the Committee's letter, I was not convinced that I would be treated with much respect or understanding when I reached Washington. In these types of situations, one usually hires an attorney to handle communications with Congressional staff, which I did. Even so, the reports from my attorney over the following few weeks were not encouraging, and they painted a picture of the Financial Services Committee as woefully unsophisticated regarding U.S. MBS and the securitization markets.

One staff member had asked where I got off saying that I had a contract with the banks. Through my attorney, I explained that there was such a thing as a contract called a PSA, which was publically available on the SEC website under the EDGAR tab, and which governed the parties' rights and obligations with respect to MBS. My lawyers explained the rights of the investors and the responsibilities of the servicers pursuant to these contracts. The staffers asked how I could possibly keep track of my rights in these deals when some of the PSAs ran over one thousand pages. In response, I provided the Financial Services Committee with a large file for each transaction in which I had an economic interest, with the twenty to thirty most important sections highlighted.

I found it more than a little disconcerting that this group of staffers, which had presumably been involved in the passage of several mortgage resolution bills, continued to opine publicly about mortgage securitization issues when they had never heard of a PSA, let alone read one. As the scheduled date of the hearing approached, and the staffers realized that I understood these contracts inside and out and had selected certain transactions in which to participate based on the provisions in those contracts, their questions and their desire for me to testify seemed to wane. The Committee's leaders had no interest in having me explain fundamental principles of contract law and mortgage securitization to Congressmen who had intended to call me to task for defending those very same principles. Soon, their staffers called my attorneys to ask me not to testify.

On November 12, 2008, the scheduled date of the hearing, I traveled to Washington, not expecting to testify but prepared to do so if necessary. My prepared statement, which was taken into evidence, appears in appendix III, and I'm happy to report that the statements made therein remain as true today as they were when I wrote them. Despite indications that I would not be called, I decided to attend the hearing, just to see what our elected officials were up to and to assure myself that the Committee would not place my name card at an empty desk and announce to the world that I had refused its public invitation.

As it turned out, I was not asked to testify, and it quickly became obvious that these hearings were not designed to be fact-finding missions but instead were "made for C-SPAN" events, staged to create the appearance of productive leadership. C-SPAN viewers could not see Committee members reading newspapers, working on their computers, and often ignoring the people testifying. In fact, for most of the hearing, the majority of Committee members were not in attendance—they simply left the room. Key members dropped in from time to time to give well-crafted "outrage" speeches before taking off again. I left Washington with the impression that these hearings were "sound-bite opportunities" for the local TV station back home, not real efforts to get to the heart of the problem.

My experience convinced me that the individuals charged with crafting legislation to extricate our country from the mortgage crisis not only lacked expertise, they did not know where to start. It was not that they were stupid; quite the contrary. The representatives had done something extraordinary with their lives: they had been elected to go Washington to serve their constituents as members of Congress. Surely, they were good people by and large, and they had my respect and admiration. However, it terrified me that these same individuals were being asked to solve the complex problems plaguing U.S. financial markets, as they did not seem have the expertise to be up to the task.

The Launch of a Legal Battle

Shortly after the Congressional hearings, I made good on my promise to sue the servicers that violated any contract to which I was a party. On October 6, 2008, the then-Attorney General of California, Jerry Brown, announced with great fanfare that Countrywide had agreed to settle predatory lending actions by multiple Attorneys General to the tune of over $8.6 billion. As part of this settlement, Countrywide had agreed to modify the terms of roughly four hundred thousand mortgages for struggling borrowers by lowering monthly payments, principal amounts or interest rates. The Attorneys General hailed the deal as a model for the rest of the country in solving the housing crisis.

The deal hammered out by Countrywide managed to settle a series of serious charges in a few months' time. The only problem with this deal was that while Countrywide had originated the four hundred thousand loans it had agreed to modify, it had sold off nearly 90 percent of them into securitizations, retaining only the servicing rights.[6] This meant that most of these loans were now owned by entities other than Countrywide, entities that essentially would be forced to pay Countrywide's fine for its bad behavior by absorbing the costs of these

---

loan modifications. Mortgage bondholders, who had invested in the securities backed by these loans and who had carefully negotiated protections against unfettered loan modifications, would now be on the hook for nearly 90 percent of the $8.6 billion of aid to distressed borrowers promised by Countrywide.

On reviewing the deal, it appeared to me that the Attorneys General failed to understand securitization (i.e., that the bank that originated the loans and put the deal together no longer owned the underlying collateral once the transaction was completed). This impression was reinforced when I compared the text of the press release from the Attorneys General to the text of the settlement: they did not match up. I have since been asked by numerous people why the Attorneys General would make such an agreement. Was it lack of sophistication or corruption? Judging by their reaction to my lawsuit, which I will discuss later, it was the former; the Attorneys General simply did not understand the securitization market and had been outwitted by Countrywide.

I sued Countrywide on December 1, 2008. The reaction was severe, to say the least. I was vilified in the press by the same politicians who were at the helm when the seeds of this crisis were planted. Four hundred protesters showed up in my front yard on a Sunday afternoon. They dragged furniture onto my lawn and claimed that I was kicking them out of their homes.[7] Attorneys General and politicians from around the country made statements to the effect that I was interfering with efforts to help struggling homeowners. Connecticut Attorney General Richard Blumenthal had this to say about Countrywide's settlement and my lawsuit: "Countrywide was very wise to reach the settlement that it did with Attorneys General because it is in the interest of its own investors as [well as] the homeowners whose mortgages will be restructured. And Countrywide has informed us of the lawsuit and its intent to vigorously defend against it, as it should."[8] I had done nothing more than take a politically powerful bank to court to force it to honor its contract. Moreover, I had framed my case as a class action to protect the interests of ordinary citizens whose pension funds, retirement funds, life insurance funds, and other investments were being used to pay the costs of Countrywide's misbehavior.

Though a wiser man may have been dissuaded by the public reaction, I found the criticism to be encouraging. It revealed that rather than being corrupt or beholden, lawmakers had little understanding of the direct and unintended consequences of their actions, including the impact these actions would have on the availability of private money for home mortgages in the future. Since then, I have spent significant time explaining these issues and organizing MBS investors from around the world to make a concerted effort to force lenders, securitization underwriters, and servicers to honor contracts they would rather ignore.

This has been a long, uphill battle. Impediments have come from a lack of information regarding who owns the underlying collateral, as well as the challenges of getting large and diverse groups of investors to present a unified front. Taking such a stand may be politically unpopular, but these organizations need to muster the courage to do so in order to comply with their fiduciary duties to their own investors. The amazingly complex process of organizing these institutions has shaken my view of some large investors while strengthening my assessment of others. It is fair to say that there is a wide variance in understanding and courage to act among major financial players in the U.S. markets today, despite their essentially identical interests and fiduciary obligations.

The Launch of a Lobbying Effort

Though the servicing banks had long had a presence in Washington and were familiar with how the wheels of politics were greased, investors arrived relatively late to the party. Significant bondholder lobbying efforts did not get underway until March 2009, when a conference of fixed-income investors was held in Washington DC. I was on a panel at that conference, along with David Grais, my attorney in the

Countrywide lawsuit, and Laurie Goodman, a managing director of Amherst Securities.[9] The meeting was attended by about seventy-five investors, representing most of the major fixed income investors in the country. The topic of our talk was the proposed servicer safe harbor legislation that had been included in HR 1106 (discussed in detail in chapter 6). This bill had passed the House and was currently being discussed in the Senate. The section of the bill that was the topic of our discussion was the portion that would have given servicers immunity from investor suits if they modified a securitized loan, regardless of what the governing PSA said. The concern was that this would allow the servicers to modify first liens without touching the second liens they owned. To many, this was the obvious intention of the bill.*

I have had the privilege of speaking at a number of gatherings over the last several years in locations around the world, but never have I experienced the reception that this panel received from this audience—ranging from shock to outrage—when it finally sank in that the purpose of the Servicer Safe Harbor provision was to destroy their securities to benefit the banks that originated the loans and caused the mortgage problem. Following the conference, which received significant media attention, I was asked by *The Washington Times* to write an op-ed piece on this topic. The result was published while the debate over the Servicer Safe Harbor was raging in the Senate. It sums up the impact on the middle class as succinctly as I have ever put the argument, and it is available online for anyone who wishes to delve further into this matter.[10]

Over the course of the next several months, I had the enlightening experience of lobbying against the Servicer Safe Harbor. For those unfamiliar with the lobbying process, as I was at the time, it turns out that one rarely gets to meet with any elected officials. Instead, each

---

* As we will discuss in chapter 6, issues surrounding second or junior liens have been driving all of the actions (and inactions) of servicing banks for several years, and will continue to do so until the banks are forced to recognize and absorb losses on these assets.

official is usually represented by a young adult with a freshly minted law degree who, while ostensibly well intentioned, is a self-described "policy wonk" with little experience in the subject matter. Invariably, the first question out of the person's mouth is, "Why didn't you come here sooner? The banks have been in here for six months asking for this legislation, and SIFMA thinks that it is a good solution." I spent a lot of time explaining to staff members that investors never knew they had to lobby to avoid having their assets seized and that the Security Industry and Financial Markets Association (SIFMA) was dominated by the large servicer banks. I also spent a lot of time trying to dispel the myth perpetuated by the banks that investors were greedy and careless while the banks were trying to save the country by helping struggling homeowners.

Though I did my best to help the lawmakers on Capitol Hill climb the steep learning curve surrounding securitizations, I found that leading them through even the first steps was shockingly difficult. (Even today, I speak with few people in Washington who truly understand the dilemma faced by investors and the United States.) It did not help that few large investors joined me in my lobbying efforts. During the debate surrounding the Safe Harbor, the only major investor to speak publicly on this issue was T. Rowe Price. Mary Miller wrote a letter to all one hundred Senators, explaining why this legislation was not in the interest of investors and the country.[11] This letter was an act of leadership that I have not seen again from major investors. Miller has since taken a senior position in the U.S. Treasury. It is nice to know that at least one major investor will speak up when the funds it oversees are threatened.

When all was said and done, though our lobbying efforts succeeded in encouraging the Senate to water down the Servicer Safe Harbor, investors were woefully unprepared to confront the powerful and experienced lobbying efforts of the major banks. I think that most investors, including me, were surprised that a lobbying effort would even be necessary to prevent the U.S. government from expropriating our assets. The premise is so foreign to investors that many still have not come to grips with the reality that the government attempted to execute a closet bailout of the nation's largest banks with assets owned by institutional investors. In addition, the banks were clever, in that they wrapped this closet bailout of their problematic second lien loans in the cloak of a euphemistic bill called the "Helping Families Save Their Homes Act," which was ultimately signed into law by President Obama on May 21, 2009.

Evaluating the Fallout from the Mortgage Crisis

I have been bearish on the overaggressive expansion of non-prime lending in the U.S. mortgage market for years. Indeed, I never put together a transaction using subprime collateral—defined as mortgages where the borrowers had lower credit and were more likely to default than prime borrowers. In addition, I had stopped structuring deals with alternative-A (Alt-A) paper—usually referring to loans with reduced documentation requirements and/or less than prime credit histories—by 2002. This was because I was skeptical of the quality of both of these loan products. Since the onset of the mortgage crisis, I have been asked frequently why I chose not to get involved in non-prime mortgage markets. Though I would like to claim extraordinary clairvoyance or analytical prowess, the answer is simple: in 2000, when I was thinking about whether to get involved in structuring subprime deals, I flew to Orange County to visit some prospective loan originators. These firms were just getting started and were desperate for vehicles through which to sell their products. I felt that basic due diligence was in order and that I should meet the management of those firms before deciding whether I should be one of the firms that would fill that role.

My most poignant memory of that trip is of meeting the CEO of a then-nascent mortgage originator, which later became a large (and infamous) subprime originator. Rather than wearing a suit or even a collared dress shirt to the meeting, the CEO arrived wearing a colorful polyester shirt, opened to the navel, with a half-dozen gold chains around his neck and gold rings on all of his fingers. The outfit did not convey the impression of an experienced banker exercising prudence in lending practices; in fact, I left the meeting feeling in need of a shower.

Even with this experience, I still underestimated how corrupt the origination and securitization system would become during the housing market boom years of 2004–2007 (the Boom Years) and how poorly the U.S. government would react to the mortgage crisis. While I cannot say that I was shocked by the onset of the mortgage crisis, I never expected that, in responding to this disaster, the U.S. government would so readily abandon the hallowed principles of contract law on which this country was built. Indeed, the sanctity of contracts has been the cornerstone of every successful economy since the Magna Carta.

On the latter point, my experience in Russia made me particularly sensitive to the problems with the political response to the U.S. mortgage crisis. To be sure, my own financial holdings and business dealings in the mortgage market would be adversely impacted by responses that abrogated contracts as per the government's initial response in 2007. However, I was also hypersensitive to the long-term implications of such a political response. I knew from my experience in the Russian MBS transaction that the single greatest investor concern was whether the government would respond to a crisis by disregarding contract rights and resorting to crony capitalism.

Unfortunately, this is exactly how the U.S. government responded to the mortgage crisis, and it has been nothing short of disastrous. The upshot of nearly every idea dreamed up by Congress is that the banks should take money from the mortgage trusts to recapitalize themselves, borrowers should be given many more months to live in homes while not paying their mortgages, and investors should suck it up. Cheating the investors in mortgage trusts has become a national pastime. Based on my experiences in Russia, I understood early on that by treating executed contracts as if they could be swept aside in the name of political and financial expediency, certain politicians were destroying the future of the U.S. mortgage market—the largest fixed income market in the world—without understanding the extremely complex financial instruments with which they were dealing or the basic implications of their actions. The legislative and economic results of misguided pieces of mortgage reform legislation suggest that U.S. government officials have been a party to widespread crony capitalism that has benefitted the large commercial banks at the expense of every American taxpayer, worker, retiree, and investor.

Of course, we cannot blame our political leaders for this mess without looking hard at our role as American citizens. Putting aside for the moment the borrowers who chose to live beyond their means, we must first direct our scrutiny to our role as voters. The American system of representative democracy allows U.S. citizens to participate in the political process, and thus, any legislative efforts related to the mortgage market, by electing the individuals who will represent our interests. As voters, we have repeatedly made the decision *not* to replace the very individuals whose business practices and legislative policies have brought this country's economy to its knees.

No politician involved in this mess should retain his or her governmental post, and my condemnation applies to leadership on both sides of the congressional aisle, the executive branch, and the quasi-independent government entities with oversight responsibility. These elected or appointed individuals have appeared generally more interested in rewriting historical facts to hide their own culpability in this mess than in fixing mortgage problems. Their supposed "cleanup" efforts have done nothing but make these problems worse. These individuals lack both the track record and the objectivity necessary to provide effective leadership in solving such an important national problem in the future. In fact, many of the individuals most responsible for this mess have been promoted, and are now key policymakers.*

Moreover, we cannot criticize the political response to the mortgage crisis without recognizing that the crisis was caused, in large part, by the reckless and oftentimes fraudulent conduct of our nation's largest financial institutions. We will examine their actions in more detail, but it is clear that the four largest banks—Bank of America, Wells Fargo, Citibank, and J. P. Morgan Chase, and these institutions' various subsidiaries—have conducted themselves in a manner that should offend the conscience of every law-abiding American. As originators and underwriters, they created and sold billions of dollars' worth of loans that should never have been made. As servicers, they have flagrantly disregarded contractual responsibilities and essentially stolen money out of securitization trusts.

Such conduct has been enabled by other banks serving as securitization trustees. These trustees have chosen to look the other way, despite obligations to police these trusts on behalf of investors. Further allegations have surfaced that banks have taken steps to cover up origination fraud and obtain additional profits on the back end by squeezing settlements out of loan originators—a practice known as "double dipping." For example, one bond insurer's lawsuit against EMC Mortgage Corp. and Bear Stearns & Co. Inc. (now known as

---

* The reader might wonder why I am not quoting or referencing specific politicians. The answer is that I do not want to turn this book into a political tool for either party and, as such, have mentioned few political or business leaders by name. YouTube is a wonderful tool to research politicians' statements, and I wholeheartedly recommend that reader take the names of the most prominent political leaders of the last decade, type their names into YouTube or any search engine, and see what they had to say about Freddie Mac, Fannie Mae, and subprime loans, both before and after this mortgage mess. Some of these individuals likely believed that they were doing the right thing by supporting homeownership before the crisis and that they did everything in their power since then to fix the mortgage problem. Regardless, any politician who had a significant role in engendering the mortgage crisis should be replaced. It would be foolhardy to think that we can be led out of this financial mess by those who led us into it.

J.P. Morgan Securities Inc.) alleges that J.P. Morgan continued to per-petuate fraud with respect to toxic Bear Stearns MBS after it acquired Bear Stearns:

> JP Morgan's duplicity also is patent from the repurchase demands it made against the suppliers of the loans in the Bear Stearns securitizations pertaining to the very same loans that [bond insurer Syncora] submitted for repurchase from [Bear Stearns subsidiary] EMC...JP Morgan advanced Syncora's positions in attempting to recover from [loan originator] GreenPoint, while simultaneously rejecting Syncora's positions in denying its repurchase demands...The conflicting and incompatible positions that JP Morgan asserted on EMC's behalf exemplifies its bad faith strategy to reject legitimate repurchase demands by financial guarantors in order to mask any exposure to those claims on its financial statements – while at the same time attempting to generate recoveries from the entities that originated and sold EMC the defective loans.[12]

Though the true extent of this sort of unscrupulous behavior with respect to U.S. MBS will be fully understood only after this financial knot is unraveled, I believe that it will, over time, be recognized the greatest financial fraud and largest looting of private wealth in American history—fraud that will make Bernard Madoff look like a rank amateur.

The course of action chosen by our politicians and financial institutions has its consequences. To see why, ask yourself a simple question: "Would you invest in an asset where the issuer, with the help of Congress, had a history of reducing or eliminating your interest in that asset when it was politically or financially expedient?" I wouldn't. Bailing out the banks at the expense of mortgage investors is a one-way street toward undermining two of the most important pillars of investor confidence: the enforcement of contracts and the rule of law.

This ultimate legacy of the mortgage crisis will stay with the United States for years to come.

The impact of these problems has not been confined to the United States. The days when problems in the U.S. housing finance sector were exclusively an American problem are long gone, as the size of the U.S. MBS market and the demand for AAA-rated dollar denominated assets by foreign institutions mean that "our" problem is also Europe's problem. Foreign institutions that bought U.S. residential mortgage assets encountered two problems: 1) a lack of liquidity, as U.S. MBS were no longer accepted as collateral for short-term credit lines and 2) losses or write-downs as the MBS were downgraded and cash flows decreased.

In the summer of 2007, as short-term funding lines dried up, the Federal Reserve Bank of New York extended discount window access to foreign institutions. Almost $1.7 billion was loaned through this discount window in late August and early September. In November 2007, Germany's Deutsche Bank received $2.4 billion, while in December 2007, France's Calyon (a commercial and investment bank) used $16 billion of collateral to receive $2 billion in loans. In the latter part of 2008, this lending increased dramatically in size. For example, Belgium's Depfa Bank and France and Belgium's Dexia Credit together received over $50 billion of funding from the Fed *in one day*: November 4, 2008. Dexia has since been bailed out by the Belgian and French governments and recently reported over a 4 billion Euro loss for Q2 2011, much of it related to U.S. MBS.

Foreign institutions have also begun initiating litigation, as well as becoming the target of litigation, in connection with U.S. mortgage bonds. In January 2011, Dexia teamed with TIAA-CREF, one of the largest U.S. pension funds, and a group of insurance companies, in a suit against Bank of America, Countrywide and Countrywide's CEO, Angelo Mozilo, accusing the defendants of perpetuating "massive fraud" in the sale of MBS.[13] In July 2011, in a lawsuit between two European banks over assets backed by U.S. mortgages, Dexia sued

Deutsche Bank alleging fraud in the origination and sale of MBS.[14] In late July 2011, the Federal Housing Finance Agency (FHFA), as conservator for Fannie Mae and Freddie Mac, sued Swiss bank UBS for almost $1 billion over loans packaged by UBS and sold to the GSEs.[15] This government action followed on the heels of the U.S. Department of Justice suing Deutsche Bank in May 2011 for more than $1 billion in damages for misleading the Federal Housing Administration (FHA) into believing that many low-quality mortgages issued by the German bank's Mortgage IT unit qualified for FHA insurance.[16]

Based on the foregoing, it is no surprise that there is a complete lack of private capital being invested in the U.S. MBS market today. By mid-2010, the proportion of new mortgages supported by the government (i.e., the proportion of the mortgage market sponsored by Fannie Mae, Freddie Mac, and the FHA) had reached 96.5 percent.[17] As of the writing of this book, the conditions remain dire: there is no private securitization market to speak of, and the government has stepped in to guarantee virtually all new mortgages in the United States. It is apparent that it will be a long time before there will be any private investors returning to the "private label" or non-government-backed MBS market, especially if they are unable to enforce their contracts or if politicians intervene in the loss recognition process set forth in those contracts. As it exceeds the U.S. Treasury market and the largest banks in size, the private securitization market is far too vital to the economic success and prosperity of America to languish in disrepair.

My experiences in Russia and during the U.S. mortgage crisis have taught me two major lessons. First, a financial system is based on trust—trust that is incredibly fragile. Once that trust has been violated, it takes many years to earn it back. I was terrified for the future of my country at the outset of the mortgage crisis when I saw the U.S. capital markets turning into a game of political roulette. I fully believed at the time that such policies had the capacity to destroy the supply of private capital to the U.S. mortgage market. I regret to say that my fears have proven to be correct.

Second, other countries are perfectly capable of learning from America's mistakes and designing a better system—one that is internally stable and removes the systemic risk and internal conflicts that contributed to the U.S. crisis. Such a system will never be risk free, of course, but it can reduce the risk of a systemic problem to a minimum. The pitfalls that the United States continues to uncover while exploring the securitization frontier should be noted by Russian officials and all other countries seeking to establish a stronger mortgage market that would provide their populations with access to affordable home loans. This can be done, it has been done, and it should be done. It is important to recognize that if such a system were to be built in a country other than the United States, it would compete directly with U.S. MBS and other securities for the international capital desperately needed to propel the American economy.

It saddens me to contemplate how the United States has veered so far off course. I am also deeply disappointed that I have not been able to do more to help U.S. policymakers to understand the repercussions of their actions, remove politics from the mortgage resolution process, and stop protecting the very powerful banks that contributed mightily to the crisis. We must also face the fact that, without having received such protections from the government, the banking system could well be insolvent today based on its mortgage-related liabilities. Clearly, we must find a way to ensure the ongoing viability of our banking system if we have any hope of moving forward from our current economic problems. At the same time, we cannot seek to have MBS investors recapitalize the U.S. banking system by having their assets expropriated by the nation's largest banks. It is a dire situation indeed.

The purpose of this book is not to attribute blame to participants but rather to examine the underlying structural deficiencies in the mortgage finance and MBS markets as they have existed historically and discuss ways to structure future mortgages and securitization systems to ensure stability and efficiency. In what follows, I draw from my experience in this industry to lay the groundwork for building better mortgage finance systems in the United States and abroad. In doing so, I draw heavily on lessons about the successes and failures of both the U.S. mortgage system and other mortgage finance systems around the world.

I begin with a brick-by-brick approach to understanding mortgages and the U.S. mortgage market, starting at the most basic level: a home loan to an individual borrower. I then discuss what happens to that loan after it is made. In that context, I walk through the process of securitization and the roles and responsibilities of originators, banks, servicers, underwriters, trustees, arrangers, rating agencies and regulators.* I also examine the economic repercussions of the political decisions and tax incentives that have helped shape the U.S. MBS market. What is the proper role for government? If the government wishes to encourage people with low and moderate incomes to participate in the housing market, how can it structure those programs to realize those goals without placing the economy at risk?

As for the mortgage crisis, I offer concrete suggestions as to how the U.S. government can react to the short-term securitization and foreclosure problems in a manner that will mitigate damages for the entire economy while preserving the sanctity of contracts. In the later chapters, I roll out a blueprint for a new mortgage system that is free from internal conflicts and mitigates exogenous systemic risk. I believe that the enactment of this proposed system will result in a more

---

* The reader may note that I do not mention the role and responsibility of investors for the reason that if they choose to repeat the buy-side mistakes of the first decade of this century, including the outsourcing of due diligence to conflicted third parties, they will automatically pay a price in the form of credit losses. At the same time, it is clear that potential MBS investors must be reassured that the conflicts of interest and abuses so prevalent in the underwriting of individual mortgages, and in the structuring and rating of MBS before 2007, have been addressed and resolved. Indeed, once investors decide that a market is rigged against them, as many have now concluded, there will not be a viable market until significant structural changes are made. It is one thing to expect investors to perform due diligence; it is another to ask them to do so when they view other market participants as actively working against transparency.

transparent and stable mortgage market, thus providing private investors with the confidence to invest in this market once again.

At the end of the book, I have included a section on some of the special challenges facing countries lacking developed capital and mortgage markets. Many of these challenges should make Americans thankful that our system, although stressed and in need of repair, was a viable system until recently and can be made viable again with the proper reforms.

While not everyone will agree with all of the opinions expressed here, I hope that my readers will recognize this book to be a serious effort to assess the past and offer lessons for the future, without regard to political ideologies or entrenched financial interests. While the United States has fallen dramatically from its perch as the beacon of financial dependability, it is not too late to right the American financial ship. The twenty-first century can and should be known as the century in which America set an example for the world to emulate. For policymakers who care to listen, I offer my thoughts on this dilemma in the hope that America does not look back on this period as "The Disaster Called the Twenty-First Century"—a time when the largest suppliers of private capital in the United States had their trust sacrificed at the altar of political expediency. Think of this as the Congressional testimony I was never able to give.

Part I:
The Boom and Bust of the
Great Mortgage Machine

"Yes, our capital markets are big. Indeed, they're global. And it would be very easy to look at your role as an often anonymous participant in these enormous, faceless financial markets, and to conclude that you don't have any responsibility to consider the consequences of your actions on the market as a whole... But if you look at what would happen if most others in your position took that same view - what would happen to the market, and more importantly, to the society that depends upon it – you've got to conclude that you simply can't ignore the bigger picture. The truth is, unless we all think of the bigger picture, not only the rule of law but the entire notion of free, fair, and competitive markets will be at risk."

—Former SEC Chairman Christopher Cox, in a speech to the securitization industry on June 7, 2006

CHAPTER 1

Introduction

In August 2007, the world became aware of major structural deficiencies in the way that the United States had originated and financed mortgages. News emerged of perverse incentives in both the way that mortgages had been made to individuals and the manner in which those mortgages had been turned into bonds and sold in the international capital markets. While much has been written about the contribution of various firms to the mortgage crisis, I am aware of no objective analysis of the fundamental flaws in the existing mortgage finance system and the reasons that otherwise rational market participants funded loans they knew could not be repaid. There has been little discussion as to why rational homeowners leveraged up their principal assets to unsustainable levels. No one has looked at the existing tax, regulatory, and financial structures of the U.S. mortgage market to understand what steps must be taken to minimize the chances of a similar crisis down the road.

At the heart of the mortgage crisis of 2007 is a complex and often misunderstood financial vehicle known as securitization. By efficiently linking the suppliers and consumers of capital, the mortgage securitization market became the shining example of American financial ingenuity, serving as the primary source of capital for aspiring homeowners in the United States for over a generation. This system, however, must have been deeply flawed if millions of people suddenly decided (or were encouraged) to make misrepresentations in loan applications where few had done so in the past, while loan originators and bankers suddenly stopped caring whether the loans they were making would default. The reality is that the mortgage crisis did not stem from a simultaneous and total breakdown in the underlying morality of millions of people. A deeper dive into the history of the securitization market reveals that the system evolved in a patchwork manner, such that it failed to anticipate or account for extreme events. When confronted with an extreme event such as an unprecedented rise in housing prices, this securitization system produced improper economic incentives, leading to disastrous results. Thus, while there may have been some bad actors, *the crisis resulted primarily from good people responding rationally to improper economic incentives.*

The U.S. mortgage market must be rethought and rebuilt from the ground up if private capital is to flow once again into this important sector of the economy. Never again should the economy be held hostage to poor credit underwriting because economic incentives are poorly aligned. Never again should our financial system be exposed to excessive risk by a small number of overleveraged firms that stand to reap enormous profits in good times, while forcing the U.S. taxpayer to bail them out in bad times, all the while blaming the down economy rather than their own imprudent behavior for their troubles.

However painful the mortgage crisis has been, it is not the only economic crisis in recent U.S. history that was caused by mortgages and how they were financed. As we will discuss in chapter 2, the savings and loan crisis (the "S&L crisis") in the 1980s was also caused by mortgage problems stemming from an extreme event—an unparalleled period of high interest rates. By contrast, the 2007 crisis was caused by an unparalleled period of low interest rates. There are lessons to be learned from both experiences. For this reason, I will examine both the S&L crisis and the current mortgage crisis, including the failures of Fannie Mae and Freddie Mac, and with an eye toward rebuilding the U.S. mortgage finance system so that it provides a steady supply of capital to the American homebuyer without exposing the American economy to excessive and unnecessary risk.

To proceed further, it is important to establish exactly what securitization is and what it was intended to do. Securitization is a legal structure that links the providers of capital with the consumers of capital. It was developed to help normalize the risk of mortgage lending and create safer investments out of residential mortgage loans, which were historically volatile and a headache to own. This was because a bank or other owner of a mortgage loan faced several risks, including these: 1) the borrower might default on the loan, forcing the holder of the loan to conduct a costly foreclosure to recoup some portion of the investment; 2) interest rates might rise and leave the loan holder inadequately compensated with a below-market rate on the loan; or 3) the borrower might refinance or pay back the loan all at once (known as a "prepayment"), which happens most frequently in periods of decreasing interest rates, putting the holder of the loan in the undesirable position of having to find someplace else to invest this money at the most inopportune time.

Securitization, as recounted memorably in Michael Lewis' book, *Liar's Poker*, was Wall Street's solution to this problem. The idea was to buy up large numbers of mortgage loans and sell securities backed by the cash flows from these loans to investors. These securities made it possible for investors to hold a piece of a diversified pool of several thousand mortgages that would theoretically have a more predictable rate of return. This solution proved to be far more efficient at linking the various market participants and spreading risk than the traditional banking system, and it quickly developed into a huge piece of the U.S. financial market.

The securitization of mortgages had one critical flaw: the market became too efficient at providing capital, while allowing securitization participants to distance themselves from the risks inherent in mortgage lending. This feature, combined with an exceptional period of U.S. home price appreciation, led to enormous moral hazard; the originators, underwriters and servicers of securitizations were no longer motivated to ensure that mortgages performed. These players began abdicating their responsibilities for credit underwriting, pool-level due diligence, and proper servicing of mortgage loans post-origination.

At the same time, securitization investors, the purchasers of MBS, failed to understand that the economic incentives for the banks and the other deal participants encouraged them to get as many deals completed as possible, regardless of the quality of the resulting investment products. If investors had understood these concepts, they might have bargained for better contractual protections in the securitization agreements or structured these transactions with more logical economic incentives. Indeed, securitization is flexible enough to incorporate these proper economic incentives into its structure and, with the benefit of hindsight, it can be rebuilt and restored to its role as the most efficient and lowest-cost provider of capital to prospective homeowners.

Some readers may question the wisdom of bringing back mortgage securitization, as they believe that it is the root of the mortgage crisis and the recession that followed. These readers may recall that, in the 1930s, the United States suffered through a depression blamed largely on the excesses of the stock market, its crash, and the resulting fallout. The United States had two possible courses of action: to understand, expose, and stop those excesses or to eliminate the stock market altogether. In choosing the former, the twentieth century unleashed an unprecedented period of industrialization and a corresponding increase in the standard of living for all sectors of the U.S. population, funded largely by the sale of equities in the stock market.

Similarly, while it is true that securitization has taken its share of criticism during this crisis, it is important to understand that securitization is simply a legal mechanism—one that is invaluable for its ability to efficiently allocate capital and risk. Like any other tool, it can result in abuse if not used properly. In the case of the mortgage crisis, the primary cause of this crash was not securitization itself but its application. More specifically, poor choices by deal participants—loan originators, deal sponsors, rating agencies, servicers and investors—created an environment of misaligned economic incentives in which participants were encouraged to routinely ignore their contractual responsibilities. When politics and a misunderstanding of mortgage problems were thrown into the mix, it made for a combustible combination.

Later in this book, I will discuss in detail the steps we must undertake to resolve troubled securitizations in such a way that the contract rights of securitization participants are not eroded and our national reputation is preserved as a country that honors its written agreements. Suffice it to say here that the problems with mortgage securitizations, however severe, can and should be addressed within the securitization structure rather than by throwing the baby out with the bathwater.

Without a private securitization system, we face a bleak future for the U.S. mortgage market. As of mid-2011, since the disappearance of private securitization, virtually all new mortgages are processed through government agencies, primarily Fannie Mae, Freddie Mac, and the FHA.[18] The resulting government securities have been, or will be, sold to either the Fed (through its recently completed $1.25 trillion MBS Purchase Program), to the Treasury, or back to Freddie Mac or Fannie Mae. The respective roles of these agencies are explained in chapter 2, but the important point is that *there is so little private money available for mortgages today that nearly all mortgages are guaranteed or financed by the U.S. government.*

To put the importance to the United States of the securitization system into perspective, at the end of 2007, the outstanding value of U.S.-based securitizations was $11.6 trillion.[19] In comparison, at that time, banks in the United States had combined assets of just over $13 trillion.[20] Meanwhile, the total amount of U.S. corporate bonds outstanding was $5.9 trillion and the total government debt held by domestic and foreign investors amounted to $4.5 trillion, each a fraction of the securitization market.[21] What is clear from these numbers is that the U.S. banks lack sufficient capital to fulfill the demands of the U.S. economy. For consumers, the lack of capital stemming from the demise of the securitization market will manifest itself in higher interest costs for homeownership and less capital for other consumer credit demands. Thus, securitization has become essential to the U.S. economy, and the loss of this avenue of finance will restrict the flow of capital for decades to come.

Furthermore, without private securitization, the U.S. mortgage market will become dependent on the government and the banks for funding. In 2002, when I was researching the benefits of creating a Canadian securitization market, I determined that a mortgage market without competition from a securitization market created an oligopoly for the banks and easily added 1 percent to the annual interest rate of every mortgage (thereby increasing monthly mortgage interest cost about 25 percent in today's mortgage interest rate market). It also has the effect of concentrating the interest rate and the credit risk of mortgage lending in the nation's largest financial institutions, making those institutions—and thus the U.S. economy—more vulnerable to ordinary interest and unemployment rate fluctuations, credit risk, and other systemic risks. If we deem certain banks "too big to fail" due to their importance to the overall economy, it is even more critical that we protect the securitization system, which is far bigger than even the largest banks and critical to the safety and survival of financial institutions as a whole.

We are at a critical juncture in our nation's history where we must decide if we are going to have a private sector mortgage market or a *de facto* government-controlled mortgage market. It is my firm belief that private investment is essential to the success of any MBS market. Historically, the private sector has been the financier of choice for the United States, but the stigma of the mortgage crisis has tarnished the system's reputation. Today, the private securitization market is frozen, not because of a lack of demand for home loans but because investors believe that the risks of investing in U.S. MBS are so large and unquantifiable that government guarantees are required. Few would dispute that it is both impractical and unsustainable to have the U.S. government guarantee all future mortgages in this country. To resurrect and fund a private label market, we must win investors back with a system that is honest and transparent and that does not create perverse incentives or allow participants to defraud one another.

Returning to the theme with which I began this chapter, the purpose of a mortgage origination and intermediation system is to provide an efficient bridge between the consumers and the providers of capital, not to enrich the banks or the arrangers of transactions. To accomplish this, the economic interests of all parties must be better aligned and no participant—originator, investor, arranger or homeowner—should automatically "win" just by showing up, at the expense of other participants in the transaction. Instead, the objective is to create a mortgage finance system where participants win only if they ably perform their particular function in creating a viable investment. If structured properly, such a system will be stable and will not add significant systemic risk to the economy. However, given the size of the mortgage market, any weak point or logical flaw in such a system has the potential to cause harm to other parties and the economy as a whole. In short, securitization is far too important to leave up to politics or chance. Given that non-government supported mortgage securitization activity in the United States, as well as the rest of the world, has virtually ground to a halt, the time to deal with these issues and build a more logical and efficient mortgage system is now. The mortgage intermediation system that finances the hopes and dreams of America is *way too big to fail*.

"Those who don't know history are destined to repeat it."

—*Edmund Burke*

CHAPTER 2

The History of the US Mortgage Market

The United States has had a functioning mortgage credit system since the early 1800s. While there have been periods when the cost of mortgages and/or the requirements to qualify were prohibitively high, such as during the Great Depression and in the early 1980s, credit has generally been available to those with the desire and the means to finance a home at a reasonable rate of interest. To understand why this has been the case, we first explore the key elements of any functioning mortgage credit system. We then examine the history of the U.S. mortgage market to understand how it developed certain flaws that contributed to the mortgage crisis.

Mortgage Basics

The first requirement of a successful mortgage system is a legally supported method for recording the ownership of real property—the collateral that is backing, or securing, individual mortgage loans. This element is critical because purchasers of real property and the financiers of such purchases must be able to determine with a high degree of certainty who owns the property and gain comfort that no third party will appear after the purchase and challenge the validity of the transfer. The United States has a strong title system that originated during the colonial period and was formalized with the land grants and homesteading expansions of the 1800s.* This system constitutes the legal foundation for home ownership in the United States, and while it has been challenged and is under tremendous pressure, the basic system has held up.

The second requirement of a functioning mortgage credit market is a system enabling the enforcement of legally binding mortgage contracts. A mortgage is nothing more than a contract between a lender and a borrower for a loan that will assist the borrower in purchasing or financing a piece of real property. The contract spells out loan repayment terms and what happens if the borrower defaults or is unable to pay back the loan. In all mortgage contracts, the property serves as collateral, meaning that if the buyer is unable to repay the loan, the lender has the right to seize the property, sell it in a foreclosure sale, and recoup the funds it lent from the proceeds of that sale. Thus, to induce lenders to provide affordable capital to prospective home buyers, it is critical that they be able to enforce such contracts and limit the downside risk of mortgage lending.

Another important characteristic of a working mortgage system is the availability of long-term mortgage credit. The longer the term of a mortgage, the lower the borrower's monthly payments or, to put

---

* The United States currently has an outdated deed recording system that, in many localities, still relies on physical books created in the days before computerization. While not a direct contributor to the mortgage crisis, the existing title system does contain inefficiencies that led to the creation of Mortgage Electronic Registration Systems, Inc. (MERS), a national electronic mortgage registry created and used by banks to save costs—some would say to cut corners—in the physical deed recording process. The emergence of MERS as the dominant method of mortgage record keeping (it serves as the mortgagee of record on over 60 percent of outstanding residential mortgage loans) contributed to the onset of a foreclosure crisis in 2010, in which questions emerged over who actually owned and had standing to foreclose on the properties at the heart of the mortgage crisis. These challenges led to a temporary freeze in foreclosures by all four major servicers, a spike in the legal costs arising out of the foreclosure process, and the launch of an investigation by all fifty state Attorneys General into the foreclosure process in October 2010. Later in this book, we will discuss ways to overhaul this system and prevent these problems from cropping up again.

---

it another way, longer term mortgages allow borrowers to finance the purchase of a more valuable home for the same monthly payment. The standard mortgage term in the United States is thirty years, a long time for investors to have capital tied up. As discussed in chapter 1, there are many risks to mortgage investors stemming from such factors as changes in interest rates, home values, politics, contract enforcement, etc. In many countries, investors are generally unwilling to provide capital for long-term mortgages, especially in nations with weak title laws or legal systems that do not enforce contracts.

By contrast, the United States has historically been viewed as a stable environment with a stellar record in honoring contracts, so Americans have had the luxury of abundant long-term mortgage credit—credit that Americans have come to take for granted. Indeed, it is crucial to understand that *it is the sanctity of the mortgage contract in the United States that has engendered the ample supply of long-term credit for mortgage loans.* While Americans have come to expect cheap credit as a fact of life, if we destroy investor confidence in the U.S. legal system, these investors will no longer be willing to make long-term mortgage loans. The private market that has provided this type of credit to homeowners in the past will disappear for good if we do not take immediate corrective action.

The Role of Mortgage Finance

Proper legal safeguards for home ownership and mortgage lending form the foundation for a functioning mortgage market. Even with the proper legal safeguards in place, there would be an extremely limited market for first-time home buyers if there were no effective system for financing those mortgages. Without a mortgage finance market, there would be only two ways for someone to buy a house: pay cash or obtain financing from the seller. Those who already owned homes would be limited in their ability to "trade up," as it would likely take years or even decades to get enough capital out of one residence to buy the next one. Those who did not already own homes would rarely have enough capital in the bank to buy them. It does not take much imagination to realize that without mortgage finance, the dream of home ownership would only be possible for the wealthiest few.

The primary tool of mortgage finance has been, and remains, securitization. As readers will recall, securitization is the process of pooling individual assets, aggregating the cash flows from these assets, and creating securities backed by those cash flows that can be sold in the capital markets. The introduction of this structure allowed investors to hold a diversified piece of a large pool of mortgages, rather than absorbing the considerable risks that came with holding individual thirty-year home loans on their books. Because investor demand for securitized mortgages has generally been higher than demand for raw mortgages, securitization has led to competition among investors, thereby lowering homeowners' borrowing costs. The U.S. homeowner has benefited substantially from readily available and attractively priced mortgages since securitization was introduced. A brief overview of U.S. MBS market history illustrates the dramatic impact that mortgage finance has had on the accessibility of affordable credit.

The Creation of Government Mortgage Agencies

Mortgage lending in the United States was originally handled exclusively by local banks. As community members saved money and deposited it into savings accounts in their town's bank, those funds would be made available to others in the community through loans from the bank. Community members who were qualified were able to get loans, while those who maintained savings accounts benefitted by receiving interest on their savings. This local system had certain advantages: local banks generally had plenty of information about the creditworthiness of the borrowers in their communities, and because banks were forced to hold loans on their books until maturity, they were motivated to lend money only to those who were likely to repay. In most communities, however, it was rare that the demand for mortgage loans consistently equaled the amount of funds the bank had available for mortgage lending. In some cases, a bank had more savings on deposit than it could prudently lend out, causing the bank either to lend money imprudently, or simply sit on its cash, foregoing returns. In other cases, the demand from borrowers surpassed the availability of capital from local savers, meaning that the bank could charge higher interest rates on its mortgage loans and screen out all but the wealthiest community members during the application process.

As the U.S. population grew and migrated to the West and South, the demand for mortgage credit in those areas grew. At the same time, the East was experiencing a lower demand for mortgage credit but growing deposits. As the gulf between local demand for capital and its availability grew wider, it put strains on the historical model of local mortgage lending by local banks. This imbalance was solved in high growth areas by selling individual mortgage loans to banks and other whole loan investors in slower growth areas. Money flowed to the West and South, providing financiers with suitable investments and borrowers with the funding necessary for home purchases.

In the 1930s, the U.S. economy collapsed into the Great Depression and the value of homes fell precipitously. This crisis led to a dramatic rise in foreclosures and a series of bank failures, just as the nation would experience during the mortgage crisis some eighty years later. The government attempted to alleviate the mortgage problems stemming from the Great Depression by introducing new legislation, including the National Housing Act of 1934, which established the FHA. The role of the FHA was to provide mortgage insurance to private lenders to induce them to begin lending money again. This meant that when an approved lender made a loan that conformed to FHA interest rate and mortgage term standards, the FHA guaranteed the credit performance of that loan.

In 1938, as part of FDR's New Deal, the government created Fannie Mae, a government agency that also had as its purpose the promotion of private mortgage lending, especially to the middle class. Fannie Mae's primary method of encouragement was to purchase FHA-insured loans in the secondary market, thereby freeing up private lenders to originate more loans.[22] From 1938 to 1968, Fannie Mae was by far the largest institution buying mortgages from banks in the secondary market; it continued to play a major role in the U.S. mortgage market up to the mortgage crisis of 2007, and contributed significantly to that crisis, as we will explore in more detail later.

In 1968, Fannie Mae was split into two entities: an ostensibly private version of Fannie Mae (the publicly traded and stockholder-owned corporation that we now know) and government-owned and financed Ginnie Mae.[23] Fannie Mae, being publicly chartered but now privately owned, became known as a Government-Sponsored Enterprise (GSE): it had no explicit government guarantee but was believed to carry an implicit guarantee that the government would not allow it to fail. Ginnie Mae was chartered as another vehicle for encouraging home ownership, primarily by supporting the liquidity of FHA-insured mortgages.[24]

To accomplish this purpose, Ginnie Mae underwrote the first major effort to securitize mortgages in the United States in 1968 by creating a new financial instrument that involved pooling qualifying mortgages into trusts that allowed the cash flows from borrowers to be passed through to investors.[25] This financial instrument became known as a "pass-through security." Under the contracts governing these new financial products, Ginnie Mae "wrapped" or guaranteed these pass-through securities, meaning that if borrowers defaulted on their mortgages, the government would reimburse security holders for their losses after foreclosure.

To ensure that Fannie Mae and Freddie Mac were not taking on excessive risk, the GSEs established criteria for the loans that would be eligible for their programs. Loans that met all of the requirements, including size and underwriting standards, were called "conforming" loans. "Jumbo" loans, meaning loans that exceeded the agencies' size restrictions, were categorized as "non-conforming" loans, along with any loan that did not meet all underwriting standards. Because they were standardized and well understood, conforming loans were generally used as the collateral for the agency mortgage instruments sold to investors, resulting in the creation of standardized and well-understood securities.

These investment vehicles had significantly lower transaction costs associated with their sale than the underlying mortgages and were backed by Fannie Mae and Freddie Mac, which were considered to have U.S. government agency credit risk. These vehicles were less risky and more fungible than unsecuritized mortgages (also known as "whole loans"), allowing investors to trade them easily and obtain a more predictable rate of return. As a result, the market for conforming loans trading as agency pass-throughs quickly became, and has remained, more liquid and more efficient than the market for unsecuritized conforming loans. The introduction of government guarantees and the concurrent standardization of mortgage lending was thus a critical first step in the creation of a mortgage backed securities market in the United States.

Another significant step in the development of this market was the creation of Freddie Mac to compete with the now-private Fannie Mae and further promote the growth of the MBS market in 1970. Freddie Mac was originally owned by the Federal Home Loan Bank System, but it was later spun off, like Fannie Mae, into a GSE. In 1971, Freddie Mac issued its own mortgage securities (known as participation certificates) backed by privately originated mortgages.[26] Fannie Mae followed suit in 1981, issuing pass-throughs that were called, for the first time, "mortgage backed securities."[27]

In the fallout from the S&L crisis in the 1980s, discussed in further detail later in this chapter, many different types of loans that had been held by failed thrifts were in need of financing by the private sector. The nascent mortgage securitization market was there to serve as the vehicle for transferring ownership of those loans to the public markets. However, a method for dealing with the varying credit risk of the different loans had to be developed, and the "senior/subordinate" structure was the solution.* The senior/subordinate structure was a system that designated certain classes of securities as senior to others, meaning that they were entitled to payment priority over the junior or subordinated classes. This structure allowed the pool of mortgages to "self-insure" by asymmetrically splitting the credit risk and directing the credit losses to the subordinate class or classes of the securitization. The senior classes received a AAA (triple-A) credit rating from the rating agencies, while the lower, subordinated classes received lower ratings. The lowest classes were not rated at all, as they were the riskiest bonds and were essentially the equity in the transaction. Any losses in the pool of mortgages would be allocated first to the lowest class bond, commonly called the "first loss bond," before being allocated to each successively senior class.

The senior/subordinate class structure was a creative and welcome innovation. Though refinements to this basic senior/subordinate structure such as reserve funds and other so-called "credit enhancements" were introduced over the years, basic subordination has remained the preferred manner of financial alchemy used by Wall Street to obtain a triple-A credit level for the senior securities in its securitization

---

* In addition to senior/subordinate structure, there are a large number of permutations of risk distribution that the market has or could have adopted in structuring securitizations, several of which are presented and discussed in more detail in appendices V and VI.

---

trusts.* By definition, this method also requires the creation of junior securities that carry the bulk of the credit risk in the pool. Thus, as we will see, the senior/subordinate structure created the potential for major mortgage finance problems down the road, in that the originator was able to sell off entire classes of subordinated securities and their associated credit risk to other investors. This meant that a mortgage originator no longer had any financial stake in the loans it originated or the securitizations it produced.

In 1983, Freddie Mac issued the first Collateralized Mortgage Obligation (CMO),[28] a structure that facilitated the senior/subordinate structure and the division of bonds into different slices or "tranches" with varying risk characteristics to appeal to the preferences of different types of investors. Many of the agency pass-throughs also began to be structured as Real Estate Mortgage Investor Conduits (REMIC) by Wall Street. The REMIC structure took advantage of a section of the IRS tax code that allowed loans to be owned by a trust without being subject to "double taxation" or other negative tax implications.

These structural innovations opened the market to non-traditional mortgage investors by allowing traditional mortgages to be structured into a variety of securities with favorable tax treatment and customized risk characteristics. These features, when combined with the presence of an "agency" wrap or implied government guarantee, assuaged investor credit concerns regarding vast pools of conforming collateral, making this asset class far more attractive.

---

* It is interesting to note that the market structure that became standard in the industry during the late 1980s and early 1990s consisted of investors purchasing subordinate securities at a discount. This meant that in a scenario in which many homeowners prepaid or refinanced their mortgages rather than paying them off over time, the subordinate bonds would prove quite lucrative, as subordinate investors would receive any interest paid to date and have their principal paid back at par. This windfall would be due to a prepayment event, not good credit analysis.

The Birth of the Non-Agency Market

The combination of Ginnie Mae, Fannie Mae, and Freddie Mac was thus able to provide a steady supply of mortgage credit to the conforming sector of the mortgage market, but there remained large pools of collateral—the so-called "non-conforming loans" that did not meet strict GSE loan criteria—for which there was no mechanism for achieving such cost savings, risk reduction, or liquidity. Lenders holding such loans were forced to either keep them on their balance sheets or trade them as whole loans. The lack of guarantees associated with these loans meant that lawyers and property inspectors had to be hired whenever a whole loan was traded, pushing transaction costs even higher.

This all changed in the 1980s, when the first successful securitizations of non-conforming loans converted these historically illiquid assets into public securities. These successful securitizations of jumbo loans demonstrated that it was possible to create non-agency mortgage backed securities that would be attractive to investors. Almost overnight, a two-tiered market for trading mortgage loans emerged: agency MBS and non-agency or "private label" MBS.

Additional techniques were developed to bolster the credit quality and attractiveness of private label instruments and allow them to keep pace with their agency brethren. Private label MBS began to take advantage of both the REMIC section of the tax code and the credit enhancement of the senior/subordinate structure to offer a wide variety of attractive investment vehicles to investors. Private label underwriters also began to take advantage of another form of credit enhancement called the credit wrap or guarantee, generally provided by private guaranty or mortgage insurance companies, which guaranteed the performance of the non-agency securities.[*] The private label market

---

[*] These companies, just like the quasi-governmental entities they emulated, have all experienced significant financial difficulties as a result of the mortgage crisis of 2007.

was now able to create securities out of non-traditional mortgage loans that provided high returns to investors, while reducing credit risks and tax consequences to acceptable levels. The non-conforming sector of the mortgage market could thus take advantage of large, liquid capital markets that had previously existed only for agency paper.

The 1980s and the S&L Crisis

Savings and loans or thrifts are depository institutions created in the first half of the nineteenth century in the United States to help promote and facilitate homeownership for the working class. The original business model of this industry was to take short-term deposits and use that money to originate and hold fifteen- or thirty-year fixed-rate loans for aspiring homeowners. This was a simple business model that, with interest rates remaining constant, worked well for more than a century. But when the United States was hit with a period of historically unprecedented interest rate increases starting in the 1970s, it brought this system to its knees and resulted in the S&L crisis of the 1980s.

A closer look at the causes of this earlier crisis will reveal some striking similarities and lessons for evaluating the current mortgage crisis. Historically, the thrifts were limited in what they could pay to depositors for their demand deposits by a regulation known as Regulation Q (Reg. Q). Consequently, in the 1970s, when interest rates began to spike, savers had a profound economic incentive to move their savings from the local thrift and invest those funds in money market funds that paid a substantially higher rate of interest. As savers moved their money out of their bank accounts, the resulting disintermediation created a liquidity crisis for the thrifts. The interest ceilings that Reg. Q placed on savings accounts were ultimately relaxed in the 1980s, so the thrifts could again compete with the money market funds for investors. However, when thrifts began clamoring to pay market interest rates to attract deposits, the banks had to pay more for these deposits than they were earning on the many loans on their balance sheets. The thrifts proceeded to absorb this negative margin or interest rate spread as a direct loss, causing them to "bleed to death."

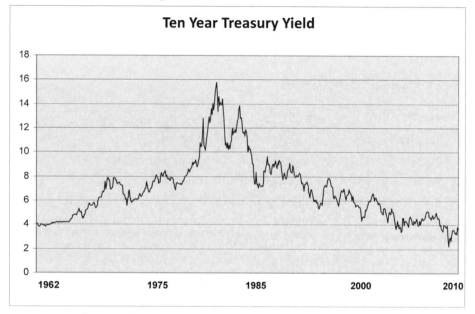

SOURCE: BLOOMBERG L.P., CUSTOM GRAPH, INDEX: GT10,
GENERATED USING BLOOMBERG TERMINAL ON APRIL 15, 2011.

The federal government responded to the resulting thrift liquidity and solvency crisis by encouraging the healthy thrifts to acquire those in distress. In addition, the Federal Savings and Loan Insurance Corporation (FSLIC), the government entity that insured savings and loan deposits, ran out of cash, so the government allowed the banks to count goodwill—an intangible asset—as an asset for capital purposes. While this helped bring the thrifts into compliance with their capital requirements, it did not put cash into their hands and meant that they were operating without any real capital. Nevertheless, the hope was that this would buy the thrifts time to "earn their way out" of the problem.

To help the thrifts return to profitability, the government also relaxed the regulations limiting the thrifts' permitted investments. This had the intended effect of allowing the thrifts to put capital into higher margin lines of business such as construction and commercial loans. As would be expected given the higher margins, these loans also carried with them much higher levels of risk. Many of the thrift owners had little expertise in evaluating these types of riskier investments, but it mattered little to them, because they had little or none of their own capital or their customers' capital at risk. Instead, given the chance to play with other people's money (i.e., government-insured deposits), they eagerly invested in high-risk ventures in the hope of returning their institutions to solvency. In hindsight, the high likelihood that this "double-or-nothing" strategy would lead to a financial debacle is obvious. Unfortunately, it was not so obvious to banks and regulators in the early 1980s.

By the end of the 1980s, the S&L experiment had ended very badly, and 296 thrifts had failed. By the mid-1990s, 747 thrifts had failed. All in, these failures cost the taxpayers a total of $125 billion and resulted in the government takeover of $519 billion of assets from failed thrifts.[29] It was, as everyone thought at the time, the financial debacle to end all financial debacles. As recent events have illustrated, when history is not well understood, it will surely be repeated.

The Rapid Rise and Fall of Subprime Lending

During the decade from 1995 through 2005, the United States experienced one of the greatest periods of home price appreciation (HPA) in its history. Fueled by such factors as an investor exodus from stocks after the dot-com bust in 2000, historically low interest rates, and an influx of foreign capital, this housing bubble created a perfect storm that exposed the flaws in the senior/subordinate securitization structure. Borrowers who might have encountered trouble paying their mortgages were able to either refinance their homes at historically low interest rates, or "flip" their properties (buy and sell them in a short period for a profit). Median home prices continued, year after year, to rise to dizzying new heights (see the charts that follow). The result was an extended period of suppressed delinquency rates in the United States based on the frequent prepayment of mortgages.

During this period, some hedge funds reaped outsized returns from their investments in subordinate MBS tranches. This success attracted significant attention and these hedge funds received massive inflows of capital. Other hedge funds and investors also sought to get in on the action, and even investors wary of this new product had to join in or be left in the dust by the returns achieved by their competitors. This had the effect of both driving up the demand for additional credit risk and driving down the cost of credit enhancement. There were two ways for lenders and other market participants to respond to this increased demand: make a greater volume of loans to qualified individuals or make riskier loans to less-qualified individuals. The markets responded in the early 2000s by doing both.

In addition to pounding the pavement in search of additional prime lending candidates, originators began to relax their guidelines to create more lending opportunities. With investors demanding a greater and greater volume of mortgage backed securities, Wall Street was more than willing to provide investments based on, and intermediate the credit risk of, these new, riskier loans. With Wall Street investment banks now willing to buy up any loans they could get their hands on to serve as the raw materials for securitization, originators gladly began arranging loans for a new group of prospective homeowners: those with low incomes and weakened credit ratings. "Subprime lending" became an avenue for the creation of such loans, broadening a class of low- or no-documentation loans formerly reserved for wealthy individuals who did not wish to disclose all of their income. These subprime loans did not necessarily require substantial down payments from borrowers or verification of the borrower's stated income. Borrowers, who

Home Price Appreciation and Related Trends

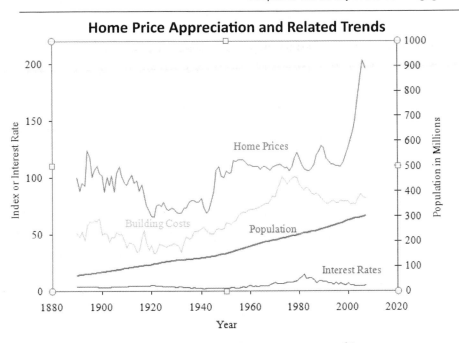

SOURCE: ROBERT SHILLER, *IRRATIONAL EXUBERANCE*, 2ND ED. (PRINCETON: PRINCETON UNIVERSITY PRESS, 2005), FIG. 2.1. DATA UPDATED BY AUTHOR 2007, HTTP://WWW.IRRATIONALEXUBERANCE.COM/FIG2.1SHILLER.XLS. (ACCESSED APRIL 12, 2011)

Median and Average Sales Prices of New Homes Sold in the United States

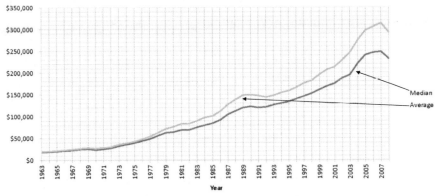

SOURCE: U.S. CENSUS BUREAU, "MEDIAN AND AVERAGE SALES PRICES OF NEW HOMES SOLD IN UNITED STATES—ANNUAL DATA," 2009, HTTP:// WWW.CENSUS.GOV/CONST/USPRICEANN.PDF (ACCESSED APRIL 12, 2011).

could not have qualified for any loans a year or two before, could now qualify for jumbo loans simply by writing high income numbers on their loan applications.

Under these conditions, and as a result of the senior/subordinate structure, mortgage originators, the former gatekeepers of credit quality, stopped caring as much about whether these loans were being made wisely (i.e., to borrowers who had the ability to repay the loans). Instead, lenders began originating ever-increasing volumes of loans regardless of the credit risk—loans that they could immediately turn around and sell to Wall Street, which could likewise turn around and sell slices of that risk to investors. As long as HPA continued at its torrid pace, and investors were protected by the senior/subordinate structure and other forms of credit enhancement, this game of "hot potato" proved very profitable. The game was so dependent on the idea that housing prices would continue to rise and interest rates would remain low that when HPA leveled-off, the music stopped, and prepayment rates plummeted.

Securitization participants soon learned that when loans are not repaid, everyone in the deal is in trouble. Up to then, the innovation of the senior/subordinate structure had allowed for the deceptively oversized returns in the late 1990s through the mid-2000s, fueled the unsustainable growth in demand for mortgages, and concealed the cracks in the foundation of mortgage securitization. Because lenders and securitizers (also referred to as deal underwriters, issuers, or arrangers) could effectively sell off the entire credit risk of a transaction to someone else, concern for credit quality went out the window, creating substantial moral hazard. In addition, the outsized returns created a large flow of capital into subordinated mortgage securities, making it even cheaper to pass off the credit risk in an MBS transaction. It is important to recognize that while the housing bubble's burst would likely have caused a short-term depression in mortgage returns in any event, the senior/subordinate structure linked to protracted payment events led directly to the long-term disintegration of the entire mortgage market.

In addition to the creation of the senior/subordinate structure, Collateralized Debt Obligations (CDOs) also had a hand in the explosive and unsustainable growth in mortgage credit demand. A CDO took a portfolio of securities from different MBS trusts that had similar credit ratings and pooled them into a new security. The logic was that if there were a diversified portfolio of uncorrelated credits, the pool could sustain a credit loss from some of the underlying securities and still retain the credit integrity of its senior classes. The same hedge funds that were purchasing the MBS subordinates were also purchasing the riskiest credit classes from the CDO bonds. The senior bonds, generally viewed as virtually riskless, were often retained by the same Wall Street firms that brought these transactions to market.

As the market later learned, this process also had disastrous consequences. The entire underlying premise of the CDO securitization—that these risks were uncorrelated—was incorrect, as all of these risks proved dependent on the common factor of sustained HPA, but so long as U.S. home prices continued their meteoric rise, the market for CDOs created demand for additional subordinate mortgage credit that in turn spurred on the creation of additional risky mortgage loans.

The Post-Apocalyptic Mortgage Market

To put the mortgage crisis in perspective, it is important to reiterate that the total par value of outstanding securitizations at the peak of the market was approximately $11.6 trillion,[30] making it more than twice as large as the entire U.S. Treasury market. It is therefore not surprising that the collapse of the mortgage market had devastating repercussions for the nation's financial health. According to the FDIC, from 2001 through 2007, twenty-four banking institutions failed.[31] In 2008 alone, twenty-five U.S. banks went bust.[32] This number spiked to 140 failed banks in 2009,[33] followed by a whopping 157 lenders in 2010.[34]

The mortgage crisis had devastating effects on the entire economy, not just the participants in mortgage finance.

Nevertheless, private institutions were not the only ones hit hard. Fannie Mae and Freddie Mac were also devastated. As GSEs, they were not backed by the full faith and credit of the United States, even though it was widely assumed that the government would not let them default. On September 7, 2008, this assumption was confirmed when the FHFA placed both Fannie Mae and Freddie Mac in conservatorship, where they have been operating ever since. As of March 31, 2011, there was approximately $2.4 trillion of Fannie Mae-guaranteed fixed rate MBS outstanding and approximately $1.5 trillion of Freddie Mac-guaranteed fixed-rate MBS outstanding.[35] Ginnie Mae, operating as a U.S. government-owned GSE within the Department of Housing and Urban Development (HUD), does carry the full faith and credit of the United States. As of March 31, 2011, there was approximately $1 trillion of Ginnie Mae guaranteed fixed rate MBS outstanding.[36]

The delinquency rates on the loans underlying this vast pool of government-backed mortgage securities have been staggering. The GSEs, and thus American taxpayers, will suffer greatly from the mortgage crisis for years to come. According to *Mortgage News Daily*, as of the third quarter of 2010, "Fannie Mae and Freddie Mac have drawn down a total of $148 billion in Treasury funds since [they] were placed in federal conservatorship in August 2008."[37] Aside from the losses suffered by investors and taxpayers, another important consequence of the mortgage crisis has been the contraction of the market for new mortgages. In 2010, GSE issuance was about $1.4 trillion, down from $1.7 trillion in 2009.[38] Non-agency issuance of new loans has been virtually zero since 2008,[39] and any material issuance is not likely in the foreseeable future.

In addition to the GSEs that are regularly discussed, several other financial institutions have been placed into conservatorship by agencies of the U.S. government. The U.S. Central Federal Credit Union was akin to the "Fed" of the credit union world. Rather than providing services to consumers, U.S. Central provided services to other corporate credit unions, in essence acting as a credit union for credit unions. On March 20, 2009, the National Credit Union Administration (NCUA) placed U.S. Central into conservatorship.[40] Many of the large "corporate credit unions" have also been merged or taken over. It is safe to say that the credit union system is massively stressed and would have failed without the government bailout initiated in January 2009.

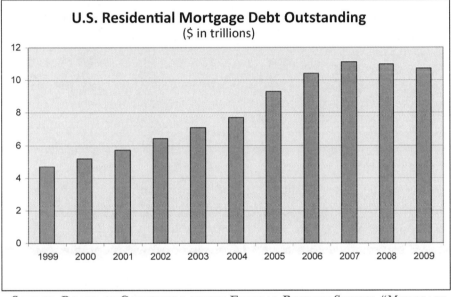

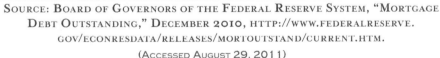

SOURCE: BOARD OF GOVERNORS OF THE FEDERAL RESERVE SYSTEM, "MORTGAGE DEBT OUTSTANDING," DECEMBER 2010, HTTP://WWW.FEDERALRESERVE. GOV/ECONRESDATA/RELEASES/MORTOUTSTAND/CURRENT.HTM. (ACCESSED AUGUST 29, 2011)

Takeaway: The Dangers of Undercapitalization

The S&L crisis resulted in large losses for investors and the U.S. government. This calamity, which took the form of credit losses from loans made by institutions, had its genesis in the interest rate movements of the 1970s and 1980s. Several lessons should have been learned after the S&L crisis but were not, as they were repeated during the onset of the recent crisis. We will return to these lessons during our discussion of how to fix this country's broken financial system, as they must be taken to heart if progress is to be made.

The first is that when the government provides guarantees, depositors become less concerned about the solvency of their depository institutions, meaning that banks can take on more risk without fear that depositors will leave and take their money to more conservative or safer institutions. The evidence thus suggests that deposit insurance creates a classic moral hazard problem. The safety net brings about the harm it was intended to prevent, because it actually encourages riskier behavior.[41]

Second, when capital requirements are relaxed, struggling institutions take on even greater risks as they try to earn their way out of their problems—the "double-or-nothing" approach. When these marginal banks later fail, the societal costs are much higher than if those banks had failed sooner.

The third lesson is that interest rate movements affect the way people and institutions behave. When there is a large interest rate movement, some players will be on the losing side. While having market players fail from time to time is entirely acceptable, it is not acceptable for numerous market participants to arrange their balance sheets so that with periodic changes in interest rates, their firms become insolvent. In this situation, failure is not acceptable since the costs are borne by the taxpayers or the general economy if the failure becomes systemic.

The final lesson is that accounting is not a real-time metric by which to assess risk. Owners and managers of institutions know when their capital is being depleted well before accounting reports indicate that their capital positions are at risk. They react to this information in rational ways, which is to say that they take large risks when their capital and solvency are in jeopardy. We should be careful that we do not allow those who are losing money to make a bad situation worse.

"The most important single central fact about a free market is that no exchange takes place unless both parties benefit."
—Milton Friedman

CHAPTER 3

The Mortgage Loan Cycle

For the purpose of evaluating the mortgage crisis and the path to recovery, it is also important to drill down and examine the building blocks of the mortgage system: individual mortgage loans. While obtaining a mortgage may seem straightforward to a consumer, the reality is that, from 2005 to 2007, the typical loan passed through many entities, each having different functions and motivations. Understanding the life cycle of these relatively straightforward debt instruments will allow the reader to appreciate why fixing the mortgage mess will be no simple matter.

The mortgage loan cycle begins when a prospective homeowner decides to buy a house and needs to borrow money to pay for it. The individual likely decides to go to a local mortgage originator and apply for a loan. Ordinarily, the individual must provide income, credit, and other financial information. If it is doing its job properly, the originator will verify all of this information for accuracy and adequacy. An independent appraiser must also verify the value of the home to be purchased. The borrower, with the help of the originator, considers what type of loan to take out from a range of options, such as a fixed- or variable-rate loan. The borrower must also decide how much of the purchase price to borrow and how much to pay up front in the form of a down payment. Historically, the most common U.S. mortgage has been the thirty-year fixed rate loan for 80 percent of the value of the home, with the borrower supplying the remaining 20 percent as a down payment on the property.

Once the value of the house is confirmed to meet the price offered, and the borrower is qualified for the size and type of loan selected, the loan is approved, the loan contracts are signed, and the prospective homeowner purchases the house on the closing date. When the loan is made, a lien on the property in the name of the lender is recorded at the county clerk's office. From the homeowner's perspective, this marks the conclusion of the bulk of the mortgage process, and from that point forward, the homeowner's only role is to make his or her monthly payments. However, if the lender elects to sell the mortgage into a securitization (as was the case with most first lien mortgages originated during the Boom Years), the closing date is only the beginning of the mortgage's journey. Most homeowners are unaware that mortgages travel through many different hands and are structured into a variety of securities with varying credit risk, prepayment risk, and payment duration. With the securitization market in full swing, it truly "took a village" to originate, administer, and transform a mortgage into a tradable security.

Let's run through the primary members of this "village" and their roles in the mortgage loan cycle. As mentioned earlier, the originator lent money* to the borrower for the purchase of the home and was expected to verify or "underwrite" the loan file (not to be confused with the underwriting of a securitization transaction) to ensure that the value of the underlying property was supported, the loan complied with all laws and regulations, and the borrower was likely to pay the loan back.

---

* I have phrased this description of the mortgage loan cycle in the past tense because, at the time of writing, no private mortgage securitization market is in existence, for all intents and purposes. I remain hopeful that this market will come back, but it is far from certain that it will.

While some mortgage loans remained on originators' books after they were made, the majority were sold to GSEs or Wall Street firms that pooled many loans with similar characteristics. These firms, referred to as underwriters, arrangers, or "sellers and sponsors," were successful if they arbitraged the market, thus earning fees for arranging the transactions. If arrangers could not sell mortgage securities for more than they paid for a pool of mortgages, the prospective mortgage transaction would not happen, as arrangers would lose money.

When a loan was conforming, it was usually sold to Fannie Mae or Freddie Mac to be wrapped and sold as a simple pass-through security or structured into a REMIC.* If the loan was non-conforming, it was likely aggregated with several hundred or several thousand similar loans and placed in a pool of loans in a private label REMIC trust. As a general rule, the homeowner would not have been aware that his or her loan had been securitized or that the ownership had changed. The homeowner still remitted the same monthly payment to the servicer of his or her loan.

The servicer of the loan was often the bank that originated it, but the servicer could also sell or transfer its servicing rights to others. Servicing rights are valuable because servicers receive a portion of the monthly interest earned on the loan and took out this fee before the proceeds were distributed to the owner(s) of the loan. In return for this fee, the servicer was responsible for sending an invoice to the homeowner each

---

* As discussed in the previous chapter, a REMIC is an investment vehicle that is granted federal tax-exempt status by the IRS (though the income received by bondholders is still subject to federal income tax). However, the term REMIC is used more generally to refer to a pass-through in which the risk associated with the underlying collateral is divided up in an asymmetric manner. For example, some REMICs are composed of long-term payment securities and short-term payment securities derived from the same pool of loans. Though REMICs do not create or eliminate risk, as the classes of a REMIC must aggregate to the exact collateral of the underlying pool, they are effective at tailoring risk levels to the tolerances of different investors. Though the private label bonds issued by Wall Street firms have been given several names over the years, including Collateralized Mortgage Obligation (CMO) and REMIC, I use the term REMIC, where possible, for consistency.

month, collecting the homeowner's payments, and distributing the funds to the ultimate owner(s) of the loan. For example, if the loan was owned by a bank, the servicer remitted the borrower's payments directly to that bank. However, if the loan was sold into a mortgage pool used to create bonds, the servicer remitted the money to a paying agent whose function was to distribute the correct amounts to various bondholders. The servicer was also contractually obligated to take action when the homeowner failed to make a monthly payment and, ultimately, to foreclose on the property if the homeowner defaulted on his or her mortgage obligation.

The investors in mortgage bonds, also known as certificate holders or bondholders, were typically money managers, hedge funds, life insurance companies, college endowments, pension funds, IRA investments, banks, or sovereign wealth funds, among others. Different investors purchased different classes of REMIC bonds, and investors typically had no interest in purchasing an entire mortgage securitization. Instead, they bought bonds with the timing and risk characteristics that best fit their investment needs.

To feel comfortable that what they were buying carried the appropriate level of risk, investors relied on rating agencies to analyze mortgage bonds and assess their likelihood of repayment. Rating agencies looked at the different classes of bonds in a structure and assigned ratings to each. The most secure bonds were rated AAA, the second most AA, then A, BBB, BB, and B and so on. Many investors bought only bonds that were considered investment grade, meaning bonds rated BBB or higher. Because bond prices varied directly with ratings, arrangers structured deals to create as many highly rated bonds as possible.

The level of seniority of the various classes of bonds determined the order in which investors would be repaid and the order in which investors would absorb any losses to the securitization. How soon investors were repaid depended on the cash flows coming into the trust from the underlying mortgages. Cash came into the trust when borrowers made their monthly mortgage payments of interest and principal or sold or refinanced their homes and paid off their loans early. Bondholders then received payments from these cash flows based on seniority.* If borrowers defaulted on their payments, this caused losses to accrue to the trust, which were then allocated to the most junior bondholders first. Most private label MBS structures were set up so that the most junior class of bondholders absorbed all of the credit losses until its principal was depleted, at which point the next most junior class of bondholders took the next set of losses and so on, up the credit stack to successively more senior classes of bonds. When losses reached the top or most senior class of bonds, that bond would absorb all of the remaining losses. This hierarchy of cash disbursements and allocations of loss is called a "credit waterfall."

In addition to relying on the ratings given to their bonds, investors also sought comfort regarding their MBS investments in the form of representations and warranties provided by the originator(s) and arranger(s) of a deal. Typically, an originator would make representations ("reps") and warranties regarding the quality of their origination practices and the risk characteristics of their loans, including a representation that they would follow their own published underwriting guidelines. An arranger of a trust would often adopt the reps and warranties of the originator(s) as their own or make a separate set of representations regarding the quality and risk characteristics of the loan pool. Most trust agreements provided bondholders with the right to force originators or arrangers to repurchase or "cure" any loans found to breach these reps and warranties or to substitute properly originated loans in place of defective ones. As

---

* Note that prepayments can affect bondholders in different ways, depending on the structure of the MBS transaction. Often, junior bondholders stand to benefit most from a high rate of prepayment, because they bought their bonds at a discount based on credit risk, while senior bondholders that paid a premium for their bonds with the goal of being repaid over a longer time horizon would be harmed by a high prepayment rate.

we will see later, while these so-called "repurchase rights" appeared quite strong on paper, enforcing them would prove to be difficult for bondholders.

If a loan was sold into a securitization trust, the ownership of the loan was officially transferred to that trust. When the cash flows from those loans were structured into securities and sold to investors, the ownership of the trust and its contents was effectively transferred to those investors. At that point, the originator no longer had any ownership position in the underlying mortgage loans, though it may have still held servicing rights to those loans. This complete transfer of ownership was so important that, for mortgage bonds to be rated by the rating agencies and accepted by investors, REMICs also received a "true sale opinion" to this effect from a reputable law firm. This law firm would provide a letter containing its legal opinion that the owner of the underlying collateral was now the REMIC trust rather than the originator.* The transfer of ownership of the loans, the collection and distribution of payments through the waterfall, and nearly all other steps of REMIC formation described earlier were overseen by the trustee, an entity that was charged with acting as the fiduciary of the bondholders or investors in the REMIC trust.

These processes and all other aspects of the operation of the securitization were detailed in the PSA, the all-encompassing legal document that specified the rights and responsibilities of the deal participants.† This document typically incorporated by reference agreements between homeowners, originators, servicers, trustees, and other deal

---

* As we will discuss, the lack of understanding on the part of lawmakers regarding the results of this process and who ultimately came to own the loans at issue has been one of the biggest reasons that government efforts to mitigate the mortgage crisis have failed miserably.

† These documents tended to be derived from a common template and, as such, featured many similarities across different trusts, especially those issued by a common underwriter. However, each PSA had its own unique elements, depending on the intent of the particular parties to that contract, making broad generalizations about the terms of these agreements difficult.

participants. For the mortgage market to operate, it was critically important that contracts bound each of the deal participants together and ensured that all participants would perform as agreed. I cannot stress enough how important the concept of respect for contracts has been to the success of mortgage transactions in particular and of our private ownership society in general.

The biggest challenges for mortgage securitizations have, invariably, surrounded the handling of missed payments, extra payments, or prepayments by borrowers. That is, if enough borrowers in a particular trust are delinquent on their mortgages or prepay their mortgages faster than anticipated, MBS cash flows are impacted, and losses begin to accrue to the securitization and its investors. If the underlying loans default, these losses are passed through to investors. If the underlying loans are prepaid too fast, likely as a result of a decline in interest rates, investors' principal is returned sooner than anticipated and must be reinvested in a lower interest rate environment. If, on the other hand, interest rates increase, the underlying mortgages prepay more slowly than bondholders anticipated, preventing investors from redeploying capital at the higher market rates. Each of these outcomes imposes losses on mortgage investors.

Let's go back and view the life of a mortgage from the perspective of the homeowner, examining each of the several choices with which that individual is faced. The homeowner is contractually obligated to remit and owes a monthly payment on his or her mortgage, but this does not mean that he or she is without choices. Every month, the homeowner decides among several options for dealing with the loan, each of which is covered by the homeowner's mortgage contract. These choices include the following:

1. The homeowner can make his or her regular monthly mortgage payment covering interest on the loan, taxes, insurance, and principal reduction. As the homeowner makes each successive monthly payment, he or she will slowly pay back or "amortize" the loan over

time. If the homeowner continues to make payments until the loan is paid off, the mortgage lien is retired (and the homeowner can host a mortgage burning party).

2. The homeowner can make higher payments than the regular monthly payments. The excess amounts will be applied to the principal balance, and the homeowner will have the "mortgage burning party" earlier than stipulated in the mortgage loan.

3. The homeowner can pay off the loan all at once, because he or she has sold the property, refinanced the loan, or come into enough cash to be able to pay it off. In the standard thirty-year mortgage in the U.S., a homeowner can pay off a mortgage at any time without penalty.

4. The homeowner can cease making full payments. If the homeowner can later make up those payments and any late fees incurred during delinquency, the mortgage will be brought current, and the homeowner can return to making regular payments. However, if the homeowner cannot make up those payments, the foreclosure process will eventually be initiated and the property auctioned off on the steps of the local courthouse. The lien holders and the servicers will then be paid off, to the extent possible, from the proceeds of the foreclosure sale. If any money remains after these parties are paid, the former homeowner will receive the balance. In the event that the proceeds are insufficient to pay the loan off in full, the trust takes a credit loss, and the loss flows through the credit waterfall in the securitization. In this case, the loss is allocated to the most junior class of securities still in existence.

Besides this last option, two other options are available to the homeowner who cannot make regular monthly payments or pay off the debt. Neither of these options is covered by the original mortgage contract, so they must be negotiated by the homeowner.

First, the homeowner can sell the property for less than the unpaid principal balance of the mortgage in a process known as a "short sale." This option is available only with the consent of the servicer (and usually the trustee) as the representative of the investors. The advantage to the homeowner of completing a short sale is that his or her credit rating might be less adversely affected than it would be in a foreclosure, and the borrower might receive a cash payment from the lender to expedite the resolution of the defaulted loan. This is often called "cash for keys."

Second, the homeowner can renegotiate the terms of the mortgage and reduce the principal balance or monthly payment amount, a process called a loan modification or workout. A mortgage note can be restructured only if the owner is willing to agree to the changes. If the entire note is held by one entity, such as a bank, this is a straightforward process: the borrower meets with the owner of the mortgage note to discuss his or her ability to pay and to negotiate modifications to the mortgage. However, if a securitization trust owns the mortgage note at issue, there is often no contractually easy or practical process by which to modify the terms of the note.

During the mortgage crisis, when a record number of borrowers began defaulting on their mortgage obligations and facing foreclosure, voters placed tremendous political pressure on government officials to mitigate the foreclosure rate. This prompted officials to undertake numerous initiatives aimed at fixing this problem, all of which turned to loan modifications as the panacea. At first, they passed legislation offering cash incentives to servicers to modify loans held in securitization. However, because most servicers had no contractually viable method, under the terms of their PSAs, to effectuate the workouts urged by Washington, these programs failed to result in substantial modifications. Politicians responded by encouraging servicers to ignore the terms of these PSAs with legislation attempting to provide legal safe harbor or legal protection to the servicers if they should succeed in modifying loans.

These efforts were the result of a fundamental misunderstanding by politicians of the ownership structure of securitized loans, as described in this chapter, and the interests of the parties involved. In particular, these purported solutions ignored the fact that the servicers responsible for determining whether a loan should be modified *did not own these loans*. Servicers were contractually obligated to service loans in the best interests of the ultimate bondholders, but lacked economic incentives to determine whether a loan modification would be in the best long-term interest of those investors. Instead, as we will see, servicers had significant conflicts of interest that caused them to act contrary to bondholder wishes and interests. These conflicts, and government officials' failure to recognize them, led directly to my lawsuit against Countrywide in 2008.

"Cheating is more honorable than stealing."

—*German proverb*

CHAPTER 4

The Mortgage Crisis of 2007

Now that we have developed an understanding of the history of mortgage finance and its key players, we have a framework for evaluating the environment and events that led up to the mortgage crisis. In particular, we must look at each of the participants, their incentives, and how they reacted to an unprecedented period of low interest rates at the beginning of the twenty-first century.

Though the mortgage crisis came into public view in the summer of 2007, its roots took hold many years earlier, after the collapse of high-tech stocks in 2000. When the stock market crashed that year, the Federal Reserve reacted by cutting short-term interest rates, a defensible move in that environment. But the Fed then continued to hold rates at historically low levels for several years after the dot-com crisis had passed, including holding them as low as 1 percent for two full years. This added economic fuel to the U.S. economy, but it also sowed the seeds for another bust, which eventually manifested as the U.S. mortgage crisis.

In a nutshell, here's how it happened. Sharply lower federal funds rates caused a corresponding decrease in mortgage rates. Even after the economy had recovered, the Fed held interest rates at rock-bottom levels for an extended period. Home prices appreciated because the economy was growing while the cost of financing a home was dropping. At the same time, restrictive land use regulations in certain metropolitan areas artificially decreased the supply of available housing in the more desirable markets, sending housing prices in those key areas skyrocketing.[42] Many new home buyers, for whom the dream of homeownership was suddenly within reach, entered the market, while others traded up from modest to pricier homes. Soon, the protracted period of home price appreciation and low mortgage rates attracted speculators who saw the opportunity to turn a quick profit by flipping properties. Even homeowners who stayed in their houses enjoyed the boom. Those who were able to refinance their mortgages at lower rates did so, and as rates fell, there were massive and repeated mortgage refinancing waves. Many chose to take cash out of their homes and increase the size of their mortgages. In 2002 to 2003, the mortgage refinancing index hit levels impossible to imagine (see the chart that follows) as the entire home-owning population had the opportunity to refinance whenever interest rates dropped.

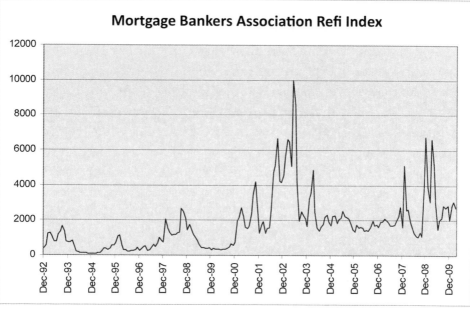

SOURCE: BLOOMBERG L.P., CUSTOM GRAPH, INDEX: MBAVREFI, GENERATED USING BLOOMBERG TERMINAL ON AUGUST 6, 2010.

Borrowers also began entering into oversized mortgages that were well beyond their means to repay, expecting to either refinance later at a lower rate or flip the home if they could no longer afford it. When interest rates began to spike in 2004, refinancing was no longer an option. The Wall Street mortgage machine that had expanded its capacity to meet the oversized demand for housing in the first half of the decade had run out of prime candidates to keep its wheels turning. Next, it turned to less-creditworthy borrowers to fuel the process. While home prices continued to appreciate for a few years longer, common sense began to take hold as many realized that the housing market had become a bubble supported by easy subprime financing. Eventually, rationality returned to the housing market, as investors and home buyers began to doubt that home prices would continue upward forever.

When this unprecedented run of HPA came to end and home prices finally leveled off, many borrowers found they could not make their mortgage payments, refinance at lower rates, or recoup the unpaid principal balances of their loans by selling their homes. Those who had enough equity in their homes to try to sell rushed to do so, causing a flood of houses on the market. Soon, the supply of houses for sale exceeded the number of potential buyers. House prices that had leveled off now began to fall, and millions of people who could pay their mortgages stopped paying them because they were "underwater," meaning that the mortgage exceeded the current value of the house, resulting in negative equity. Once it was clear that millions of mortgages would not be paid off, panic gripped the financial markets, and the mortgage crisis of 2007 was in full swing.

As the housing market collapsed, the nest eggs of many homeowners shrank and consumers responded by cutting spending, thereby dragging the entire U.S. economy down further. Institutional investors watched in horror as their investments in mortgages and MBS started to suffer credit problems. Many who had invested in mortgages were highly leveraged, meaning a small percentage drop caused a disproportionate drop in wealth, and soon entire firms and banks were either collapsing or at risk of collapsing. It would not be long before the federal government was forced to step in and bail out numerous financial firms with billions of dollars of taxpayer money.

In the simplest terms, the mortgage crisis can be traced to a large number of borrowers failing to make their mortgage payments, but how did the United States get to the point where millions of people were suddenly unable to honor their contractual obligations? And how were these bad mortgages allowed to drag down major financial firms followed by the entire U.S. economy? To answer these questions, we must view the years leading up to the mortgage crisis through the eyes of the key players in the mortgage finance market.

Homeowners

The demand for mortgages springs from two sources: people who want to buy homes and people who want to refinance the homes they already own. During the years preceding the mortgage crisis, unusually low interest rates combined with a strong economy to create a huge demand for houses. Home prices appreciated quickly—so quickly, in fact, that they created a self-reinforcing cycle. Buyers were eager to buy houses before prices got even higher and mortgage interest rates went back up. Many people who had never owned homes before, and even those with poor credit and low incomes, decided to enter the housing market. A new type of mortgage product called the subprime loan was made available for the poor credit, low-income segment of the mortgage market. This product was riskier than a prime loan, but the voracious investor appetite for mortgage credit risk that existed at the time ensured that plenty of mortgage capital was made available to fund this new segment of homeowners.

Subprime loans had to be structured differently than prime loans, because the borrowers had less financial wherewithal. For example, subprime borrowers typically did not have the money to make down payments. Historically, U.S. homebuyers make a down payment of at least 10 to 20 percent of the home price. By contrast, in the subprime market, down payments were cut to 5 percent or even eliminated altogether. Banks began to make two mortgages on a property at one time. The first would be a mortgage for, say, 90 percent of the value of the house, and the second would be a mortgage for the remaining 10 percent. The second mortgage, as the junior lien, was considered the riskier mortgage and thus carried a higher interest rate. Typically, banks kept the higher-paying second mortgages on their books and sold the first mortgages into the securitization market.

Another strategy to attract subprime borrowers to the market was to offer low teaser rates. With this feature, the borrower would pay a low interest rate during the first twelve to thirty-six months of the mortgage, after which the rate would reset to a higher level. Many borrowers could make the initial payments but would have trouble making the higher payments when the rate went up. Homeowners and mortgage originators proceeded under the assumption that the house would appreciate in value and allow the borrower to sell the house for a quick profit or refinance into a new mortgage with another low teaser rate down the road. This strategy worked as long as housing prices went up and homeowners held onto their jobs.

Lenders also offered a loan product called the pay-option Adjustable Rate Mortgage (ARM), also known as the "pick-a-payment" loan or simply the "option ARM." This structure allowed homeowners to decide how much they were going to pay on their mortgage each month. The minimum payment was often substantially below the accrual rate on the loan, and any deficit would be added to the principal balance of the loan. If a borrower made only minimum payments each month, the outstanding balance could grow to between 110 percent and 125 percent of the original balance before it hit the maximum limit on negative amortization, at which point the borrower would be underwater. Once that limit was reached, the borrower's next monthly payment would be at a rate that fully amortized the ARM over its remaining term. This often resulted in substantial "payment shock" for the borrower, placing the borrower at great risk of being unable to afford further mortgage payments. Most borrowers who took out this type of loan counted on the ability to refinance to avoid experiencing payment shock. This meant that without continuing home price appreciation, this loan was virtually guaranteed to default.

Still another non-prime variant was the Alt-A loan. This product was generally characterized by reduced documentation requirements. Unlike conventional mortgage applications, these so-called "stated income" or "no doc" loans did not require the borrower to produce a W-2, income tax return, or any other form of income verification. Instead, the applicant could write down whatever income number came to mind without having to provide any supporting documentation. Mortgage originators frequently advised the applicant as to what income number needed to appear on the application to qualify the borrower for the mortgage. The temptation for income manipulation proved irresistible, and these came to be known as "liar loans."*

Though there were many variations on the theme of alternative mortgage products, all were intended to entice marginal buyers into the market. At the height of the origination boom, homeowners were even able to get a home without a down payment and walk away from the closing table with cash—*effectively financing homeownership at over 100 percent*! Because it is rare in most states for the borrower to be required to pay for any deficiency from a foreclosure sale out of personal assets, such products have the economic effect of creating a free option for the homeowner to bet on real estate. If home prices go up, the borrower can flip the property for an instant profit. If prices go down, the borrower can walk away from the property with no financial injury save for a tarnished credit score.† It is thus no wonder that millions of first-time buyers entered the real estate market during this time.

---

* Though Alt-A paper was designed bear a credit risk somewhere in the middle between prime and subprime, the limited documentation feature of Alt-A and the concomitant temptation to falsify income moved the credit risk associated with this product, and the ultimate delinquency rate on these loans, much closer to subprime.

† Furthermore, even after borrowers stopped making payments, they got to continue living in the home rent-free until foreclosure. Historically, foreclosure sales took six months to two years to complete. In the economic and political climate of the

The Boom Years also affected those who already owned homes. Home prices rose materially faster than home buyers' incomes. This appreciation in home prices provided homeowners with the opportunity and incentive to take cash out of their homes by refinancing. This was called "cash-out refinancing," and it was a way to obtain additional tax-advantaged debt, because in the United States, mortgage interest payments may be deducted from taxable income. Low interest rates and the opportunity to take cash out of one's home combined to create the same economic effect as a massive tax cut for the home-owning sector of the population. For homeowners who chose not to refinance their mortgages, there was the yet another way to take cash out of their homes: home equity loans that allowed mortgagees to borrow against the equity they had accumulated.

The net effect of all the mortgage activity was a massive increase in the debt levels of millions of Americans. So many highly risky loans were made to borrowers who were not creditworthy that, inevitably, there were many who could not make their payments. When foreclosures followed, the market was flooded with a glut of homes for sale, putting downward pressure on home prices. In turn, falling home prices created a negative feedback cycle, as many more borrowers began to find that it was not worthwhile to pay their mortgages. Many of these defaults were "strategic" defaults: the borrowers could have made the payments but elected not to, because they would have lost equity in the deal. Why make mortgage payments on a $300,000 mortgage when the house was worth only $250,000? Unless you expected housing prices to increase materially in the near future, you were throwing your money away. While some may levy a moral judgment against borrowers who took on debts they could not repay, the hard truth is that most of these borrowers were acting rationally to maximize their economic interests when faced with perverse incentives. Given the opportunity to take on

---

post-mortgage crisis era, foreclosures commonly take two years or longer. Many homeowners have now been living in houses for years without having made a down payment, many monthly mortgage payments, or any rent payments.

cheap, non-recourse debt against properties that might appreciate in value, and given that there was nothing inherently illegal about taking on excessive debt or risk, many borrowers could not resist.

While alternative mortgage products were often heralded during the Boom Years as furthering the American dream of homeownership, they ultimately resulted in an unimaginable nightmare for subprime borrowers, American taxpayers, and the entire global financial system. The net effect of the extended period of low interest rates and the financial edifice of mortgage securitization was thus to encourage overinvestment and overconsumption in housing. It is now clear that most subprime mortgage loans should never have been made, as they were unlikely to be repaid except by refinancing into a new loan or by selling the underlying property. As we will discuss later, if lenders choose to make these types of risky loans in the future, they should be forced to hold them in their own portfolios—that is, the loans should be ineligible for private label securitization. Otherwise, there is too much risk to both the homeowner and the investor.

Mortgage Originators

We should not place all of the blame for the mortgage fiasco at the feet of borrowers who had blemished credit records at the outset without recognizing that someone else had to be willing to make all of those risky loans. Who was minding the mortgage store? In principle, it should have been mortgage originators, the commercial and mortgage bank entities responsible for seeking out prospective borrowers, helping them through the loan application process, and verifying that these borrowers were qualified for the mortgages they sought. In other words, the loan originators, as the providers of capital to prospective homeowners, should have been the gatekeepers of mortgage finance.

In turn, this begs the question: if mortgage originators were responsible for providing the mortgage funds to borrowers, why were they so willing to make loans to borrowers who were unlikely to pay them back? The answer lies in the dispersion of risk that resulted from the process of securitization. In the years leading up to 2007, originators could sell every single mortgage loan they made, earning a fee on each, regardless of the loan's risk. Though they were producing a risky product, they could offload every bit of that risk onto others,* earning profits that allowed them to make and sell additional risky loans. Thus, mortgage originators were also acting rationally, given that their economic incentive was to maximize the fees they earned by originating and selling as many loans as possible.

In addition, these originators had to compete with the scores of other originators in the same market. They knew that if they refused to make a loan, a potential borrower would walk down the street to their competitor, who likely would make the loan because there was a market for it. Most originators therefore took the view that if someone up the mortgage finance food chain was willing to buy a product, that originator, rather than its competitor, should be the one to provide it. Who were they to tell Wall Street—the masters of risk diversification—which loans were too risky? Instead, their incentives encouraged quantity over quality, thereby contributing to the explosive growth of the subprime market.

The key players in the mortgage origination market were the origination arms of the "Big Four" banks—Bank of America, Citibank, J.P. Morgan Chase, and Wells Fargo—and the origination arms of the major investment banks—including Lehman Brothers, Merrill Lynch, Morgan Stanley, Goldman Sachs, Credit Suisse, and Bear Stearns. In addition, a number of independent mortgage lenders (the so-called "shadow banks") such as Countrywide, New Century, and IndyMac Bank, played a role. Many of the shadow banks and investment banks that fueled the housing boom either no longer exist or have been

---

* Later in this chapter, we discuss how originators retained some risk of being forced to repurchase loans that did not meet quality control guidelines, but due to structural flaws in the way securitizations were set up, the enforcement of these repurchase provisions was so difficult that most originators viewed the threat of significant repurchases to be remote.

absorbed by the Big Four. In fact, the majority of all mortgages are serviced today by one of the Big Four.

The surviving banks that acquired large subprime originators, such as Bank of America, which acquired Countrywide and Merrill Lynch, and J.P. Morgan, which acquired Bear Stearns and Washington Mutual, face significant contingent liability based on their prior origination activities. Originators set their own origination and underwriting standards. When they created loans and aggregated them into pools to be sold into securitizations during the Boom Years, these originators made contractual guarantees, called representations and warranties, regarding what standards they had followed and the fundamental characteristics of the loans they were selling. These reps and warranties were incorporated by reference into securitization agreements for the benefit of the other parties to the deal. Most PSAs stipulated that if a loan was later found to materially deviate from these representations, the loan would be subject to being repurchased by, or "put back" to, the lending bank. *Without being able to perform their own due diligence on the underlying loans, the investors' only assurance regarding the quality of their loan pools rested in these contractual guarantees.*

Unfortunately, the evidence emerging from subprime originations shows that originators largely ignored their standards and representations when they sold loans during the Boom Years. One could assume that these lenders thought they would be protected against repurchases by the high procedural hurdles investors face before they can enforce these obligations (which we will discuss in detail later). However, as of the completion of this book, banks are beginning to realize that they can't ignore this liability forever, and are being forced to deal with it.

For example, an interesting development is occurring as the final version of this book is being sent to press: a group of 22 investors is trying to settle claims with respect to 530 Countrywide trusts with an original balance of $424 billion and a current outstanding balance of $221 billion. These investors, some of whom are extremely influential in the money management and banking worlds, have the cooperation of Bank of New York, the trustee on the majority of Countrywide securitizations. Bank of New York, as part of this proposed settlement, has received full indemnification from Bank of America (Countrywide's alleged successor-in-interest after its purchase of the lender in 2008) against any suits arising from the proposed settlement. This proposed settlement is subject to judicial review and has already been challenged by several groups of investors and the Attorneys General of Delaware and New York, many of whom feel the terms of the settlement are too generous to Bank of America. New York Attorney General Eric Schneiderman has gone so far as to seek judicial leave to sue Bank of New York of fraud for its role in negotiating this settlement as trustee for the bondholders.

Many of the conflicts that we will discuss in detail in this book are highlighted by this proposed settlement: disparate interests among different investors; dependencies and complex interrelationships between investors, trustees, and servicers; disagreements over potential remedies; and vastly different calculations as to damages. While some form of large settlement will be necessary to help put the mortgage crisis behind us and move on to the next generation of mortgage securitization, such settlement(s) should be transparent and in the best interest of the damaged parties, not the perpetrators. A settlement that places expediency as the foremost goal will likely just prolong the mortgage crisis, as potential investors will feel as though the game is rigged against them and remain reluctant to invest their capital in the future U.S. housing market.

Indeed, as much we would like to put the problems of the mortgage crisis behind us, we cannot ignore the fact that the banks appear to have sold mortgage products that did not come close to matching the descriptions in the documents that they filed with the SEC or the documents they used to market these deals. Recent litigation has alleged that a large number of subprime loans originated in 2006 and 2007 contained material misrepresentations or deviated significantly from what was represented in legal documents filed with the SEC; in some cases, more than 50 percent of the loans in a given pool were allegedly defective.[43]

Dick Bowen, the business chief underwriter for correspondent lending in the Consumer Lending Group of Citigroup Mortgage, a man with thirty-five years of underwriting and structured finance experience, was in charge of evaluating the risk of Citibank's origination activities. Bowen testified before the Financial Crisis Inquiry Commission that even prime mortgages originated during this time largely failed to meet underwriting standards. The numbers cited in his testimony are astounding:

> The delegated flow channel purchased approximately $50 billion of prime mortgages annually...In mid-2006 I discovered that over 60% of these mortgages purchased and sold were defective. Because Citi had given reps and warrants to the investors that the mortgages were not defective, the investors could force Citi to repurchase many billions of dollars of these defective assets. This situation represented a large potential risk to the shareholders of Citigroup...I started issuing warnings in June of 2006 and attempted to get management to address these critical risk issues. These warnings continued through 2007 and went to all levels of the Consumer Lending Group... We continued to purchase and sell to investors even larger volumes of mortgages through 2007. And defective mortgages increased during 2007 to over 80% of production.[44]

As the originators, the banks were on the front line of the loan origination process. As the gatekeepers of mortgage credit, they could have most easily avoided the problems that led to the mortgage crisis. The importance of providing proper economic incentives to these parties so that they follow their own representations and warranties in any future mortgage system cannot be overstated.

Investors

Before turning to discuss the Wall Street firms that bought the mortgages and turned them into securities, it is important to understand the investor mentality prevailing at the time. Wall Street arrangers are essentially intermediaries, and although one can argue that part of their role is as trusted advisors, it is important to understand what investors—their customers—wanted at the time.

Many institutional investors such as insurance companies, pension funds, and other firms that invest for the long term are heavily regulated and may purchase only investment-grade securities, meaning those rated BBB and higher. For years, investment-grade MBS had provided these firms with secure investments that generated returns far higher than other investment-grade securities such as U.S. Treasuries. Investors were content to purchase the senior tranches of MBS deals, knowing that the subordinate bonds would take the earliest credit losses and preserve the performance of their investments. As we will discuss later in this chapter, the rating agencies failed to assess correctly the risks of MBS and CDOs by a wide margin.*

The big problem in creating MBS was what to do with the subordinate mortgage bonds that took the first credit losses via the senior-subordinate structure. There would have been no buyers for subordinate securities if they had been priced at their face value or par, so Wall Street solved this problem by pricing subordinate securities at a discount to par. The discounts were largest for the more deeply subordinated securities. The logic was that, while the coupon, or interest rate, might be only 6 percent, the investor could expect to capture a much higher return if the bond did not default and ultimately paid off at par or anything close.

---

* It is now apparent that rating agencies labeled many classes of MBSs as investment-grade when in fact the underlying mortgages could not deliver the quality implied by the ratings. At the time, these agencies were thought to be experts in assessing risk. It is interesting to consider whether investors can be faulted for trusting the determination of these so-called risk-assessment professionals.

Several boutique hedge funds had large holdings in subordinate mortgage bonds in the years leading up to the mortgage crisis. While these investors were credit experts, these bonds also provided them with a type of interest rate option. If interest rates went down and there was a prepayment wave, the investors received a windfall. If interest rates rose or remained constant, the investors hoped that the borrowers' credit quality would ensure that the bonds would continue to perform and the investors would receive their coupon payments. Thus, if an investor was comfortable with the credit on the underlying pool of loans, he or she made the decision to purchase the subordinate securities, believing that losses from the mortgage pool would be small and the investor would be amply rewarded for taking on such risk.

As noted earlier, the 2000s ushered in the largest prepayment wave the United States had ever experienced, and these deeply subordinated bonds performed in spectacular fashion. Bonds that were purchased for 20 cents on the dollar (or 20 percent of par) were, in some cases, paying off at par within a year or eighteen months. This payoff was in addition to the interest payments that subordinate bondholders had received during these twelve to eighteen months. These spectacular returns allowed small hedge funds with credit expertise and funds available for investment to grow exponentially. Some of the small funds had multiple years with triple-digit returns. Some funds saw their assets under management increase by a factor of one hundred. This provided those funds with inflows of new capital, which they were eager to turn around and invest in more subordinate MBS. This success attracted other funds with less credit expertise into subordinate MBS investing, and even they were successful, as virtually any investor in deeply subordinated bonds was rewarded when the prepayment wave hit. All this added up to a major infusion of cash into a relatively small sector of the MBS market, creating the demand for this market to expand rapidly.

The ability to intermediate the deeply subordinated securities had always been a challenge for private label MBS bankers, but suddenly, it became easier and more profitable for Wall Street to unload this type of risk. Given that there were new-found eager buyers of these securities, Wall Street obliged by creating massive numbers of new mortgage structures, each with massive credit risk, most of which was based in some part on the performance of newly minted subordinate securities.

Though every investor is familiar with the mantra that past performance is no guarantee of future results, it is understandable that so many investors flocked to throw money at the subordinated MBS that had provided such exceptional results in the years during the prepayment wave. As they watched their competitors post triple-digit returns years after year, it became harder and harder for investors to stand by and watch, even if they did not believe in the fundamentals underlying subprime securities. A logical retort to this was that investors, acting rationally, could choose *not* to invest rather than purchase credit-intensive securities that were overpriced and poorly underwritten. I note (not in the interest of self-promotion, but to show that it was possible) that I declined to put any subprime deals together or invest in any subprime securities, because I did not trust the underlying collateral.

Of course, I was investing my own funds, while most hedge fund managers handle other peoples' money, a distinction that changes the incentives dramatically. While it may have been sensible to avoid this subordinated subprime debt, one need only look at the economic incentives of the fund manager to understand why they did not. Fund managers are typically paid a 2 percent annual management fee based on the amount of principal under management, plus 20 percent of any profits. This compensation structure provides the fund manager with strong incentives to take additional investors' money, even when they know they can not effectively deploy it. Balancing out this quest for profits is another investing mantra with which most investors are familiar: markets can stay irrational a lot longer than they can stay solvent. Investors could be correct in predicting that subprime loans would blow up someday, but if they sat on the sidelines for three years waiting for that to happen, they could find themselves out of a job.

By examining these incentives, we can understand why I was in the minority of investors in choosing to abstain from subprime securities.

I am hesitant to blame particular participants for their actions in the mortgage crisis, because if we accept the economic theory that people are fundamentally motivated by self-interest, they are doing what economics predicts they will do. Rather than seek to change this fundamental quality of human nature, it makes more sense to change the incentive structure built into a financial system, so that it channels ordinary human motives into socially productive behavior. This philosophy is at the heart of the reforms to the traditional structured finance model that I propose in later chapters.

Wall Street

When the market began to demand greater amounts of mortgage debt, there were two options for meeting that demand: increase the number of mortgage loans or boost the amount of risk per loan. Around 2003, Wall Street, as the arrangers of the transactions, decided to do both. While firms continued to package and sell prime loans, they also began greatly increasing their production of subprime loans. To put this increase in perspective, in 2000, Wall Street securitized less than $25 billion of Alt-A assets; by 2005, that number had grown to more than *$300 billion*.[45] At the same time, what came to be labeled "prime" in 2005 would not generally have been considered "prime" in 2000. What was labeled as "subprime" in 2005 would never have been made at all in 2000. The underwriting standards that dictated these characterizations were being loosened, creating more credit risk per loan concurrently with the increased production of subprime loans.

With this change in risk appetite came a number of new financial innovations, each creating more risk for the investor while making it easier for prospective homeowners to get credit approval to purchase a home. The massive demand for bonds linked to mortgage credit fueled an equally massive overleveraging of the American home along with a glut of mortgages that could not have been made but for Wall Street's ability to sell mortgage credit risk to insatiable investors. Wall Street created new and creative ways to slice and dice mortgages into derivative upon derivative that leveraged the risk inherent in subprime loans (and ultimately amplified the harm caused by their failure). In particular, Wall Street firms created additional derivatives called Credit Default Swaps (CDSs), which allowed investors with no ownership stake in the underlying assets to place trillions of dollars of side bets on the success or failure of mortgage derivatives and the banks that created them.[46]

The Wall Street machine continued to hum along, churning out private label mortgage derivatives in ever-increasing numbers through the end of 2006. In early 2007, the collapse of two Bear Stearns hedge funds signaled to many that subprime mortgages had a high risk of not being repaid and would generate substantial losses upon foreclosure. Wall Street responded through the first half of 2007 with a frenzy of securitization of existing mortgages in the pipeline. The goal was to move rapidly souring mortgages off of the books of the financial institutions before the music stopped. In August 2007, as delinquencies spiked, the mortgage markets virtually froze. This brought a dawning of awareness that a significant problem was on our hands, though the extent of that problem was still unknown.

Warren Buffett had called derivatives "financial weapons of mass destruction" in 2002,[47] and his prophecy came true a few years later, even if he may not have foreseen the manner in which it would play out. When borrowers inevitably defaulted on the imprudent loans backing these trillions of dollars of derivatives, they knocked over the financial dominos that cascaded into the mortgage crisis of 2007. As alternative mortgage loans continued to unravel, they pulled down the entire U.S. economy, and people started to lose their jobs. This in turn created more people who were unable to pay their mortgages, further depressing housing prices in a vicious cycle of wealth disintegration.*

---

* It is important to note that the U.S. government introduced a number of programs to slow the mortgage collapse, but none of the programs encouraged homeowners to make their payments. The programs instead made it less expensive for homeowners to default, thereby making the crisis worse.

As banks and financial institutions revealed their massive holdings of mortgage-related investments and securities during 2007 and 2008, it became apparent that much of this mortgage credit exposure was concentrated in a small group of firms and funds. When these institutions were forced to write down the value of their distressed assets, many could not meet their capital requirements, and business-to-business lending started to dry up. The most highly leveraged firms, Bear Stearns and Lehman Brothers, ceased to exist, as the former was absorbed into J.P. Morgan Chase while the latter was allowed to fall into bankruptcy. As the banking system seized up due to lack of capital and fear of counterparty insolvency, the U.S. government interceded with financing and bailouts in an effort to prevent the collapse of the entire U.S. financial system.

As the details of this calamity came to light, a slew of claims began to be levied against Wall Street, ranging from the suggestion that these issuers were acting with insufficient transparency to accusations that Wall Street was blatantly defrauding its customers. Recent lawsuits include allegations that issuers' MBS offering documents did not accurately disclose the true nature of the underlying collateral, that issuers omitted material information about the inaccuracy of published bond ratings, and that issuers concealed their due diligence findings from investors that would have shown that loan pools contained massive deficiencies.[48] These allegations call into question the familiar refrain, heard time and again from Wall Street institutions, that they were "just giving their customers what they wanted."

Rating Agencies

Prior to the 1970s, rating agencies were paid to vet a particular security by the investors considering a purchase of that security. The security's issuer could not select the rating agency, and thus could not affect the rating of its securities. Issuers paying for a rating would have been viewed as an unacceptable conflict of interest. The business model of investors paying for ratings worked well until the advent of the Xerox machine. Once it became easy to copy and distribute reports, investors could easily get copies of reports without paying for them. Accordingly, in order to survive, the rating agencies had to find new sources of revenue. In the 1970s, the business model changed, and issuers began to pay the rating agencies. In this way, the conflict of interest previously viewed as unacceptable became the norm.

Today, rating agencies are hired and paid by the investment banks arranging the transactions or the issuers that hire the investment banks. Rating agencies are paid whether a deal is completed or not, so, in theory, an agency could refuse to rate a transaction or refuse to give it the rating the issuer wants. The reality, of course, is that this rarely happens, as each rating agency competes with the others for business. How much more business would a rating agency get from an issuer if a less-than-stellar rating kept a deal from being completed?

The fact that there were three major nationally recognized rating organizations vying for Wall Street's business, when only one or two would usually be used on a transaction, created perverse economic incentives for the agencies' treatment of MBS. Wall Street's primary goal was to generate as many AAA-rated bonds from a pool of mortgage loans as possible with the least amount of subordinated bonds, thereby maximizing profits by fetching the highest possible price for these bonds. Wall Street firms regularly "shopped" rating agencies to see which would optimize their deals. Accordingly, instead of competing on price or service, the rating agencies began to compete on what they would view was the least amount of subordination necessary to achieve an AAA rating on the rest of the bonds. This created a classic "race to the bottom" scenario where the agency willing to give the best ratings on the worst underlying collateral were favored, forcing others to match these standards to survive. This system frequently created absurd results. For example, it was not unusual for a single MBS deal during the Boom Years to have two rating agencies rating the senior securities and determining the subordinate level to achieve AAA ratings, while the other rating agency rated the subordinate bonds and decided on the appropriate "splits"—the division between the BB- and the BBB-rated bonds.

It is not hard to see how this system puts rating agency professionals in an untenable position. Bankers understand that they control the revenue stream of the rating agency and have the ability to stunt a rating agency professional's career growth. What young professional at a rating agency would want to stand up to a senior banker from a major firm, especially one that is telling the young professional that he doesn't understand what he's doing and is at risk of losing all future business from the bank? What about when, as is often the case, the young professional aspires to someday work for one of the large investment banks or hedge funds, which offer the most lucrative and venerated jobs on Wall Street? The young professional is overmatched; the lack of objectivity and the opportunity for pressure within such a system is unavoidable.

Government-Sponsored Enterprises

Fannie Mae and Freddie Mac had a regulatory requirement to maintain a balance between the interest rate exposure of their assets and their liabilities. However, as we have discussed, the historically low interest rates of the early 2000s resulted in massive and repeated prepayments of fixed-rate mortgages. This refinancing activity put stress on the GSEs and other financial institutions that expected their senior MBS assets to remain outstanding for a materially longer period. While this may sound trivial because prepayments result in these institutions having their principal repaid in full, a large prepayment wave creates a material economic event, especially if that institution is levered twenty or thirty to one. When an entity borrows five-year money to fund a five-year asset and that asset pays off in three months, the institution must reinvest those funds at a rate 1 percent or 2 percent lower than it was receiving before. If an institution's funding costs exceed its asset returns, this will cause financial bleeding, and if this goes on long enough, the institution will bleed to death.

The United States experienced this identical problem during the S&L crisis, but then it was caused by rising interest rates that left thrifts borrowing new money at rates much higher than they could recoup from their existing loans. This time, declining interest rates meant that Freddie Mac and Fannie Mae, whose liabilities were generally based on a longer time horizon than their assets, owed high rates of interest on their existing long-term liabilities and had trouble finding new investments that offered a comparably high rate of return. Of course, when the duration of assets and liabilities are matched, there is no problem—interest costs and interest income fluctuate at the same rate and offset one another—but in the early 2000s, mortgages prepaid faster than anyone anticipated and left Fannie Mae and Freddie Mac with reported funding mismatches that hit dangerously high levels in July 2002.[49] This was despite the fact that the GSEs determined their own methodologies for spotting mismatches and had the flexibility to amend the methodology on an as-needed basis.

The extent of the problems at the GSEs first became public in June 2003, when Freddie Mac announced that its earnings for the past three years would have to be restated by some $5 billion.[50] The purported reasons for this understatement included a "lack of sufficient accounting expertise and internal control and management weaknesses" as well as efforts to "smooth out" or reduce volatility in reported earnings.[51] Fannie Mae's regulator made similar disclosures regarding the larger GSE in September 2004,[52] which were soon followed by an agreement between the regulator and Fannie Mae to address these accounting issues.[53] Provided with an opportunity to clean up this mess behind closed doors, Fannie Mae did not file timely financial results or hold shareholder meetings from 2004 to 2007, and only in mid-2007 did Fannie Mae begin to report on its $6.3 billion dollar profit *overstatement*, which dated back to 2001.[54] Similarly, Freddie Mac did not release quarterly financial results between 2002 and 2007 and only began to report on its profit understatement, which dated back to 2000, in late 2007.[55] These accounting fiascos provided

Fannie Mae and Freddie Mac with several years to take risks that they hoped would help them "earn their way out" of their financial problems.

In the meantime, there was significant "financial innovation" in the mortgage industry, and Fannie Mae and Freddie Mac decided to participate. They had watched their share of the U.S. mortgage market drop due to their lack of involvement in the non-prime mortgage products being developed and securitized in the private label markets. Accordingly, Fannie Mae and Freddie Mac began taking credit risk on loans that previously they had decided were too risky to guarantee. We know from our study of the S&L crisis what happens when institutions are in financial trouble and have the opportunity to make double-or-nothing-type bets to earn their way out—they take those bets. Conveniently, it was about this time when the accounting systems for both firms were suddenly found to be inadequate and upwardly biased regarding the firms' underlying financial strength and stability. Fannie Mae and Freddie Mac were thus able to take on large amounts of credit risk under the cover of accounting darkness in the form of mortgages with lower credit quality and looser underwriting standards. This was the same strategy tolerated by the goodwill accounting policies promulgated in the 1980s during the thrift crisis. This double-or-nothing strategy that had simply postponed and exacerbated the S&L crisis had the same impact on the mortgage crisis, only this time it ended in even more dramatic fashion.

Trustees

Each securitization has a trustee that oversees the mortgage trust. That trustee is contractually obligated to ensure that each deal participant does what it is supposed to do over the thirty-year life of the securitization. The current mortgage crisis has made it crystal clear that there are massive conflicts of interests among the participants in a securitization. These are discussed in detail in the following chapter; the key point to remember is that under the structure of existing transactions, there is little economic incentive for banks and other deal participants to maintain high standards of integrity. This fact would not be so problematic if the securitization trustee—the party charged with overseeing the conduct of the deal participants—actually had any incentive to seek out or punish banks or other deal participants whose conduct had fallen below agreed-on standards. Instead, under most PSAs, the trustee is indemnified by each of the deal participants against any liability stemming from those participants' wrongdoing. Thus, the trustee risks nothing by sitting on its hands rather than making sure the rules of the transaction are followed. Further, because the trustee is paid a monthly fee regardless of any actions it takes (and due to the lack of new securitization activity, it need not compete for future business), it makes little economic sense for a trustee to spend much effort policing a deal. True to this incentive structure, trustees have done as little as possible to help resolve distressed MBS deals since the onset of the mortgage crisis, instead remaining content simply to collect their monthly fees.

Servicers

Servicers have a contractual responsibility to the bondholders and the mortgage trust, and they are obligated to maximize the value of any mortgage loan for the benefit of the bondholders. However, servicers are also subject to powerful conflicts of interest, due to the fact that they formerly wore a different hat: they were the originators of many of the loans they now service. Of all the conflicts alluded to thus far, servicer conflicts have become particularly problematic for resolving distressed MBS deals and have led to massive and systemic servicer misconduct. This misconduct has been the primary factor preventing delinquent loans from being liquidated, modified, or otherwise resolved. Though some criticism for the failure of loan modifications may be directed at the structure of securitizations, the servicer controls the underlying documentation and has the authority to implement loan modifications. Due to their conflicts of interest, the Big Four banks, which are also the biggest four servicers, have been slow in releasing that information to investors seeking to enforce their rights to put loans back to the originator when the description of the loans and the actual collateral differ. We examine this issue in detail in the next chapter.

Document Custodian

Document custodians are contracted to retain all of the legal and related documents that demonstrate that the trust is the owner of the loan. Generally, the document custodian is also the trustee. However, this is a possible conflict in that the trustee must initiate litigation against itself if it fails to properly retain the documents. This has resulted in very lax industry standards for the retention of documents. Going forward, the document custodian should be independent from the trustee and independent from all other parties in the transaction.

Securitizations

Mortgage securitization has been vilified by many as the culprit for the mortgage crisis, but as we have discussed, securitization is just a mechanism for dividing up a set of cash flows into securities designed to meet the varying risk appetites of a range of investors. Securitization served an important function by opening up the mortgage market to large public sources of capital, making mortgages readily available at attractive levels to more U.S. homeowners. Why has securitization attracted such negativity?

Part of the answer lies in the way that securitizations themselves have been organized. Recall that securitizations are supported by PSAs, the detailed trust documents that explicitly describe how participants in the securitization are to perform. Most of the criticism levied against securitization stems from the way that these trusts have been carried out through their organizing documents. One such criticism has been that securitizations were not structured to be transparent enough to allow investors to determine the credit quality of the underlying loans, either before or after they purchased their securities. Another criticism is that the mechanism in the PSAs for investors to enforce repurchases when loans are found defective—including the requirement that at least 25 percent of certificate holders band together—is unduly restrictive and creates free rider and holdout problems. This effectively relieved originators and issuers from having any "skin in the game," as they were unlikely to be held responsible for the loans they arranged and sold.

Yet another particularly vexing problem has been that PSAs have either no provision or limited provision for restructuring a mortgage, should the homeowner get into financial trouble. Loan restructurings were not generally anticipated in securitizations. The typical solution in the past was to foreclose, but foreclosure carries with it significant costs for the borrower and the holder of that specific loan, as well as for the market in general, especially in an environment of falling home prices. In such extreme situations, extensive modification of mortgages may be preferable, allowing borrowers to keep making payments and remain in their homes, providing an increased expected return to investors versus foreclosure, and keeping a glut of homes off the market.

Given that a securitization typically has dozens, or even hundreds, of investors, all with different investment goals, there is no easy way to modify a mortgage for a homeowner and then process that change through the deal, unless the rules are agreed upon in advance. If one investor has a bond that pays only interest, he or she will object to a modification that decreases the interest that the homeowner pays. Another investor holding significant principal would prefer that a modification be comprised of a reduced interest rate rather than a reduction of principal. Thus, securitization did not cause the mortgage crisis, but the way it was used did make it unnecessarily difficult to restructure or resolve a loan held within a securitization trust. These inefficiencies have certainly intensified the current crisis and must be resolved if we are to have a functioning non-governmental mortgage finance system going forward.

The Structure of the Conventional Thirty-Year Mortgage

Thus far, we have talked about how securitizations and their participants contributed to the mortgage crisis. We must also consider one more factor: the structure of the conventional U.S. thirty-year mortgage, the basic building block of our mortgage securitizations. Though they may seem like two separate items, the structure of the underlying mortgage notes and the performance of the mortgage securities market are closely linked. The reason stems from the prepayment option contained in the conventional mortgage. As discussed, a conventional mortgage loan can be prepaid by the borrower at any time without penalty. If the borrower exercises this option, it usually results in a loss for the mortgage investor. As we will discuss in more detail in chapter 8, such losses are only minimally troublesome when viewed in isolation, but when they are absorbed en masse, as tends to be the case with large interest rate moves, they can cripple the financial system.

The prepayment option embedded in the conventional mortgage structure is actually at the heart of both the S&L crisis and the mortgage crisis. During the S&L crisis, a spike in interest rates meant that borrowers elected not to prepay their long term debts, causing the S&Ls to lose money. This created an incentive to speculate in projects they did not understand in an attempt to right the ship. Leading up to the mortgage crisis, low interest rates caused a prepayment wave in the early 2000s that allowed subordinate MBS investors to make massive profits—profits that fueled an insatiable appetite for additional mortgage credit risk.

The structure of the conventional U.S. mortgage creates enormous interest rate exposure for the entire investment community, exposure that cannot be properly hedged given the size of the mortgage market. This interest rate exposure will eventually wreak havoc on financial institutions and cause them to do what they've done in the past: dump the losses from extreme events on the U.S. taxpayer. The prepayment option thus turns a loan into a lottery ticket; though a few may win, the cumulative losses far outweigh the gains. If the government's role is to remove systemic risk from the financial system, there is no logical reason to allow free prepayment options to be a standard feature of U.S. mortgages. In later chapters, we will discuss some subtle but important features that could be added to the conventional mortgage to ameliorate the harmful effects of interest rate fluctuations.

Part II:
The Obstacles to a Rapid Recovery

*"A man is usually more careful of his money
than he is of his principles."*

—*Ralph Waldo Emerson*

CHAPTER 5

A Market Collapse Compounded

We examined previously the environment and factors that led directly to the housing crash and the collapse of the MBS market in the United States. The problems described collectively as the "mortgage crisis" did not stop there. In fact, the mortgage crisis has been particularly devastating because it is two crises rolled into one.

The first crisis, as I described, surrounded the collapse of the mortgage market in 2007 stemming from homeowners, especially subprime borrowers, defaulting on their mortgages in record numbers. This kicked off a downward spiral of declining home values, reduced consumer spending, economic contraction, and job losses. Though this first crisis would have created a significant setback to the U.S. economy on its own, the setback turned into the worst economic calamity since the Great Depression because of severe structural problems and inappropriate actions by key market participants.

In particular, failures by certain homeowners to make mortgage payments they could afford, failures by mortgage servicers to modify troubled loans or foreclose on loans for which no workout was possible, failures by originators and investment banks to stand behind their reps and warranties as to defective loans, and failures by fund managers to pursue loss mitigation strategies on behalf of their investors, all threw a wrench into the machinery put in place to deal with toxic loans, distressed borrowers, and the allocation of mortgage-related losses. This second crisis prolonged the cleanup process with respect to the first and created a lingering drag on the U.S. housing market that continues to this day. Indeed, there is no end in sight.

The fact remains that, as of March 2011, 8.32 percent of all mortgage loans outstanding in the U.S. are delinquent,[56] and the problem is getting worse. Even though the U.S. economy is stabilizing, additional mortgages go into default every day. As the mortgage market continues to fold in on itself, we are left with the fundamental realization that *these losses will continue until the structural problems within the mortgage markets are resolved.*

From politicians and homeowners to banks, investors, and servicers, everyone is saying that they want problem mortgages to be resolved, but it is not happening. Just as improper economic incentives created the first crisis, we now find that we do not have the proper economic incentives to resolve this secondary crisis. Even though all participants in the mortgage system signed contracts that defined how they would perform, most now find that complying with these agreements is not in their best economic interest. Hence, they are choosing to ignore their contracts. This is true of homeowners, servicers, and banks, and though they were never participants in the deals, even politicians are ignoring the contracts that underlie mortgage securitizations. Examining the reactions of each of these players in the aftermath of the collapse of the housing market should allow us to understand why this crisis persists years after its onset.

Homeowners

By 2007, Americans held unprecedented levels of mortgage debt. When real estate prices started to fall that year, borrowers who had purchased their homes with the thinnest of margins found that they were underwater. Such negative equity constituted the single most important factor driving mortgage defaults during the mortgage crisis, causing more defaults than the factors of unemployment and upward mortgage rate resets combined.[57] In fact, though only 12 percent of all mortgages featured negative equity, they comprised 47 percent of all foreclosures during the second half of 2008.[58] The problem has only gotten worse: as of March 2011, 23.1 percent of U.S. mortgagors held negative equity in their homes.[59]

When homeowners owe more on their homes than the properties are worth, they have a dilemma. They cannot sell because they cannot recoup enough money through the sale to pay off their mortgages. If they continue paying their mortgages, they are losing money with each payment. On the other hand, if they stop making payments, they will eventually lose their homes altogether. If a mortgage is held by a bank on its own balance sheet, the homeowner has a good chance of being able to renegotiate the terms of the mortgage through a loan workout, but if the mortgage is held in a securitization, modification is difficult and sometimes impossible.

Thus, two borrowers with the same credentials and the same loan terms may obtain completely different results when they ask for a loan modification, based on nothing more than the luck of the draw as to which entity is currently holding or servicing their mortgage. As Federal Reserve Board Governor Sarah Raskin noted during a housing conference presentation in February 2011, "The consumer is really not part of the contract between the servicer and the set of investors," and thus has little control over whether a loan workout takes place.[60]

The upshot of this is that the borrowers who are unable to renegotiate the terms of their mortgages are stuck with contracts that ostensibly require them to act against their economic interests. What do these borrowers do? They compare the cost of default to the cost of paying their mortgages, and many decide to walk away from their homes when it is cheaper to default than it is to pay the loan. When homeowners default even though they can afford to make mortgage payments, it is termed a "strategic default."

Strategic defaults can be measured by looking at the credit of those who default on a mortgage. If a borrower defaults on a mortgage, but is current on his or her car loans, credit cards, and other consumer debt, it is most likely a strategic default. Strategic defaults had a negligible impact five years ago, but a report published by Experian Information Services, Inc. found that they grew to 19 percent of total mortgage defaults by mid-2009.[61] These voluntary defaults are particularly troublesome because the collective action of millions of borrowers *who have the ability to pay but choose not to* is dragging down the value of U.S. real estate and the economy as a whole.

To be sure, the housing market has also been plagued over the last few years by a high number of defaults where the borrowers simply did not have the money to make their mortgage payments. However, we can't ignore that many others have *chosen* not to make mortgage payments because they would lose money with every check they wrote. Often, homeowners took on excessive debt because they wanted to get in on real estate before prices went higher. Their houses became too expensive only *after* the dream of creating wealth through house appreciation faded. Other homeowners bought houses with the intention of living in them for an extended period only to find that it was no longer economically viable to make their payments and that they could live with the relatively minor financial and legal consequences of default.

The impact of this last factor cannot easily be dismissed. In the aftermath of the mortgage crisis, the proportion of U.S. loans that were seriously delinquent (defined as mortgages past due for ninety days) as of February 2011 was 8.2 percent, of which 4.6 percent were in the foreclosure process.[62] However, the United States is not the only country to have experienced a dramatic rise and fall in housing prices over the last several years. England saw its property values spike and then collapse in similar proportion to the United States. If negative equity was the only factor driving strategic defaults, one would expect to see default rates in England approaching those experienced in the United States. Interestingly, England's mortgage delinquency rate was just under 2.5 percent of all mortgage loans in the second quarter of 2009 and declined each quarter thereafter through 2010, according to the U.K. Council of Mortgage Lenders.[63] Meanwhile, repossessions (the U.K. term for foreclosures) remained steady at around one-tenth of one percent during 2009, and that number declined by nearly a quarter in 2010.[64]

Why the astounding difference in foreclosure and delinquency rates between the two countries? The answer is that many U.S. states prohibit or severely restrict recourse to borrowers' other assets in the event that foreclosure sales do not fully satisfy mortgage debts. English law, on the other hand, holds borrowers personally liable for paying off their mortgage debts and allows deficiency judgments to be executed against borrowers who fail to pay off their debts, even after they have defaulted and left the property.

Another factor affecting homeowners' decisions on whether to pay their mortgages is the length of time it takes to foreclose. Homeowners will consider how many months they can live in a house free of charge (that is, neither making mortgage payments nor paying rent) when considering whether to go into default. As the old saying goes, "Why buy the cow when you can get the milk for free?" Foreclosures routinely take one to two years in the aftermath of the mortgage crisis, providing enough of a free ride to convince some who are able to pay to stop making mortgage payments.

State and federal governments have introduced several programs since the onset of the crisis that they hoped would help alleviate some of these problems, yet none of these, interestingly enough, encouraged borrowers to pay their mortgages. Instead, they discouraged payments and increased the number of strategic defaults by providing borrowers with incentives not to pay. The three general categories of government programs and their impacts on defaults are summarized here:

- Both state and federal governments have established programs to extend the foreclosure process. They have done this through foreclosure moratoriums and by inserting additional procedural steps into the foreclosure process. In some states, sheriffs have refused to evict people who have run out of legal options to stay in their houses. These policies have created a moral hazard, in that they encourage homeowners to live in a home for years without paying. *When the government extends foreclosure timelines, more people will decide it is in their best interest to default on their mortgage.*

- Many programs require that homeowners be delinquent on mortgage payments in order to be eligible for government assistance. For example, many loan modification programs require that a borrower be delinquent or in default to be eligible for a government-sponsored workout. *If borrowers perceive that they can reduce their mortgage payments through a loan modification that requires that they be delinquent, they are more likely to stop making payments so that they can qualify for the program.* Again, this creates a clear moral hazard.

- Early in the mortgage crisis, the federal government changed the tax code to alleviate the tax burden on those who defaulted on mortgages.[65] Previously, the tax code treated debt that a borrower failed to pay back as income, meaning that the borrower had to pay income tax on that debt. In late 2007, the federal government changed the tax code so that borrowers no longer had to treat unpaid mortgage debt as income. Once the tax liability for unpaid mortgage debt went away, the number of strategic defaults skyrocketed. *By reducing the economic consequences of default, the government further encouraged strategic default.*

Economic theory dictates that borrowers will act in their perceived best interests when deciding whether to write a mortgage check each month. Based on the perverse economic incentives at play in the aftermath of the mortgage crisis, this has often meant that borrowers *choose* to default on mortgages they can afford to pay. In turn, this leaves the institutions that loaned money to these borrowers, or the investors that bought securities backed by these loans, holding the bag. Why would government stand up for people who are not paying their bills while ignoring the interests of the investors who made huge amounts of capital available for U.S. mortgages in the first place? As we will see, politicians have their personal interests to look after as well.

———

Politicians

The government in the United States has had a longstanding goal of increasing home ownership rates. Until recently, when property values stopped increasing and the marginal homeowner began defaulting, this policy was never seriously questioned. Now that the American dream of homeownership has turned into a nightmare for the millions of homeowners in default and the financial firms that lent them money, many are beginning to argue that we have pushed home ownership too far. Indeed, it would seem that, for at least some portion of the population, home ownership is not a realistic goal.

Nevertheless, statements such as this remain political hot buttons, as most would like to believe that the American dream of home ownership is still within reach for the majority of citizens. As a result, politicians tend to tiptoe around this sensitive subject, wary of alienating constituents by telling them that they would be better off renting. Policymakers continue to advocate extending the American dream to as many people as possible, despite the burden these policies place on the rest of the population, as we have seen in recent years. The following highlights some of the key political issues spawned by the mortgage crisis and this divergence between the ideals and the realities of home ownership:

- Millions of individuals and families are losing their homes to foreclosure. Even though many of these people made little or no down payment on their homes, and they all signed contracts that stated that they would lose their homes if they did not make their monthly payments, they continue to complain to their elected officials in large numbers. These affected individuals vote, and politicians are eager to respond to their concerns.

- Besides affecting the individuals losing their homes, the high foreclosure rate experienced by the United States in the years following the mortgage crisis has dragged down the housing market and the entire U.S. economy. If homes are to be kept from falling into foreclosure, it must make economic sense for homeowners to continue making payments. The actions of the U.S. government have been aimed at providing economic incentives to accomplish just that, but they have repeatedly backfired, providing incentives for homeowners to default. Realistically, the only way to make sure that people stay in their homes is to provide them with equity and an affordable monthly payment, thereby reducing the chances of re-default and keeping large quantities of housing inventory off the market.

- It is politically untenable, not to mention potentially unconstitutional, for Congress to pass a law offering distressed homeowners a gift of equity in their homes, because the mortgage notes on these homes are actually owned by others with the legal right to take title to the properties in foreclosure. Politicians have thus sought creative ways to pay for this transfer of equity, which usually means shifting the cost in some manner to the investors who own the mortgage bonds. Such efforts are in direct violation of investor contracts and, in the opinion of many, the Takings Clause of the Fifth Amendment of the U.S. Constitution, but these legal risks have not stopped the federal government from trying to move in that direction.[66]

- Mortgage losses are large enough to threaten the solvency of many U.S. banks, especially the largest ones. Congress does not want these banks to become insolvent, as this would require the FDIC to take large losses (not to mention putting a dent in campaign contributions). It would put politicians in a sticky situation to have to choose between bailing out the banks and bailing out the FDIC. Either choice would put members of Congress at risk of losing their seats. Thus, Congress seeks ways to shore up the banks, including by forcing investors to shoulder a disproportionate and unwarranted share of the losses the banks would otherwise suffer.

All these issues provide legislators with political incentives to introduce and enact legislation that attempts to shift the costs of the mortgage problem from the banks to the investors and taxpayers. Indeed, several federal programs have been put in place to compensate servicers for modifying loans that they do not own or have the right to modify, including the Home Affordability Modification Program, the Hope for Homeowners Program, and the Helping Families Save Their Homes Act. These loans are held by investors through securitization, and thus servicers are receiving cash compensation to shift losses from banks to investors. Making matters worse, these servicers often originated the same problem loans they are now modifying, meaning that they are being paid to fix the mess caused by their irresponsible lending practices. Banks are more than willing to go along with these legislative efforts to shift losses off their books.

Banks

The large banks originated trillions of dollars of U.S. mortgages over the past decade. By the end of 2007, over $11 trillion in residential mortgages were outstanding in the United States.[67] The banks set the underwriting guidelines for every mortgage loan that they originated. The banks were also responsible for quality control—including verifying borrower income and credit rating, appraising the value of the real estate, determining the debt to income level of the borrower and so on—that any reasonable underwriter would complete during the application process before lending money to an individual. The banks then sold most of these loans to others through securitizations, and in doing so, made a series of representations and warranties regarding the underwriting guidelines and processes they had followed.

One of the representations and warranties that originators commonly made regarding their loans, and which was demanded by banks purchasing these loans for securitization, was that the ratio of the value of the loan to the value of the underlying property (also known as the loan-to-value, or LTV, ratio) was less than or equal to 90 percent. However, many homeowners were able to buy houses during the Boom Years with little or no down payment. How was this arranged? The originators made two mortgages simultaneously: one large mortgage for the first 90 percent of the value of the home and a second mortgage for the remaining 10 percent. The second mortgage was subordinated to the first, and thus considered riskier, but it generally carried with it a higher interest rate to compensate for that risk. The most common practice during the Boom Years was for originators to sell most of their first mortgage loans to others, while keeping virtually all of the second mortgage loans on their books (i.e., for their own portfolios).

Even though the originators sold most of their first mortgages to others, the servicing rights to the loans were generally split from the ownership rights and not transferred along with the loans. Instead, the originators usually retained the servicing rights as to the first and the second mortgages they originated. As servicers, they received a monthly fee for collecting payments from homeowners, distributing those funds as required, and foreclosing when needed. Servicers are thus at the center of the mortgage problem, because they are responsible for processing mortgage defaults. Servicers also have an overarching obligation, as mentioned previously, to service loans in the best interests of the ultimate bondholders. However, the biggest servicers have massive conflicts of interest based on their prior origination activities, creating incentives that encourage them to enrich their own interests over those of the bondholders that they're contractually obligated to protect. *These conflicts constitute the key economic force driving bank conduct today and the primary reason that the mortgage problem seems so difficult to resolve.*

Though these conflicts of interest all stem from banks' dual roles as originators and servicers, they fall into three distinct categories, each of which has hampered the cleanup from the mortgage crisis in a distinct manner. Let's look at each of these in turn.

Conflicts Related to Delinquent Loans

Though banks have a contractual obligation to act in the bondholders' best interests when processing loan modifications for distressed loans, they are often pulled in a different direction based on their economic incentives to protect their own assets. These incentives have a demonstrable impact on whether servicers decide to implement loan workouts. This impact may be seen most conspicuously in the difference in servicing conduct for loans that servicers hold in their own portfolios compared to loans that they are servicing for others.

The Office of the Comptroller of the Currency and the Office of Thrift Supervision Mortgage Metrics Report from the third quarter of 2009 found that, "[s]ervicers continue to modify more loans held in their portfolios than they did [*sic*] for the GSEs, government-guaranteed loans, or for private investors…Loans serviced for the GSEs accounted for 18.7 percent of all modifications despite making up 63 percent of the servicing portfolio."[68] Thus, when a bank owns a mortgage that is in default, the bank acts according to the principle that "it is better to get half a loaf than no bread at all." In these cases, the banks frequently choose to modify or otherwise resolve the loan in an efficient manner. However, when a loan is held by others in a securitization or as a whole loan, the bank earns higher servicing fees if that loan remains in a state of delinquency rather than being modified or liquidated. For each month that a borrower remains delinquent on mortgage payments, the bank receives late fees and is able to charge the loan trust (and ultimately the investors) for delinquency expenses that it often pays to affiliated companies. The bank is thus able to make money every month that a loan remains in limbo. *In other words, it is more profitable for servicing banks to keep non-owned mortgages in "delinquency purgatory" than to resolve those problem loans.*

Conflicts Related to Second Liens

When banks control the servicing for the first and the second lien, and especially when they own the second but not the first, there is additional economic incentive for mischief. In these situations, banks are motivated to encourage borrowers to pay their second (and bank-owned) lien in lieu of paying the first, which is owned by a securitization trust.* This strategy accomplishes two things. First, the banks will be the direct beneficiaries of the cash flows from the second lien mortgage. Second, the banks will earn higher servicing fees for servicing the delinquent first lien mortgage. Clearly, they would be in no rush to foreclose on the first lien.

This approach causes a wealth transfer from the owner of the first lien to the owner of the second lien. A recent research paper by four professors at Columbia University concluded that the modification program implemented by Countrywide Financial Corporation as part of its settlement with state Attorneys General over predatory lending practices actually resulted in a substantial increase in strategic defaults on first lien loans, without a corresponding increase in defaults on second lien loans.[69] This suggests that Countrywide is acting to protect its interests at the expense of the interests of the ultimate bondholders.

The same perverse economic incentives come into play where the bank owns credit card debt or other liabilities of the homeowner. In that case, the banks are also in the position to attribute losses to the owners of the primary mortgage while effectively recapitalizing or improving the credit position of their second lien loan and their unsecured credit cards. In short, banks have the ability to turn a senior loan that is in default into a revenue stream, all the while avoiding all or part of a substantial loss on their subordinate asset, the collateral for which would almost certainly be wiped out should a foreclosure be completed. Even if a servicer in this position agrees to modify a borrower's first lien mortgage, it presents the bank with another opportunity to profit should the borrower re-default on that loan.

If servicers were to foreclose on first mortgage loans where they held a second lien, their second liens would likely be wiped out. These second lien loans are not generally securitized, so the banks are not

---

* Note that borrowers are often more than willing to go along with this plan, as second mortgages are not automatically discharged upon foreclosure. While the second lien would be technically extinguished upon foreclosure, the borrower would retain the obligation to pay off the note. Therefore, it is entirely rational for a homeowner to pay a second mortgage and not pay the first.

required to take any reserves until they are delinquent. The banks have no desire to write off the second loans on their balance sheets because their exposure to these loans is so huge. The Big Four banks have over $400 billion of second lien mortgages on their balance sheets.[70] Even though real estate prices have collapsed and many of these loans would not be paid back in the normal course, they are still held at nearly full value on bank balance sheets.

This second lien overhang is the primary source of the U.S. government's fear of bank insolvency. If these loans were held in a securitization, they would have a market value of about 30 percent to 50 percent of par—about a 50 percent to 70 percent loss compared to the value the banks are currently reporting on their books. *Should a meaningful portion of the $400 billion of second lien mortgages held by the Big Four be written off, all four banks would be driven to the brink of insolvency.*

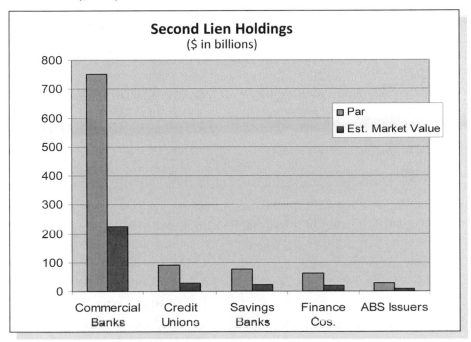

Source: Laurie Goodman, "Robosigners and Other Servicing Failures: Protecting the Rights of RMBS Investors" (presentation, Grais & Ellsworth, New York, NY, October 27, 2010), webcast available at http://video.remotecounsel.com/mediasite/Viewer/?peid=060f37 b9b28a49ac8cbbea6716c46fedid (accessed April 13, 2011).

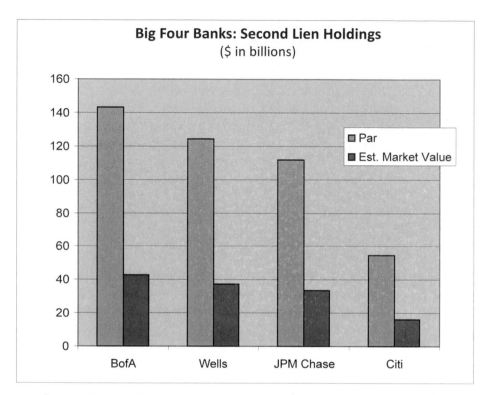

Big Four Banks: Second Lien Holdings
($ in billions)

SOURCE: LAURIE GOODMAN, "ROBOSIGNERS" (ACCESSED APRIL 13, 2011).

Conflicts Related to Loan Files

As we've discussed, originating banks made a series of representations and warranties regarding mortgage loans when they sold them into securitizations, providing investors with comfort that the loans were underwritten properly and conformed to reasonable and prudent guidelines. For investors or insurers to verify whether an originator complied with these reps and warranties, they need look no further than the loan file underlying each loan in a securitization, which documents all the steps the underwriter took and contains all documents used to verify the borrower's credit risk. Unfortunately, these loan files are usually held by the loans' servicer, which often is an affiliate of the same bank that originated the mortgages.

While servicers have certain obligations to provide those files upon request to trustees, insurers or bondholders, they have frequently resisted such efforts, because turning over these files would expose their parent or affiliate to substantial repurchase liability, should the underwriting be found defective. More than a few major lawsuits and legal proceedings have been undertaken in recent years just to obtain access to these loan files, which may be treasure troves of evidence of irresponsible or even fraudulent underwriting.[71] *Such servicer recalcitrance has acted to increase investor costs and losses and prolong the resolution of problem loans.*

In summary, the major banks, as servicers, have contractual obligations in virtually every PSA to resolve problem loans in the best interests of bondholders. However, it is hard to imagine any servicing practices more *adverse* to bondholder interests than the all-too-common practices described in the three categories above. Instead of working to resolve problem loans in a timely manner, they are purposefully delaying the process, because their economic incentives are not aligned with investors' economic interests. Indeed, they are diametrically opposed!

These delays contribute to the growth of mortgage defaults—delays, whether caused by the government or the banks, increase the economic incentives for borrowers to stop paying their mortgages. Free housing is certainly a benefit of defaulting. Worse yet, the banks are trying to work their way out of their own financial problems by manipulating the servicing of loans and refusing to turn over loan documents in trusts owned by investors. This has resulted, yet again, in the shift of losses from the banks that originated and maintain these loans to the investors who bought them. Despite contractual obligations prohibiting such conduct, the banks have chosen to ignore their responsibilities when not in their economic interests.

All this raises the question: why don't the aggrieved investors simply file suit against the banks to enforce their contracts? The answer lies in the "collective action" or "no action" clauses written into standard trust agreements, which require investors to amass a specific ownership percentage and then petition the trustee before taking action themselves. Bondholders have yet to mount any serious effort to pursue the servicers for failing to honor their obligations, in large part because of the difficulties inherent in organizing such a large and disparate group. We will now look at mortgage problems from the perspective of these investors and examine how their organizational issues have further hampered the resolution of these distressed assets.

Investors

Based on my own experience, I can confirm that investors' interests are being ignored and their contracts are being violated. By investors, I mean anybody who has invested in MBS.* It is important to understand the makeup of this diverse group, because at the heart of virtually every government or bank plan to solve the mortgage problem sits a group of investors who will bear the expense of such plan.

Who are these MBS investors that the government and the banks can so blatantly disregard? They include pension funds, insurance companies, college endowment funds, IRA funds, hedge funds, sovereign wealth funds, and foreign and domestic banks. As of the third quarter of 2010, the outstanding value of U.S. based securitizations held *outside* the U.S. banking system was $6.6 trillion.[72] In chapter 2, we talked about how Americans have been able to take the availability of mortgage credit for granted because the United States is stable and has had a stellar record of honoring contracts. It is obvious that the federal government takes these trillions of dollars of investment for granted as well. Otherwise, policymakers would not be encouraging servicers to ignore their contracts with investors, nor would the government be

---

* Because MBS are bonds, the terms bondholders, certificate holders, and investors are interchangeable.

---

looking to investors to provide equity to homeowners and to shore up the balance sheets of reckless banks.

Investors have been much maligned throughout the mortgage crisis as "the bad guys," dogged by the perception that they somehow caused the mortgage collapse by trusting the banks and rating agencies in purchasing vast amounts of MBS. Worse yet, we hear the familiar refrain that the investors are keeping mortgages from being modified or resolved because they are not willing to take any losses on their investments (see appendix II). Both suggestions are demonstrably incorrect. Though investors did purchase most mortgage loans, they did so in justifiable reliance on the representations and warranties made by the originators who created the loans, the underwriters who packaged them into securities, and the rating agencies who gave the securities their seal of approval. These were the entities closest to the original borrowers and the only ones with access to the underlying loan files that would show whether these reps and warranties were being followed.

The importance of investor confidence is soon going to become obvious. In February 2011, the U.S. Treasury issued a report to Congress entitled "Reforming America's Housing Finance Market."[73] This report discussed the importance of, and options for, gradually removing Fannie Mae and Freddie Mac from the mortgage market. This is another way of saying that private lending and securitization for the U.S. mortgage market should be restored. How successful could this plan be if there is a profound lack of confidence among private investors and the cost of capital is substantial?

Given the legislative response to the mortgage crisis, investors will undoubtedly demand a substantial political risk premium in return for investing in housing, which will ultimately be passed along to homeowners in the form of higher costs and interest rates. I cannot help but think of the saying "there's no such thing as a free lunch," popularized by Milton Friedman when he made it the title of a collection of essays on public policy in 1975.[74] The saying refers to the economic concept that a society or individual cannot get something for nothing—there are always costs to every benefit, even if hidden or dispersed. In the present case, there will indeed be no free lunch if we wish to transition from a government-backed mortgage market to one that is privately backed. Instead, politicians' efforts to allow their constituents to avoid paying their loans—no matter how well intentioned—ignore the fact that this policy harms a critically important player in the mortgage market, the investor with the money. In turn, this will translate into higher housing costs—in the form of political risk premiums—for those constituents in the future.

As for their participation in workouts and other loan resolutions, investors fully understand that as mortgages go bad, they will have losses, many of which they are contractually obligated to absorb. Investors have no interest in keeping non-performing loans on their books forever in delinquency purgatory. They would like to resolve these problem mortgages as quickly as possible, take the money they can recover, and redeploy it into ventures that are more productive. This may mean modifying a loan where the net present recovery would be greater than the proceeds from liquidation or foreclosing when no such workout is possible. The problem is that the U.S. government and the banks are trying to push losses onto investors that go well beyond their contractual responsibilities.

Again, this begs the question: why aren't investors standing up for their rights? It has to do, first, with the nature of bondholder rights and the fact that, historically, investors have not had to worry about their contracts being honored. Bondholders in securitizations are accustomed to being passive investors, buying bonds and then collecting interest and principal payments each month. The value of a bond changes when interest rates change, but bonds are far less volatile than stocks, so bondholders are not likely to monitor the details of their bonds as actively as equity holders or even corporate bondholders. Further, MBS buyers are usually investing a pension fund's money or the funds of some other third party. Their contracts require that they act as fiduciaries, but they are not paid any additional money to manage those funds actively. Accordingly, they remain passive.

Another reason that bondholders have been and remain passive is the fear of political or economic retribution. Real or imagined, many investors fear that the federal government has made a decision with respect to the allocation of mortgage-related losses, and that it would be futile to challenge that decision. Furthermore, there is often a fear of reprisals from the large banks. This is especially true with hedge funds that rely on the large banks for funding.

A third major factor contributing to bondholder inaction is, as mentioned earlier, the collective action clauses of most PSAs. These require bondholders to band together in sufficient numbers (usually 25 to 50 percent of a trust) before they can take any meaningful action to enforce their contract rights. This is a difficult proposition, because there is no public database showing who owns the classes of bonds in any particular securitization, and institutional investors tend to be reluctant to reveal their holdings, especially when it might involve a direct frontal attack on a well-connected bank.

Compounding this problem is the fact that even when bondholders have amassed the requisite 25 percent or more in a trust, they must first go through the trustee before taking action themselves. This requires dealing back and forth with a trustee that has very little incentive to assist investors, generally has many other business dealings with the securitizers, and is primarily concerned with avoiding expense and potential liability. These trustees have frequently sought cumbersome confidentiality and indemnity agreements and required bondholders to meet nearly impossible standards of proof before they will lift a finger to help these investors recover their losses from the responsible parties. Though "the ice is starting to melt" around investor actions, as more and more evidence of bank wrongdoing emerges and trustees begin to cooperate in these efforts, it has been a long and grueling process.

At the end of the day, most bondholders purchased bonds with a buy-and-hold strategy; that is, they planned to hold them for a long time, likely until they were paid off. This is why long-term investors like retirement funds, pension accounts, and college endowment funds buy bonds and are the biggest holders of distressed MBS. *When the government looks to the investors to pay for the mortgage problems, the government is effectively depleting the retirement resources of millions of Americans.* Passing the financial burden of those who bought houses with no equity onto those who have saved for their retirement is a highly questionable strategy for even the best-intentioned politician. It is happening only because bondholders tend to be passive, and most individuals do not know what is happening to their long-term fixed income investments until it is too late, especially if these assets are held in their pension funds. Combine this tendency with the procedural difficulties of bringing investor lawsuits against the banks, and it is no wonder that banks have largely been able to escape the consequences of irresponsible lending and conflicted servicing.

Even with all of these factors pointing against them, some investors are ready and willing to stand up for their rights by resisting the efforts of the U.S. government and the big banks to saddle them with the costs of problem mortgages. We will examine later what these investors may be able to do to protect themselves.

"However beautiful the strategy, you should occasionally look at the results."

—Winston Churchill

CHAPTER 6

Why Enacted "Fixes" Have Failed

Since the onset of the mortgage crisis, there have been numerous attempts by legislators to stem the fallout from delinquent loans, but no government-proposed solution has succeeded in resolving the problem. One reason is that the securitization market is one of the most complex financial markets in the world. To date, government efforts have shown little understanding of the complex and competing relationships involved in the operation of the MBS market, rendering their efforts to untangle the knot ineffective.

Making matters worse, policymakers have shown a proclivity for supporting the economic interests of servicers and certain homeowners at the expense of investors—the retirees, small investors, and insurers of the nation. Such preferential treatment has occurred in spite of the investors having negotiated agreements to protect their interests *in advance*. Government solutions have sought to abrogate trillions of dollars of contracts for the political purposes of keeping certain fortunate homeowners in their homes and bailing out the banks. These efforts may have provided temporary band aids for a handful of individuals and financial institutions, but they have utterly failed to solve the larger mortgage problem. Indeed, no proposal will succeed at solving this problem until the investors who own the mortgage assets are included in the conversation and treated in a fair and reasonable way.

The "fixes" proposed thus far have been viewed by the investment community as a closet bailout of the banking system and specifically of the Big Four banks. Make no mistake about it: the banking system is being bailed out because of government fears that requiring banks to adhere to their contracts with investors would force the banks to recognize significant capital shortfalls. Indeed, the same "too big to fail" mentality that spurred the government to bail out the banks at the onset of the crisis has caused the government to propose solutions, in the aftermath of this crisis, that released the banks from the burden of inconvenient contracts. Unlike prior government bailouts, this ongoing bailout is being paid for by a specific group—the investors who bought mortgage assets—rather than the taxpayers as a whole.

Consider the foreclosure fixes that have been implemented to date. In their desire to mitigate the dislocation and suffering caused by foreclosures, lawmakers have made it easier and less expensive for homeowners to default. They have done this by changing tax laws, slowing foreclosures, and enacting government assistance programs. Nonetheless, a functioning mortgage market must have a mechanism in place for recouping the lender's money by repossessing the house when people do not or cannot pay. It may not be a pleasant process, but it is essential to ensure that investors make money available for future home loans. Accordingly, though lawmakers may believe they are easing the hardships caused by ongoing foreclosures, they are exacerbating the long-term financial ramifications of the crisis and destroying a mortgage finance system that is *way too big to fail.*

I realize that it is politically difficult for an elected representative to ignore the pain of a constituent (and a voter) facing foreclosure and that the desire to help these constituents is a natural outgrowth of both the democratic process and ordinary human empathy.* However, if the

---

* This desire to help homeowners may have also been motivated by the idea that homeowners were misled or treated unfairly by those who originated the loans. If, as the evidence suggests, some originators deceived or tricked homeowners into loans they could not pay or higher cost loans than those for which they could qualify, it "squeakiest wheels" are to get the grease, lawmakers must understand from where that grease is coming. In the case of mortgages held in securitizations, the "grease" is being supplied by mortgage investors. Politicians must acknowledge that investors are also their constituents. Moreover, while this group has not been as vocal as the homeowner population—largely because it has yet to realize what is happening—the group is starting to organize and understand that its pensions, 401(k) accounts, and children's college funds are being raided to subsidize overzealous banks and delinquent homeowners. In this chapter, I explain how the government programs and actions that were intended to mitigate the foreclosure crisis actually work in practice, so that the costs of these programs can be viewed in the light of day and weighed appropriately by voters and lawmakers alike.

The Countrywide Settlement

On June 26, 2008, California Attorney General Jerry Brown sued Countrywide, its CEO, Angelo Mozilo, and its president, David Sambol, for deceptive lending practices, including originating fraudulent loans and using predatory lending practices to earn enormous profits by re-selling these loans on the open market. That same day, Illinois Attorney General Lisa Madigan filed a similar suit on behalf of the residents of her state. By the end of September 2008, eleven states had filed related suits against the country's former number one mortgage lender.

These suits were eventually consolidated, and on October 6, 2008, Countrywide agreed to settle all actions[75] to the tune of an announced $8.6 billion. The Attorneys General involved hailed the deal as a model for the rest of the country in solving the housing crisis, and Brown called it "the biggest mandatory loan modification in American history."[76] The settlement included loan modification assistance for an estimated four hundred thousand borrowers in danger of losing their

---

is important to remember that these predatory loans were then sold to investors, who are now bearing substantial losses as a result. Thus, homeowners are not alone in having been misled by the banks.

homes and provisions halting foreclosures while these modifications were effectuated. The logic behind this settlement was that the onerous provisions of subprime, option ARM, and other problematic loans could be remedied by simply having the loans reworked and restructured. Bank of America, which acquired Countrywide in July 2008, described the settlement as a win for investors, borrowers, and the mortgage market as a whole.

With regulators, industry executives, and commentators tripping over themselves to praise the accord, few acknowledged what a huge win the settlement was for Bank of America. Though Countrywide had originated the loans at the center of these lawsuits and the settlement agreement, it no longer owned most of those mortgages. Instead, it had retained only servicing rights to these loans, and thus it would not bear the costs of loan modifications involving lowered monthly payments, principal amounts, or interest rates. In other words, Countrywide agreed to pay a fine with someone else's money. That someone else, of course, was the group of investors that had purchased the securities backed by these loans and that had carefully negotiated protections against unfettered loan modifications in the PSAs. These investors had also been misled by Countrywide, and yet, under the terms of the Attorneys General settlement, they were to bear the overwhelming majority of the costs associated with the $8.6 billion in loan modifications that Countrywide had agreed to provide to distressed borrowers.

Furthermore, the settlement explicitly stipulated that any second liens on the properties would not be considered or modified under the settlement.[77] Remember that Countrywide—and thus, Bank of America—had an enormous position in second lien loans. These loans were junior to the first liens that Countrywide had agreed to modify, and thus should have incurred substantial losses upon the modification of the senior loans. Pursuant to the settlement, those losses were to be shifted entirely to a pool of first lien loans that Countrywide no longer owned.

These untoward consequences were completely lost on the Attorneys General, judging from their statements in the press. For example, Attorney General Richard Blumenthal of Connecticut, who had sued Countrywide for, among other things, "deliberately doctoring documents," issued a press release that stated the following:

> This settlement will cost Bank of America as much as $8.6 billion, but no cost, not a dime, to taxpayers. My hope is that this result provides a framework or template that we can convince other mortgage lenders to adopt in rescuing homeowners facing foreclosure....Countrywide must now bail out homeowners it recklessly misled into mortgages doomed to fail. [78]

Connecticut Department of Consumer Protection Commissioner Jerry Farrell, Jr. echoed this analysis, stating, "In these harsh economic times, when government is being called upon to bail out financial institutions for their unsound business practices, this settlement sends an important message to those responsible for defrauding consumers—they will be held accountable."[79]

Arizona Attorney General Terry Goddard issued even stronger statements in support of the settlement, even after he became aware of a lawsuit I filed pointing out the improper loss shifting engendered by the arrangement:

> [O]ur office continues to feel that the settlement that was reached with Countrywide's parent company, Bank of America, specifically for the loan modification program that it outlines, is a best practice for foreclosure mitigation nationwide and we hope that it is a model that will be adopted by other companies. We feel that this type of modification program is in the best interest of homeowners and borrowers, a win-win for the homeowners and the economy as a whole...and is very important for getting our economy back on track.[80]

Indeed, even after my lawsuit discussed extensively the problems with this settlement and exposed the logical flaws inherent in the settlement's remedy structure, the Attorneys General still failed to grasp the Houdini act that Countrywide had pulled to escape the costs of its deceptive lending practices. Blumenthal, after learning that his settlement had been challenged, stated:

> Countrywide was very wise to reach the settlement that it did with Attorneys General because it is in the interest of its own investors as [well as] the homeowners whose mortgages will be restructured. And Countrywide has informed us of the lawsuit and its intent to vigorously defend against it, as it should.[81]

The press coverage surrounding this settlement made clear that Countrywide was going to implement a large-scale modification program for its problem loans. Immediately following the announcement of this settlement, defaults spiked for loans serviced by Countrywide. According to research funded by The Paul Milstein Center for Real Estate at Columbia Business School, the evidence supports the theory that the Countrywide settlement induced defaults among borrowers who were unlikely to default otherwise, at least in the near future.[82] Policymakers should be encouraging precisely the opposite behavior, and their efforts, through perhaps well-intentioned, simply made this problem worse.

To reiterate, there were several problems with the Countrywide settlement negotiated by the state Attorneys General:

- It did not penalize the entity whose actions were alleged to have caused the wrongs at issue.

- It did not recognize that Countrywide lacked the contractual right to modify loans without compensating investors.

- It penalized an entity that had not directly caused the wrongs at issue and which had negotiated contractual protections against such penalties.

- It rewarded homeowners for defaulting, causing more people to strategically default, making the entire problem worse.

- It allowed Countrywide to preserve its second lien loans while modifying first lien loans, another direct wealth transfer from investors in Countrywide securitizations to Countrywide itself.

Servicer Safe Harbors

All servicers have signed contracts with investors regarding what they can and cannot do when servicing securitized loans. However, since the onset of the mortgage crisis, servicers have sought safe harbors from legal liability for taking actions outside the scope of these bargained-for agreements. The argument for these proposed safe harbors has been that they would give the servicers the legal comfort and freedom they needed to move forward on resolving problem mortgages. On the other hand, these protections also allowed servicers to act in their own economic interests at the expense of the investor interests they were contractually obligated to protect.

In one such effort, servicers obtained legal protection from investors that might be unhappy with loan modifications. This effort arose directly out of my challenge to the settlement between the Attorneys General and Countrywide discussed in the previous section. That settlement encouraged Countrywide to conduct workouts for hundreds of thousands of loans that it did not own and in most cases had no right to modify.

A few months after I filed a lawsuit challenging this settlement on behalf of investors owning some of the affected bonds, the Helping Families Save Their Homes Act of 2009 ("H.R. 1106" or the "Homes

Act") was introduced in the House of Representatives, complete with a Servicer Safe Harbor provision.[83] Ostensibly, this safe harbor was designed to eliminate "tranche warfare,"[84] which was springing up in securitizations because senior and subordinate bondholders sometimes had conflicting interests when it came to loan modifications. For example, senior bondholders generally preferred that distressed loans be modified immediately, before further losses accrued, whereas junior bondholders, whose positions already stood to be wiped out in a modification, generally preferred that the workout be delayed so that they could continue to collect interest payments due over the life of the loan. Servicers face obligations to service loans both in the interests of the trust and in conformance with the servicing protocols in the PSA, and these conflicts between tranches put them between a rock and a hard place. This is because certain servicing protocols—such as those requiring the servicer to protect the interests of junior bondholders—could be diametrically opposed to the requirement that the servicer act in the best interests of the trust.

Though the proposed safe harbor provision sought to reconcile this tranche conflict by requiring that the servicer protect the interests of the trust as a whole, the reality was that it essentially relieved Countrywide and other servicers from any liability whatsoever for complying with the settlement with the Attorneys General and performing large-scale loan modifications (i.e., even if all tranches opposed them). The safe harbor provided that, notwithstanding any contractual provisions to the contrary, so long as the servicer reasonably believed that the net present value of expected future payments from the modification of a distressed loan was higher than the net present value of expected foreclosure proceeds, the servicer would be shielded from any lawsuits arising out of its decision to modify. In other words, investors' contracts prohibiting such modification were no longer worth the paper on which they were printed. As if that were not enough, H.R. 1106 provided that servicers would be given cash incentives of $1,000 for each loan modified, as a further inducement to conduct workouts. This meant that the same servicers that had often irresponsibly originated these problematic loans in the first place *would be paid with taxpayer money to correct their own mistakes.*

H.R. 1106, largely in its original form, passed the House of Representatives on March 5, 2009. The Senate passed a companion bill shortly thereafter that provided similar protections. However, the final bill that became law contained safe harbor provisions that were somewhat weakened.[85] Ultimately, when the issue of the safe harbor was raised in my lawsuit against Countrywide, District Court Judge Richard Holwell did not accede to the expansive interpretation urged by Countrywide and Bank of America. Instead, in granting our motion to remand, he found that prior drafts of the Homes Act had "proposed more sweeping immunity for loan servicers, but Congress ultimately rejected this language in favor of the current text."[86] He thus held that Congress had not actually overridden state contract law or eliminated all liability with respect to loan modifications, as the banks had argued.

Though this legislation succeeded in largely eliminating the problems of tranche warfare, it accomplished that goal with a meat cleaver when a scalpel would have sufficed. Rather than negotiating a middle ground between the competing tranche interests, lawmakers essentially threw subordinate bondholders to the wolves. Beyond allowing servicers essentially to ignore subordinate bondholder interests when considering modifications, the safe harbor featured a number of other problems:

- It set the discount rate too low for conducting the net present value calculation. While such a calculation was supposed to determine when an investor would be indifferent between receiving the cash from foreclosure today and receiving a stream of cash flows in the future, the low discount rate prescribed in the legislation created a bias toward modification. This resulted in loans being modified that were not in the long-term interest of even the senior bondholders.

- It did not take the likelihood of re-default into account in determining whether a modification was warranted. Even if the net present value of future payments under a modified payment plan exceeded the net present value expected in foreclosure, that calculation would prove meaningless if the borrower re-defaulted on that modified loan within a short time after the workout was put in place. Such an event would result only in a foreclosure delay and a direct loss to investors.

- It ignored servicer conflicts of interest that have been the main impediment to loan modification since the onset of the crisis. The safe harbor did not take into account the fact that servicers held a large number of second liens on their books and earned large fees by having loans remain delinquent. This was the most significant problem with the legislation, and it resulted in far fewer loans being modified than lawmakers had hoped.

At the end of the day, this safe harbor achieved only a hollow victory for banks and legislators. Though it reduced the potential for tranche warfare between the seniors and the subordinates, it did so using a blunt instrument that did not promote an equitable result. Further, while the safe harbor may have removed one impediment to modification, it failed to achieve its primary goal of encouraging workouts, because it failed to appreciate the full range of servicer conflicts. This misguided legislation, if successful, would have actually rewarded banks for modifying the defective loans they had originated. It demonstrates once again the lack of government understanding of the issues raised by loan modifications, as well as the powerful lobbying forces the banks have at their disposal.

Hope for Homeowners

The Hope for Homeowners Program (H4H)[87] was a much ballyhooed government initiative that Congressional analysts forecast would "fix" some four hundred thousand loans shortly after its enactment in July 2008.[88] The idea behind this program was that if loans were written down to levels that would result in an affordable payment and provide the homeowners with equity in their homes, the default and re-default rates would be curtailed. Instead, in the five months after it went into effect, H4H helped only a single borrower avoid foreclosure,[89] leading the Secretary of Housing and Urban Development (HUD) to acknowledge the program as a failure.[90] As of January 2010, the reported number of borrowers assisted by this program was only 96,[91] and there has been no indication that this number has increased materially since that time.

Let's take a quick look at how this program was supposed to have worked. Under H4H, if borrowers qualified and provided verification of income, servicers wrote down the original loan to 90 percent of the appraised value of the property, or a 31 percent debt to income level, whichever was lower. The borrower's original loan was then replaced with an FHA loan with the lower principal balance. The lender or investor holding the original mortgage was paid off, albeit at a loss, while the homeowner would have a new, and theoretically affordable, mortgage. H4H was a program implemented with the best of intentions but was unfortunately rife with problems:

■ Whereas H4H was hailed as a program that would ultimately help investors, no mechanism was put in place to allow investors to approve its use. Furthermore, there was no attempt by any servicer to secure the approval of any investor, likely because they knew that investor approval would not be forthcoming without the removal of the underlying conflicts of interest between the servicer and the investors. In particular, investors had no way of approving writedowns as to the loans they owned, which were generally prohibited by the trust agreements governing these loans. Participants in the program thus had no way of knowing whether an investor would approve a modification under H4H or sue to enforce its contract rights. Furthermore, the terms of H4H made it possible for homeowners to retain their homes at values below market prices, thus forcing investors to hand over equity to delinquent homeowners while absorbing the resulting loss. This situation is yet another example of how the abrogation of contract rights opens up a range of unexpected issues.

- Even with better terms in a more affordable mortgage, most homeowners could not meet the underwriting requirements. The paperwork was cumbersome, and most homeowners could not qualify for a loan anywhere near the size needed for the house they were living in. There was a reason that many prospective homeowners had chosen the more expensive "low-doc" or "no-doc" application types: the income and the assets they had stated were fictitious.

- Servicers had little reason to participate. They received no economic incentive for modifying loans under H4H nor did they have any economic interest in engendering loan modifications. In fact, because the underlying PSAs generally prohibited this type of refinancing activity, servicers faced an enormous legal liability should they participate in this program. Servicers understood these economic disincentives and thus were loath to participate in the program. The only economic motivation that servicers had to participate was the benefit it would provide to their second lien portfolios. Irrespective of this small economic incentive, the program has been practically a 100 percent failure.

The H4H program could possibly have worked if lawmakers had better understood the relationships between homeowners, servicers, and investors. If they had, they might have required servicers to seek an amendment to the PSAs* to allow for this type of modification activity or provide investors with a mechanism to provide their approval for workouts that were truly in investors' interest. Given the perverse economic incentives in a securitization and the behavior of the servicers, this was not in their economic interest. Accordingly, I know of no attempt to modify any PSA contract by any depositor or servicer.

---

* Typically, the depositor in a securitization (generally an affiliate of the servicer) must approve an amendment for it to be put to a vote of the bondholders.

Home Affordable Modification Program

The Home Affordable Modification Program (HAMP),[92] announced in February 2009, evolved directly out of the failure of H4H. The approach of HAMP was to require servicers to modify loans originated before January 1, 2009 by providing them with a direct subsidy. Under this program, the servicer is the recipient of an initial payment of $1,000 for successfully completing a trial modification, another $1,000 payment for each year that the modified loan continues to perform, and an additional $500 per mortgage loan for modifications completed for at-risk borrowers prior to the loan going into default. Incentives are also provided for lenders/investors, who receive $1,500 if loan payments are reduced by 6 percent. The overarching goal of the program is to reduce a borrower's debt-to-income (DTI) ratio to 31 percent, and the U.S. Treasury will reimburse lenders/investors for 50 percent of the costs incurred to bring a borrower's DTI from 38 percent down to 31 percent.

HAMP appears to address head on some of the deficiencies identified in prior government modification programs, e.g., speaking to those who would bear the cost of modifications, creating incentives for servicers to participate, and (in program revisions discussed later) attempting to address second lien modifications. However, the initial results of the program are not promising. Though the jury is still out on the ultimate success of HAMP, to date the program is widely considered a failure. Early Treasury Reports regarding the program indicate that the average participant remains levered to an unsustainable level. For the average participating homeowner after modification, while the front-end DTI ratio (the ratio of the borrower's mortgage debt to income) was at 31 percent, the back-end DTI ratio (the ratio of the borrower's total monthly debt to income) stood at 62.4 percent as of January 2011.[93] This means that over 60 percent of the average borrower's monthly income *after* taking advantage of a HAMP modification was going to service that borrower's debt. This level of debt was unsustainable for the vast majority of borrowers. Indeed, HAMP program guidelines themselves require borrowers with back-end DTIs over 55 percent to seek housing counseling.[94]

Further, under HAMP, banks often allow borrowers to languish in trial modifications for extended periods without converting them to permanent modifications, as servicers stand to gain from extended foreclosure timelines. Because the program's incentives are weighted toward getting as many borrowers as possible into trial modifications, servicers have done just that—without focusing on creating long-term or sustainable solutions for borrowers. Thus, it does not appear that HAMP will solve the nation's foreclosure problems. Instead, it merely delays the inevitable foreclosure and therefore causes additional losses that will be absorbed by investors.

Tax Law

The U.S. tax code has always treated debt that is not paid back as income. In this way, unpaid debt becomes a tax liability, as the defaulter must pay income tax on the portion he or she fails to pay back. In 2007, the government eliminated this tax problem for those who defaulted on home loans.[95] While the intention was good, eliminating the tax burden, in practice, acts as a subsidy for defaulting. One can argue that the tax was unfair in the first place, but the impact of this change in the law was to make defaulting more economical for the homeowner. It is important to point out that other unpaid debt, when forgiven, is still considered taxable income; only home mortgage debt has been exempted. This tax change made it possible to avoid any federal tax problems engendered by defaulting on a home mortgage. Once defaulting becomes cheaper, experience and basic economic principles tell us that we will see more defaults, which is to say more strategic defaults.

Other Programs

There has been a blizzard of government programs since the onset of the mortgage crisis, each designed to address a disparate segment of the securitization process. There are several common denominators to these programs:

- They view the borrower as a victim.

- They do not provide an economic incentive for the borrower to pay.

- They act to shift losses from banks to investors.

These programs, some seemingly put together in a matter of hours by Congressional staffers with little or no experience in mortgages, attempt to deal with incredibly complex problems with impossibly simple solutions. For example, when the issue of second lien mortgages and the conflicts they created was brought to the attention of Congress, the solution conjured by the Treasury in April 2009 was a revision to HAMP called the Second Lien Modification Program (called 2MP).[96] To address the problem of subordinate liens being rendered essentially worthless when the borrower went into default on the first lien and/ or obtained a loan modification, the Treasury chose to treat those liens as equal. Though this solution was promulgated in the interests of "fairness" and was embraced by the large servicers, it ignored the credit hierarchy for these various liens set forth in initial loan agreements. Further, while principal balance reduction was encouraged by HAMP with respect to the first lien, the 2MP did not require principal balance reduction (only forbearance) on the associated second lien. The 2MP thus announced to the world that the U.S. Treasury was willing to make a mockery of contract law for short-term political gain, and it did nothing to deal with the foreclosure crisis in any logical manner.

Several other programs were also proposed and enacted in 2009–2010 that are likely to affect the economic vitality of the U.S. economy for years to come. These programs include the following:

- **Making Home Affordable (MHA).** This program, enacted in March 2009, was designed to help five million homeowners with mortgages guaranteed by Fannie Mae or Freddie Mac.[97] Second liens were explicitly excluded from this program.

- **HAMP 2.0.** In March 2010, the Obama administration announced adjustments to the HAMP and FHA programs designed to encourage principal modification, with explicit provisions for the unemployed and underemployed.[98] These adjustments for loss sharing focus on servicers of the first and second liens, but do not protect the interests of investors.

- **Home Affordable Foreclosure Alternatives (HAFA).** This is a program designed to complement HAMP by providing alternatives to borrowers unable to obtain or successfully transition into a HAMP modification. HAFA, which went into effect in April 2010, offers relocation assistance to homeowners that arrange an approved short sale or deed-in-lieu of foreclosure, thereby subsidizing default.

- **FHA HAMP.** This is the FHA version of HAMP and encourages loan modifications for distressed borrowers with FHA loans. It was provided for in the Homes Act, and it went into effect in August 2009.[99]

As we analyze this profusion of programs that the U.S. government has developed, a clear pattern emerges. When there is a problem, lawmakers "put their fingers in the dike" and hope that the problem will be solved. In reality, the reservoir must be drained and the dike reinforced for any fix to have a lasting impact. Instead of stripping away the wreckage of a failed system and building a new one from the ground up, the government has approached the mortgage problem with a slew of political placebos or band-aids. Its efforts have been consistently focused on making the foreclosure process less onerous for homeowners. Making the foreclosure process easier for homeowners encourages people to default and boosts the number of houses going into foreclosure.

I offer the following examples of borrower complaints to highlight this concept, as well as the dysfunctional nature of the relationship between mortgage servicers and borrowers in the wake of the mortgage crisis. These complaints are culled from a web forum for Countrywide borrowers that discusses their servicing experiences and issues. While far from scientific, they serve as an illustration of the environment facing struggling borrowers and the importance of proper incentives:

> I was outraged that in order to get the help we were requesting, we had to go from having an excellent pay history to completely tarnishing our record by missing 2 months of payments. I spoke to my husband about what Countrywide had suggested and we both agreed that this may be our only chance to get a reasonable rate so we better play by there [sic] rules in order to meet there [sic] criteria for the rate reduction and the loan modification. So we skipped our payments for 2 months and re-applied for the Loan Modification.

⌘ ⌘ ⌘

> We received a loan modification agreement in December, but this was after we were told not too [sic] make a mortgage payment, because if we made a payment and we were current we would not qualify.

⌘ ⌘ ⌘

> We started the process back in Oct of 2008. We have an ARM with a 8.75% rate currently. We have applied for a rate reductions but were told we would have to be delinquent on our account to qualify. That's coming from Countrywide. So, we are behind now and every time we call, we get someone different or the call center in India.

⌘ ⌘ ⌘

Then we were informed to write the hardship letter requesting assistance, told to skip our payments "because you have to be behind on payments for any assistance to be considered"…well we wrote the letters played the 29 days late [game] on the payments because we didn't want to mess with our credit and we both received letters stating the only thing they could suggest for us would be to sell our homes…We are going to try one more time since I'm understanding the president's plan offers incentives to mortgage companies for each loan modified…lets [sic] hope some cash in their pocket will be the catalyst needed for them to start helping keep some of us in our homes…

⌘ ⌘ ⌘

[C]ontacted CW 3 months before mortgage trouble they said "we can not help until you are behind" you guys already know that song and dance.

⌘ ⌘ ⌘

We would not even be behind if they did not advise us to enter into the loan modification and not send any payments in until it was approved or denied! Now they want to foreclose on us because we followed their advice!

⌘ ⌘ ⌘

I was not behind in my mortgage payments yet. I am now two months behind.[100]

Similarly, lawmakers continue to turn to the "carrot" rather than the "stick" in their efforts to induce servicer assistance with loan workouts. Namely, government programs have consistently included provisions increasing servicer compensation despite the fact that these very same institutions often created these problematic loans in the first place. These programs offer to pay servicers for "clerical costs" to reduce the principal balances of loans that they do not own. They provide various mechanisms to bail out the banks from the costs of the second lien loans on their balance sheets. In the end, the costs always seem to be shifted onto the shoulders of investors. Even so, these programs rarely provide much relief to struggling homeowners and have instead proved a consistent source of frustration and anger.

There is no better example of this desire to avoid dealing with the underlying issue of bank solvency and misbehavior that the draft of the proposed Attorney General settlement with the banks over the so-called "robosigners" scandal—referring to low-level employees hired by the banks solely to churn out foreclosure documents.* The proposed settlement contains a little collection of words called "Paragraph N." This paragraph instructs the banks to treat second lien loans in the same manner that they would treat senior, first lien loans.[101] I read this paragraph as being designed to provide political cover to the banks to lien shift (that is, transfer bad lending decisions to the pension funds of America). Keep in mind that this is a proposed settlement, put out by the Attorneys General, that purports to settle claims of misbehavior. Instead, it would convert what should be a punitive settlement surrounding outright fraud into a massive political gift to the largest banks with the ostensible purpose of masking or mollifying the impending threats to bank solvency stemming from their holdings in second lien loans.[102]

---

* The robosigner scandal broke in 2010 with revelations that major banks were cutting corners in their submission of foreclosure documentation to the courts. While an in-depth discussion of this issue is outside the scope of this book, it should suffice to understand that banks were hiring clerical workers to sign affidavits en masse claiming that these individuals had personally reviewed the documentation providing the basis for foreclosure and attesting to its existence and accuracy. Deposition testimony from many of these workers later revealed that these affidavits were false, that the workers had not reviewed the documents or confirmed the facts to which they were attesting, and were often signing the names of others.

While many can debate the wisdom of bailing out the bad lending decisions of the large banks, there should be little doubt that this is within the scope of Congressional authority. However, it is an entirely different matter to destroy a third party's assets, namely, the assets in the mortgage trusts owned by investors. The programs that bail out the banks and hence the FDIC insurance fund by grabbing assets in securitization trusts are of dubious Constitutional validity.[103] Our legislature is saying that the government may orchestrate a bailout of the banking system by usurping a third-party's assets. This short-sighted policy could amount to a violation of the Fifth Amendment's Takings Clause and cause private capital to avoid the U.S. MBS markets, and possibly other U.S. capital markets, for years to come.

"Sunlight is the best disinfectant."

—*Supreme Court Justice Lewis Brandeis*

CHAPTER 7

The Roadblocks to Resolving Problem Mortgages

To end the current economic crisis and rebuild the mortgage market, Americans and our policymakers must first understand the specific conflicts of interest that are endemic to the existing mortgage origination and securitization processes. The relationships between the main players in the mortgage market and the contract provisions that define these relationships can be complex and arcane. Just as laws and sausages are two things that one should never watch being made, the construction of a mortgage trust is not simple or particularly pretty. The answers to why mortgage problems have not been effectively resolved are buried in the fine print and contractual alchemy that form these trusts.

We are experiencing one of the greatest financial calamities in history—one that has destroyed an estimated 40 percent of the world's wealth by 2009[104]—and yet only a handful of lawsuits have been filed by trustees on behalf of investors and not a single trustee has taken a public stand on any of the government proposals that pressure servicers to deviate from the agreements the trustee is charged with enforcing. The investors, upon whom the costs of the current problem are being thrust, have remained largely silent. Why are the trustees ignoring the problems? Why are the investors muzzled? As they say, the devil is in the details.

As we've discussed, a primary cause of the mortgage crisis was the misaligned economic incentives for participants in the mortgage origination and securitization systems. These same conflicts between contractual obligations and economic interests are driving the ongoing fallout from foreclosures and distressed mortgages. Even worse, the fact that economic interests are frequently winning out over contractual responsibilities is threatening to discourage investment in any private mortgage market down the road. Later, I offer recommendations on how the mortgage market should be structured going forward, to attract investors and keep conflicts of interest from engendering another economic crisis, but to place those recommendations in their proper context, we must first discuss and understand the exact nature of the existing conflicts in mortgage securitizations.

As discussed in chapter 5, there are natural conflicts of interest that arise during the process of securitization, just as there would be with any deal that brings together a substantial number of players with competing motivations. While some of these underlying conflicts are addressed by contractual provisions, these provisions can be difficult to enforce, especially when the deal participants have the economic incentive to obstruct or ignore their contractual responsibilities. Reputable organizations might act in this manner because the losses associated with contractual compliance may be greater than the organizations can withstand. In this case, organizations cheat. The conduct of the major U.S. banks over the last several years with respect to mortgage derivatives is a prime example of how institutions will react when faced with such a scenario.

To explain these conflicts, it is useful to review the structure of a typical securitization. As you will recall, a securitization begins when a pool of mortgage loans is sold by the bank that originated them to a type of trust called a REMIC trust. The bank that sells the loans no longer has any ownership interest in them, but it still bears the responsibility for repurchasing at par any loans that fail to meet the bank's underwriting standards or the standards detailed in the PSA and prospectus. Once the loans are transferred into the trust, the cash flows are structured into bonds that are sold to numerous different investors. These loans are serviced by the trust's servicers, who collect monthly mortgage payments from homeowners and ensure the distribution of this cash in accordance with the trust documents. Importantly, these servicers are usually the same entities that originated the mortgages or purchased the loans from third-party originators. Overseeing this entire process is the trustee, whose job is to make sure that all participants adhere to the contracts they signed when the trust was created.

Given the various competing interests that must be brought together to complete a securitization, certain conflicts will arise. The PSAs governing these trusts define how those interests are to be managed, but most PSAs were not designed to handle a catastrophe as profound as the mortgage crisis. This has prevented these contracts from having their desired effect. For example, as discussed, most PSAs require investors to overcome substantial no action or collective action clauses before they can file a lawsuit. These legal hurdles were designed to limit nuisance suits; however, they are currently being used effectively to insulate servicers, securitizers, and originators from liability for bad behavior. I doubt that anyone writing a PSA, or buying securities that result from a PSA, ever considered the possibility that the most reputable banks in the country would flagrantly ignore these contracts in a transparent effort to boost revenues and avoid credit losses, while trustees stood silently by.

We focus now not on the competing interests inherent in securitizations but on the issues preventing these competing interests from being dealt with as the parties to the PSA intended. Notably, in addition to being an impediment to resolving the crisis, many of the problems that follow contributed incrementally to the conditions that brought about the mortgage crisis. After I describe each problem, I introduce in broad strokes some potential solutions. This should provide a general framework for understanding the detailed proposals presented later for revamping and revitalizing the private mortgage finance market.

The Legal Standing Problem

While the contracts underlying existing securitizations are often cumbersome, they do provide mechanisms for solving pervasive problems, such as provisions allowing investors to make changes to the trustee, the servicer, or the PSA as a whole. The difficulty is that for investors to take advantage of these mechanisms, they must overcome no action or collective action clauses to gain legal standing. This means that anywhere from 25 percent to 66 percent of all investors in a trust must locate one another and agree to act in concert before a trustee or a court will even listen, let alone take action. While these percentages may sound attainable, in practice these legal standing requirements preclude all but the most connected bondholder advocates or the largest investors from having their day in court.

One of the primary reasons that investors have been so slow to mobilize in the aftermath of the mortgage crisis, despite early evidence of systemic problems in private label MBS, is that it has been extremely difficult for investors to identify one another and amass the requisite numbers to gain standing. Remember, a securitization can have dozens or even hundreds of investors, who may have disparate interests, backgrounds, and specialties, and they are unlikely to know one another. Bond investors often hold their assets in "street name" or in the Depository Trust Company (DTC), thereby effectively shielding the names of the security holders from public view. This barrier prevents investors from determining who else holds bonds in their trusts and assembling sufficient investor representation to take action. If the U.S. government wished to introduce policies to speed resolution of the mortgage crisis, it would be wise to encourage more transparency in the ownership of MBS.

Making matters worse, bondholders are by nature passive investors, reluctant to thrust their names or their holdings into the spotlight. This reluctance is augmented by a pervasive fear among institutional investors of alienating the U.S. government and the largest banks, both of which could make their lives extremely unpleasant. This fear seems to extend across investor groups. For example, hedge funds are reluctant to sue a major bank for fear of losing their prime brokerage relationship and their leverage, both of which are generally provided by the banks that would be on the short list of potential litigation targets. Large money managers are slow to sue, because they generate substantial revenue from the management of assets linked to the U.S. government. Banks and insurance companies are regulated entities that do not wish to pursue policies that are perceived to be against "social policy."

In 2007, bondholder advocacy groups led by attorneys began emerging to enable investors to share their holdings and build coalitions anonymously. These advocates are also developing mechanisms that would allow investor coalitions to negotiate or sue without revealing their identities, as investors have proven persistently loath to sign their names to any formal letters, let alone lawsuits. As of the writing of this book, investor fears continue to be the primary factor preventing them from coming forward in truly meaningful numbers.

If investors are ultimately able to gain legal standing, four major remedies are available to them:

1. **Petitioning the trustee.** PSAs can vary, but they generally contain provisions that allow investors to petition the trustee for action when they believe that the servicer or some other participant has defaulted on its obligations. If enough investors—usually 25 percent—put the trustee on notice of an alleged default, the trustee in essence becomes an investor fiduciary, obligated to take up the fight on their behalf. At that point, the trustee would face liability should it come to light that the offending party was indeed in default and the trustee failed to act. The potential for liability should induce the trustee to demand that the offending party act in a manner as prescribed in the PSA. This could mean recouping excessive fees from the servicer, demanding that the servicer change its default

servicing practices, or requiring the originator or securitizer to repurchase deficient loans.

2. **Firing the trustee.** In the event that a trustee did not act in the best interests of the bondholders, a standard PSA provision allows investors to remove the trustee without cause, with the consent of the holders of 51 percent of the outstanding bonds in a typical transaction. Should the new trustee remain uncooperative, the investors may fire that trustee as well. A majority of the bondholders can thus control the trust through the selection of a trustee who is willing to act on investors' behalf.

3. **Firing the servicer.** The servicer must perform its job in accordance with the requirements of the underlying servicing contract incorporated into the PSA. If the servicer does not perform its job correctly, investors can request that the trustee remove the servicer and replace it with an entity that will. The request to replace the servicer can be made by petitioning the trustee, so long as investors who represent 25 percent of the bonds act together (as described earlier). However, the trustee has the right to disagree with the investors and refuse to remove the servicer. In that case, the only investor recourse would be to sue the trustee or amass a 51 percent ownership stake and replace the trustee with one willing to take action against the servicer.

4. **Amending the PSA.** If a trust is experiencing problems such as a high percentage of delinquent loans, but an underlying PSA does not allow the servicer to modify these loans, sell them in bulk, or take some other action that investors decide is in their best interest, they may modify the underlying PSA to meet these new market realities. Generally, the requirement to amend a PSA is that holders of 66 percent of the outstanding securities agree on the amendment and get the buy-in of various other parties. While cumbersome, this procedure can prove highly effective if investors choose to work together to resolve the problems plaguing their trust. This

procedure generally requires that the depositor initiate the proposed changes or at least agree with the proposed changes. Given that the depositor is usually owned or controlled by the servicer, the servicer can shield itself from having to fix the mortgage problem. This also allows the servicer to maintain its annuity of late fees and other revenue from mortgages held in suspense. For these reasons, amending the PSA is a tactic that is unlikely ever to be deployed.

Resolving the Legal Standing Problem

The intent of a no-action clause is to prevent lawsuits that are expensive to defend and would result in asymmetric settlements. The common term for these types of nuisance suits is "greenmail." Greenmail is easy to deal with: require that all lawsuits against a trust be brought on a class action basis. This way, any settlement must be approved by a judge and does not treat any single bondholder more favorably than another. This requirement removes the economic incentives for greenmail and prevents the misbehavior that will inevitably arise when parties are insulated from accountability.

Tranche Warfare—Senior versus Subordinate Bonds

Securitizations bring together disparate parties that would not normally be co-investors in the same transaction. Each investor buys bonds in one or more tranches, or slices of a deal, that match that entity's investment objectives. Since the onset of the mortgage crisis, a growing number of securitizations have been found to contain significant percentages of delinquent mortgages. Though investors in a deal can agree that these problem mortgages must be resolved, agreeing on a particular solution is another story. This is because, as discussed earlier, investors may be impacted disparately by a particular type of resolution, depending on the seniority of the bonds they hold. In particular, when a pool of mortgages starts to have credit problems, the subordinate bondholders have an economic incentive to delay the resolution process for as long as possible, while the senior bondholders are motivated to resolve these issues rapidly and move on. The resulting tranche warfare makes it difficult for problem mortgages to be resolved.

An example will help illustrate this important concept and the sources of the conflict between different classes of bondholders. Say that a securitized loan becomes delinquent, and the servicer is presented with two options for dealing with it. On the one hand, the servicer can modify the loan and recognize a loss for the trust of $25,000 today. On the other hand, the servicer can delay the modification process and ultimately recognize a loss for the trust of $50,000 when the loan forecloses in two years. Between those two options, it would be in the best interests of the overall trust to take the smaller loss today (assuming that the borrower does not re-default and end up in foreclosure anyway). The senior bondholder would be in agreement with this position, as it would result in an expedited resolution and a smaller loss to those tranches, but the subordinate bondholder would prefer to take a loss later, even if the loss might be greater.

This is because the servicer is required to "advance" or loan the trust the equivalent of any monthly payment that a borrower fails to make. The result is that the subordinate bondholder receives interest payments until a loss is recognized through modification or foreclosure. Thus, when faced with a choice between recognizing a loss immediately (and foregoing all monthly payments associated with the bond) and pushing to delay the recognition of that loss (while continuing to receive monthly payments of interest and scheduled principal), the subordinate bondholder will always choose the latter. This puts the subordinate and senior bondholders in direct conflict over the proper approach to defaulted loans. This is a defect in the underlying structure of the subordination in traditional mortgage backed securitizations. I know of no PSA that has addressed this problem.

Tranche Warfare—Short versus Long Bonds

Conflicts also arise between the front of the senior structure (the short-term investors who get their money out first) and the back of the senior structure (the long-term investors who have to wait until the short bonds are paid before recouping their investment). Some senior tranches are subdivided even further into securities that repay quickly and securities that pay over a longer term. When there is a credit loss, the front and the back have different economic interests regarding the disposition of any defaulted loans. To an investor in the front of the senior structure, a foreclosure is more attractive than a modification, even if the modification might be a better long-term resolution. This is because the front end gets all of the cash from the foreclosure and is paid off first. The back of the senior structure does not see any of the cash until the front is paid off. This means that the back end of the trust ownership has a much longer perspective than the front bonds. The front-end investors will be repaid and will have forgotten about the transaction long before the back-end investors are paid off.

Resolving Tranche Warfare

The conflicts described in this section are a natural part of the securitization process and are unavoidable. The design flaw is not that conflicts exist but that there is no easy process for investors or servicers to resolve the conflicts. The PSAs that govern the securitizations require that the servicers service in the best interest of the trust *and* that they follow the servicing protocols outlined in the PSA, including respecting the rights of each class of bondholders. However, modifications may affect each class differently, making it virtually impossible for servicers to resolve problem loans without angering some subset of bondholders. This tranche warfare problem in current securitizations has been largely eliminated by the safe harbor promulgated in the Helping Families Save Their Homes Act. As discussed earlier, this safe harbor provided servicers with legal protection to act to resolve delinquent mortgages in the best interests of the overall trust, without having to worry about legal action from one tranche or another. This was not necessarily the best way to handle this problem, as it obliterated subordinate bondholder rights rather than striking a balance between competing interests, but it essentially put the issue of tranche warfare to bed.

In the future, it would be advisable for those structuring securitizations to anticipate this inherent conflict between classes of bondholders and build a mechanism into the PSA that deals fairly with such competing interests rather than sacrificing certain investors *ex post* for the benefit of others. The easiest way to deal with this is to make the trustee the arbiter of the economics of the modification, with guidance from the PSA. For example, the PSA could stipulate a net present value test at the outset of the transaction. As long as the test is objective, it will make sense for the deal as a whole. While it is true that the subordinate investor will take an additional loss and the senior will have less of a loss, this can be priced into the securities when they are created and sold. The fact that such a mechanism was not generally included in PSAs to begin with constitutes a massive failure of imagination on behalf for the creators of these securitizations.

Servicer Conflicts

The issues we just discussed involved conflicts between servicers' various contractual responsibilities. What about situations in which a servicer's contractual obligations are clearly defined in the PSAs but are in direct conflict with the financial interests of that servicer or the servicer's parent company? We have seen time and again that when these situations arise, the financial interests of the servicer will dominate and the contractual rights of investors will be ignored. The key servicer conflicts can be grouped into the following four categories:

1. The collection of late fees and foreclosure expenses paid to affiliated companies.

2. Lien priority conflict.

3. Servicing to avoid put-backs.

4. Information asymmetry.

1. Late Fees and Foreclosure Expenses

In the years following the onset of the mortgage crisis, both homeowners and politicians have bemoaned the glacial speed at which servicers appear to be resolving problem mortgages. One of the major factors contributing to these delays centers on the payment and reimbursement of late fees.

When borrowers are late with their monthly payment, the servicer adds a late fee to the amount owed. The purpose of this fee is to cover the additional expenses a servicer incurs when a payment is late and the servicer must advance that payment to the trust. This late fee is ultimately paid to the servicer in addition to the regular monthly fee the servicer receives for servicing the loan. This has created a conflict for the servicer between earning revenue and resolving a problem loan. If the servicer resolves this delinquent loan, whether through modification, foreclosure, or otherwise, late fees will cease, cutting off this additional source of revenue for the servicer.

The "credit waterfall" in a securitization defines the order in which different parties get paid when the trust receives foreclosure proceeds or payments from borrowers. Most credit waterfalls mandate that servicers be paid before any payments are made to bondholders. This means that if a loan goes into foreclosure or is restructured, servicers are paid their servicing fees and any late fees off the top of any proceeds, thereby increasing the loss experienced by the trust. Say that a bank services a $250,000 loan for a trust and the loan goes bad. If the servicer forecloses in three months, the late fees of $200 per month might amount to $600. If the home is sold for $200,000 (net of all other expenses except late fees), the trust gets $200,000 less the $600 in late fees paid to the servicer or $199,400. If, on the other hand, the servicer waits 12 months to foreclose, resulting in late fees of $2,400, the trust receives only $197,600, because $2,400 in late fees are kept by the servicer.

Though the servicer has a contractual responsibility to place the interests of the bondholders above its own interests, this example shows that servicers have an economic incentive to do the opposite: to delay the resolution of problem loans for as long as possible. Prior to the onset of the mortgage crisis, late fees were not material to the servicer's overall revenue, and servicers thus tended to foreclose quickly, consistent with their obligations to bondholders. As of August 2010, however, 6.9 million U.S. mortgage loans were thirty or more days delinquent or in foreclosure.[105] Today, it is not uncommon for mortgage pools to experience delinquency rates of 40 percent or more. Further, given the glut of foreclosures and foreclosure problems plaguing today's market (exacerbated by robosigner and other documentation problems), some loans are taking two to three years to resolve. The huge number of delinquent loans currently accruing late fees translates into billions of dollars for the servicing industry. This is a wealth transfer from investors to servicers as a reward to servicers for ignoring their contractual responsibilities. This money is in addition to the other wealth transfers discussed earlier.

Late fees are not the only fees that come out at the top of the credit waterfall. A servicer also has the ability to engage suppliers to perform tasks such as appraisals in connection with delinquent mortgage loans. Moreover, these suppliers are often affiliated with the servicing bank or the servicer's parent company, creating an insidious conflict. If a servicer, or an affiliate of the servicer, is paid a fee for every appraisal it orders, especially when the appraisal fee is paid directly to the bank and comes out at the top of the credit waterfall, the servicer might decide that three appraisals are needed instead of one when determining what to do about a problem mortgage. These excess appraisals benefit the servicer to the detriment of the investors/bondholders.

The same conflict exists for homeowner insurance that is "force placed" on the defaulted properties. When a borrower stops making mortgage payments, including homeowner insurance premiums, the servicer may move the insurance on the home to an affiliated company that collects the insurance premiums, again off the top of the credit waterfall, while the property is in default. An example is the Balboa

Insurance Group, formerly owned by Countrywide, which handled the insurance on the underlying properties when Countrywide mortgage loans went into default. Prior to Bank of America's sale of Balboa, which was completed in June 2011,[106] Countrywide's servicing unit set the insurance fee with Balboa, and the bill was sent to the securitization trust with no accounting verification and no attempt to ensure that the insurance rate was competitive.

According to a November 2010 article in *American Banker*, many of the country's largest banks frequently engage in questionable practices with respect to force-placed insurance, potentially costing investors billions of dollars per year.[107] The article noted that force-placed insurance could be 10 times as costly as regular policies, and that servicers frequently received kickbacks in the form of "commissions" from these insurance companies for the rights to a servicer's force-placed business.[108] In other instances, servicers placed excessive or unnecessary insurance, improperly backdated these insurance policies, or received an additional cut of the premiums by reinsuring part of the homeowner policy.[109] All of these tactics pile on losses for investors and continue to do so as long as the defaulted mortgages remain unresolved. At the time of this writing, Bank of America just received regulatory approval to sell the Balboa insurance subsidiary to QBE of Australia.[110] One can only suspect that disclosure of these conflicts caused Bank of America to dispose of the subsidiary.

These problems took center stage last year when the Federal Trade Commission (FTC) announced that it had reached a $108 million settlement with Countrywide over charges that the servicer had deceived cash-strapped homeowners into paying inflated fees for default-related services.[111] According to the FTC's complaints, Countrywide set up subsidiary vendors for the sole purpose of increasing its revenues by overcharging homeowners for everything from appraisals to lawn care.[112] By funneling default-related services through these subsidiaries, Countrywide succeeded in earning substantial profits during bad economic times.[113] The FTC settlement was designed to reimburse homeowners for their losses; however, careful reflection reveals that it was actually the investor that suffered a loss as a result of these practices. When homeowners are in default and not making their mortgage payments, they most likely are not reimbursing the bank to cut their grass. Instead, these costs are included in the costs of foreclosure and passed on to the investor. The FTC settlement did not understand this basic fact of securitization: the investor absorbs virtually all of the losses from any misbehavior on the part of the servicer.

The Attorneys General might have lacked an in-depth understanding of the problems within securitizations when they agreed to the Countrywide settlement in 2008, but agreements like the FTC settlement described earlier and the proposed robosigner settlement discussed in chapter 6 can only lead to one of two possible conclusions. On one hand, policymakers might be pathetically incompetent and are being taken advantage of by the more sophisticated large banks. I do not subscribe to this view. On the other hand, policymakers may have little interest in actually resolving these matters, instead being more concerned with scoring political points. After reviewing the various government settlements that have emerged from this crisis, this second conclusion seems the more likely explanation.

2. Lien Priority Conflict

The biggest conflict of interest inherent in the current securitization model occurs when a servicer services a loan for a borrower who has other outstanding debts with the same servicer or the servicer's parent company. This may not sound serious, but it is proving to be a toxic problem in resolving delinquent mortgages. To understand the problem fully, some definitions and explanations of lien priorities are in order. The following priorities are well established and have been in place in the U.S. banking system for over one hundred years:

- **Lien.** The right of a creditor or bank to sell a property to satisfy the debt of someone who has failed to meet his or her loan obligations with respect to that property. A lien is included in every mortgage contract signed by a homeowner when purchasing a house. The purpose of the foreclosure process is to allow the creditor to execute the right secured by its lien.

- **First mortgage lien.** The senior lien on a piece of real property. This lien has the first priority in the event of foreclosure, meaning that it is paid off first. Accordingly, this lien has the least credit risk of all mortgage liens.

- **Second mortgage lien.** The next most senior lien on a piece of real property. This lien gets paid off only when the first lien has been paid in full. A second lien can be placed on a property after the first lien is placed or simultaneously with the placement of the first lien. When placed on the property at the time of purchase, a second lien is often called a piggyback loan. This loan generally carries a substantially higher rate of interest to reflect the high-risk nature of the loan.

- **Unsecured credit.** A loan to a borrower that is not secured by real estate and is the most junior or lowest priority in the homeowner's capital structure. This category often consists of credit card or install-ment loans. These loans generally carry the highest rate of interest, reflecting the significantly higher credit risk stemming from the absence of any lien securing collateral from which to satisfy the debt.

The servicer conflict involving lien priorities is significant. Securitized loans are virtually always first lien mortgages, meaning that they have the most senior lien priority. Pursuant to its contractual priority and corresponding lower rate of interest, the first lien loan should invariably be the first to be repaid. However, servicers with other outstanding loans to the same borrower prefer that these junior loans be repaid first. In fact, servicers have substantial financial incentives to favor second lien loans and unsecured credit debts over first lien mortgages, even though they signed contracts saying that they would service those loans in the best interest of the investors. Once servicers sell first lien loans into securitization, they lose any economic interest in the performance of those loans. The lien priority issue is so important because, as discussed in chapter 5, the four largest banks in the United States, who are also the four largest mortgage originators and servicers, hold over $400 billion in second lien mortgages.[114]

As with the other conflicts we've discussed, the best way to illustrate the lien priority problem is with an example. Assume that Joe Homeowner purchases a home for $500,000 and secures a $400,000 first lien loan at an interest rate of 6 percent. Concurrently, Joe takes out a second lien loan to fund the down payment of $100,000. The second lien loan, being more risky, carries an interest rate of 8 percent. The originating bank (which is also the servicer) elects to sell the 6 percent loan to a MBS trust while retaining the higher-rate loan in its portfolio. Note that in this familiar scenario, Joe has no equity in the home and has not made a down payment with his own money.

Soon thereafter, things take a turn for the worse for Joe, and he cannot afford to make his mortgage payments. We will assume that the servicer has determined that the underlying property could be sold in foreclosure for $350,000, net of expenses. If the servicer foreclosed on the property, it would cause the second lien holder (the servicer) to suffer a 100 percent loss on its $100,000 junior loan. This is because the first lien holder is entitled to recoup its entire unpaid principal balance before the second lien holder receives a dime. The first lien holder in this example would thus receive the $350,000 recouped from the foreclosure sale (resulting in a loss of $50,000), while the second lien holder would receive nothing and suffer a loss of $100,000.

On the other hand, if the servicing bank modified Joe's first lien loan and reduced the principal balance to reflect the pending $150,000 loss, the balance of the first lien could be reduced from $400,000 to $250,000 without touching the second lien loan balance. The entire loss would then be taken by the first or senior lien holder, which happens to be someone other than the servicing bank, while the bank's second lien would remain pristine. If Joe defaults again, the property would be liquidated for the $350,000 at foreclosure, with the trust or senior first lien holder receiving $250,000 and the servicer and second lien holder bank receiving $100,000. The loss in this scenario is shifted entirely from the servicer and junior lien holder to the trust/investor and senior lien holder, a phenomenon known as "lien shifting."

Another version of lien shifting occurs when the servicer reduces the interest rate on the first lien so that the borrower has the cash necessary to service the second lien. While the principal of the loan remains intact, the actual value to the owner of the senior loan decreases based on the reduction in interest flow. Again, the purportedly senior lien is being devalued for the benefit of the purportedly junior lien.

If we take into account borrowers' credit card debts and other unsecured credit, the problem gets worse. Because there is no collateral to which to turn to satisfy these debts, the servicing bank once again has an economic incentive to reduce the interest rate or forgive principal on the most senior and most secured debt in a homeowner's capital structure for the benefit of the subordinate or unsecured junior lien positions. This is clearly outside the intent and letter of the vast majority of PSA agreements, but it is being done on a mass scale with the encouragement of several government-enacted "fixes."

This lien priority conflict is precisely why PSAs that govern most securitizations carry strong prohibitions or limitations on restructurings or loan modifications. However, given the political and economic climate in the aftermath of the mortgage crisis, rational restructurings are necessary, as well as in the economic interests of investors.[*] The protections for investors contained in the PSAs should force servicers to negotiate with investors to reach a solution acceptable to all parties. PSAs are being ignored and trustees are standing idly by as servicers effect a massive wealth transfer from investors to themselves through lien shifting.

---

[*] The term "rational" here denotes restructurings that deal with junior liens in a productive and equitable manner, while still honoring contractual and legal subordination.

3. Servicing to Avoid Put-Backs

When banks originated mortgages and sold them into securitization trusts, they made numerous statements regarding the quality of the loans they were selling. The arrangers of securitizations often adopted these statements as their own and passed them along to the trust and the bondholders. These statements, known as representations and warranties, were generally made in the purchase and sale agreements between originators and securitization arrangers, and were then incorporated into the PSAs for the benefit of the trust (see example, appendix VII). The originating and securitizing banks further agreed that if any of these statements were found to be materially untrue as to any particular loan, investors and insurers would have the right to "put back" the loan to the seller, that is, to force the selling bank to repurchase the loan out of the pool at par. In this way, loans that were misrepresented or fraudulent could be removed from the pool and the corresponding loss would be borne by the firm that sold the defective loan.

Prior to the mortgage crisis, this was not a significant issue. Over the years, I have often had to research the details of a particular loan that has gone bad in a transaction to see whether it complied with the given reps and warranties. Whenever I concluded that the loan was not as represented, the banks generally repurchased the loan and made the transaction whole. It was rarely a point of contention.

It should come as no surprise that mortgage originators and securitization arrangers no longer want to absorb the losses inherent in buying back defective loans. Consequently, servicers, especially those owned by mortgage originators, are generally looking to minimize put-backs at the expense of the investors they are contractually obligated to protect. This conflict becomes particularly apparent in the way that servicers handle claims for Private Mortgage Insurance (PMI). PMI compensates the lender for a portion of its loss when foreclosure proceeds are insufficient to repay the lender on a defaulted loan. When a loan with PMI is securitized, the trust becomes the beneficiary of the PMI policy, providing investors with an avenue for recouping a portion of their losses should that loan go into default. It is the servicer's contractual responsibility to file a PMI claim.

The problem is that servicers frequently choose not to file PMI claims that would benefit the trust, because such claims often trigger investigations by the PMI provider into the characteristics of the underlying loans to determine the legitimacy of the claims. If the PMI provider were to reject a claim, the servicer would have a contractual duty to inform the other participants in the transaction. This would open the door to a potential put-back claim from investors based on the same deficiency on which the PMI carrier relied to reject the claim. Further, should the PMI company decide to rescind coverage on a particular loan based on an underwriting deficiency, the originator would be exposed to a put-back based on the standard representation and warranty provided by the originator that the loans would carry PMI.

To date, I am aware of no instance in which a servicer has notified the trust participants that a PMI provider has rejected a claim or rescinded coverage. Servicers frequently elect not to pursue PMI claims in the first place to avoid such a scenario. This is a perfectly rational economic decision from the standpoint of the servicer; the problem is that it does nothing but increase investor losses. Furthermore, such a decision is inconsistent with the servicing protocol to which the servicer agreed when it entered into the PSA with investors.

The reluctance of banks to honor their contractual obligations with respect to representations and warranties does not end with their conduct as servicers but continues up the securitization chain to their conduct as securitization underwriters and originators with contingent liabilities to repurchase loans found to be defective. This response by the banks is not surprising, given the conflicts of interest discussed here and the size of the threat to the financial industry from put-back exposure.

As we've discussed, during the Boom Years and the run up to the mortgage crisis, lenders and issuers increasingly ignored their own lending and underwriting guidelines in an effort to boost loan and securitization volume. This resulted in a massive amount of misrepresentation in the creation of securitizations between 2004 and 2008, meaning that banks now face significant put-back liability. Two comprehensive reports have been issued on the potential exposure of the banks to this liability, the first by Compass Point Research & Trading, a broker-dealer based in Washington DC, and the second by Laurie Goodman, the well-known managing director of Amherst Securities. Both have come to the same basic conclusion: the liability faced by the banks is enormous.

Compass Point calculated a base case put-back liability for the top 11 underwriters of private label transactions (that is, non-agency deals) of approximately $134 billion, including $35.2 billion for Bank of America and $23.9 billion for J.P. Morgan.[115] Compass Point applied a methodology to the different vintages and types of MBS that went through the expected percentages of deficient loans, loans that investors would try to put back to the banks, and loans that banks would actually have to buy back. Based on this and the average loss severity of loans in delinquency, Compass Point was able to generate best case, base case, and worst case scenarios for the losses the banks could be expected to suffer. The critical assumption in each analysis was the percentage of investors that would actually act to put loans back to the underwriters and the success rate of those attempted put-backs. This has been the hardest factor to handicap because it appears that most investors are reluctant to pursue potential repurchase claims through litigation, even if they stand to recover significant amounts. Still, though Compass Point's base case analysis uses the aggressive assumption that investors will successfully force put-backs on 80% of seriously delinquent and defaulted subprime and Alt-A loans from 2005 to 2007,[116] this does not alter the conclusion that the amount of potential liability faced by the banks is almost beyond comprehension.

Laurie Goodman, on the other hand, performed a detailed analysis of deficiencies in each type of mortgage class (prime, alt A, subprime and option ARM), including the subcategories of loan status (always performing, reperforming, non-performing, and paid off), and calculated the expected losses for each category.[117] Again, the critical assumption in this analysis was the percentage of private label investors that would pursue their claims. Goodman assumed that 10-15 percent of investors would successfully pursue their claims. Using this assumption and her own methodology, she concluded that the aggregate loss for the servicers solely from put-back exposure would be $97 billion. If Goodman had applied Compass Point's success ratio of 80% to her numbers, her estimate of the potential loss from put-backs would have been five to six times higher.

While I can quibble with the details and assumptions of each of these analyses, it is clear that the magnitude of the potential loss is astounding. It is for this reason that the major banks have adopted an aggressive posture toward put-back requests since the onset of the mortgage crisis, vowing to fight the requests on a loan-by-loan basis and draw out the put-back process for as long as possible. For example, J.P. Morgan CEO Jamie Dimon said during the company's 2010 third quarter earnings call that "[w]e'll just drag out [repurchase] losses as these things play themselves out." [118] He followed that statement up during J.P. Morgan's fourth quarter 2010 earnings call by saying, "[y]ou've got to do it loan by loan. This could be a long, ugly mess."[119] Echoing that strategy, Bank of America CEO Brian Moynihan said during his company's third quarter 2010 earnings call that,

> [t]his really gets down to a loan-by-loan determination and we have, we believe, the resources to deploy against that kind of a review...we will go in and fight this. It's worked to our benefit to—we have thousands of people willing to stand and look at every one of these loans.[120]

While there have been some exceptions, most investors have been reluctant to go to the mat on repurchases and take these powerful financial institutions to court when confronted with the refusal of banks to honor their contractual reps and warranties. Based in part on the reluctance of investors to pursue litigation over these failed put-back attempts, banks have avoided reserving for substantial losses from investor put-backs. Still, the magnitude of this potential liability and the possibility that the banks will have to pay a substantial portion of these claims has made it difficult for the banks to raise capital and perform the functions required of a banking system. Until put-backs and the solvency of the banking system are properly addressed, the banks will be hindered from performing their vital role in our economy.

4. Information Asymmetry

By virtue of their role, servicers have the most current information regarding the status of specific loans in a pool. In addition, they hold all of the initial contracts between homeowners and mortgage originators, as well as all of the documents used by originators to underwrite the loans. In theory, all of this detailed information is made available to the investors through guarantees in the PSA, but to obtain this information, investors must make a formal request through the trustee. Trustees have, until recently, been content to sit on their hands and ignore these requests. Even when trustees elect to pass along such requests, servicers have been notoriously slow to make this information available, and much of it is missing or outdated by the time it is delivered. The information is often delivered in a disorganized or inscrutable manner that is of little use to investors. Because the information is not checked or audited by anyone but the servicer, the information delivered is often only the information that the servicer wants the investors to see. Meanwhile, the servicer may withhold critical information including the following:

- Loan-specific information needed to discover fraudulent or misrepresented loans.

- Information on early payment defaults that must be repurchased by the originator.

- Records of loan modifications that may or may not have been legitimate.

- Evidence of the trust's entitlement to mortgage insurance proceeds that the servicer did not claim.

- Information on delinquent first liens where the servicer holds a second lien that it is encouraging the borrower to pay in lieu of the senior lien.

- Records of payments from the trusts to community organizer groups for counseling services provided to borrowers.

- Records of payments from the trusts to companies affiliated with the servicer or the servicer's parent company.

- Evidence of borrower fraud.

Again, much of this resistance to providing loan files and other loan information stems from the servicers' desire to avoid put-backs. Rather than open themselves or their parent companies up to repurchase liability stemming from breaches of reps and warranties, servicers would rather delay investor receipt of that information. By dragging their heels, servicers hope that investors will get tired of throwing money at the problem or that the problem loans will eventually be removed from the pool through foreclosure, meaning that delinquency information regarding the specific foreclosed loans will no longer be made available in monthly servicing reports. Monthly servicing reports generally discuss the status of the existing loan pool for that trust and do not discuss loans that have been "resolved," as in foreclosed or paid off. This may eliminate a potential source of red flags for some investors just looking at the current month's report.

As a result, investors are being denied timely, consistent, and accurate information regarding their collateral. While investors may petition the trustee for this information, the trustee is generally under no obligation to cooperate and may ignore the requests.[121] This lack of disclosure and access to information would never be tolerated in any other public capital markets but is par for the course when it comes to recent-vintage MBS.

Resolving Servicer Conflicts

In most securitizations, investors have the ability to resolve servicer conflicts, if they are able to organize and amass sufficient holdings to take action. Once they have banded together, investors can fire and replace the trustee or servicer, file lawsuits, and/or modify their PSAs. In future transactions, as discussed in chapter 10, investors would be wise to demand stronger enforcement provisions that would make it easier for bondholders to enforce put-backs, access information, or have input into proposed loan modifications. This, combined with stronger incentives for trustee cooperation with bondholders, would encourage servicers to respect bondholder wishes, even if it came at the expense of their bottom lines.

Under the current paradigm, the only way to resolve servicer conflicts, barring a trustee change of heart, is through collective investor action. The government could help with this process in several distinct ways. First, it could make it easier to identify the investors in each trust. Second, the government could require greater transparency through a Truth in Servicing Act. In enacting such legislation, lawmakers could require banks to report detailed information about loan pools to both the government and investors. The simple, reflexive approach of making the servicers' actions more visible would encourage servicer compliance with their contracts. Third, the government could pass legislation allowing first lien holders to have input into the treatment of junior liens. Alternatively, it could pass a law—similar to the one proposed by Rep. Brad Miller—preventing originators from also having servicing arms or prevent servicers from servicing first lien mortgages when they held an interest in the junior or unsecured debt of the same borrower. Either of these proposals would go a long way toward eliminating lien priority conflicts.

Trustee Apathy

Each mortgage securitization has a trustee that is charged with acting as a fiduciary of the trust and its investors. In practice, however, the trustee tends to remain "aggressively passive," as described by attorney and bondholder advocate David Grais,[122] because it is indemnified by the servicer under most PSAs. These agreements further provide that trustees need not act on behalf of investors until those investors manage to organize and present 25 percent of the outstanding bonds to the trustee, along with specific evidence that the servicer is defaulting on its obligations. Once a quarter of the investors gets together and petitions the trustee, the trustee has the choice of acting or simply ignoring the petition. If the trustee chooses to ignore the investor request and investors successfully sue the trustee, the servicer will pay all expenses and losses of the trustee pursuant to its indemnification obligation.*

Because the servicer agrees to pay any legal claims and fees that the trustee may face based on the actions of the servicer, the trustee faces no economic consequences for failing to do its job. This means that the entity charged with overseeing the participants in a transaction over the thirty years that the deal may be outstanding has no reason to spend any time or effort making sure that the rules of the transaction are being correctly applied. In fact, because trustees are paid little for their services—usually one basis point on the outstanding principal, or $10,000 for a $100 million transaction—trustees are better off doing nothing and avoiding having to maintain any staff or incur any costs. Accordingly, while the trustee is supposed to be the watchdog for the

---

* One could reasonably speculate that the lack of trustee activity has also been motivated by interlocking business with the servicers. Does anyone seriously think that Bank of New York will act aggressively against Bank of America if two-thirds of its trustee business is generated by B of A?

trust, it is paid to sit on its hands. The servicer, in turn, is left to its own devices, with absolutely no oversight.

Resolving Trustee Apathy

Short of legislation, the fix for this state of affairs is simple: the investors should notify the trustee that they control 25 percent of the transaction and believe that there is evidence of a servicer default. Complying with this difficult process is the only way for investors to have any hope that a fiduciary will oversee their transactions. Should the trustee refuse to act on their behalf, investors can sue the trustee for breach of contract in addition to suing the servicer and other participants for defaulting on their obligations. Whether any recovery stemming from this suit would be paid out of the pockets of the trustee or the servicer would be of little concern to the investors at that point.

A second option would be for investors to create a new independent trustee owned by the investors, which would act as a fiduciary on the existing transaction. This trustee could agree to have no business relationships with the servicing banks, except for being the trustee on future transactions. This would remove all current and future conflicts of interest for trustees. Furthermore, on future transactions, the trustee fee should depend to some extent on the credit performance of the pool or the mortgage market. If the trustee is going to have to become active, the additional costs inherent in such a role should be reflected in the fee structure of the trust services.

The Loss of Investor Confidence

The conflicts discussed so far in this chapter have helped prevent problem mortgages from being resolved. These toxic mortgages continue to hamper the cleanup from the mortgage crisis and drag down our economy. Most Americans and politicians focus on this aspect of the problem and the fact that millions of homeowners in the United States are facing foreclosure. While these issues are significant, the far more devastating consequence of these persistent roadblocks is the long-term impact they will have on the future of the private mortgage market. Namely, *the desire to invest capital in America is at risk. Without capital, our economy will languish.*

Let's be clear: the biggest problem in the U.S. mortgage market today is the private sector investors' loss of confidence in the market. The lack of private capital has turned a problem with toxic mortgages into a crisis. Providers of capital have disappeared because they lack trust in the mortgage market and the opacity of the financial system. They do not want to lend in the United States as long as the government overrides the rights of investors in order to help banks and homeowners. Americans who have enjoyed an abundant supply of private sector mortgage money for generations should remember that no law of nature guarantees a supply of capital to the U.S. markets. It is investor confidence in the financial structure and legal system that makes capital available. This confidence has eroded, and it must be rebuilt.

I can best explain the investor confidence issue by summarizing a conversation I had with a senior executive at a major non-U.S. bank at the end of 2009. The executive asked me a series of questions about the problems facing the U.S. government. I never imagined that I would have a conversation like this when discussing the United States and its securitizations:

> **Banker**: Why is your government trying to allow servicer banks to modify first lien loans before they force the elimination of second lien loans?

> **Author**: There is a problem in that the largest servicers are also the largest banks in the country as well as the largest holders of second lien loans.

> **Banker:** So if your government honors lien priority, the largest banks in the United States will be in financial trouble or possibly insolvent.

Author: Yes, that is the problem.

Banker: If the banks were to become insolvent, your FDIC would take a loss.

Author: Yes, that is correct.

Banker: And the FDIC is your government fund to honor the deposit insurance promises?

Author: Yes.

Banker: So the government is taking property from a third party so that its deposit insurance scheme does not have to pay claims.

Author: Yes.

Banker: How is this different from the situation in Iceland in 2008, when the banks were nationalized and the Icelandic government failed to honor its deposit insurance agreements?

Author: It is not substantially different.

Banker: Then why do you think that this scheme is not a sovereign default by the U.S. government?

This conversation demonstrates the magnitude of the credibility gap facing the U.S. government. *If the current mortgage securitization problems are not handled correctly, there will be much less investment in the United States in the future, and any available capital will be more expensive due to political risk.* Once investors believe that their contracts will not be honored, they will invest their capital elsewhere or demand a substantial political premium for the risk of investing in U.S. mortgages. If this happens, the efficiency and size of the largest fixed income market in the world will go the way of the dodo bird. Reform will be moot.

Before we resolve all the problem mortgages and rebuild our mortgage market, we need to agree on the goal. *The objective of any mortgage resolution strategy should be to mitigate the losses for investors in the securitizations.* Keeping homeowners in their homes should not be the objective; it is a means to an end. Homeowners should be kept in their homes only when they can pay enough to make it economically beneficial for the investor.

While this objective may sound hardhearted, one must keep in mind that the investors in securitization trusts are the country's pension funds and the investment accounts of working Americans. It is not the obligation of an investor to augment its losses to implement social policy, to provide capital to banks, or to satisfy the political needs of any politician or party. While social policy that dictates taking pity on defaulting homeowners at the expense of Americans' pension and retirement accounts may sound defensible to some when considered in isolation, it is foolhardy when the resulting harm to investor confidence is taken into account. Instead, it must be left up to the investors, who own the loans and supply much of the capital for homeownership in America, to decide how to resolve mortgage credit problems. I realize that this may be politically unpalatable, but it is essential to the survival of the mortgage market as we know it. The sooner we realize that this is correct, the sooner the U.S. economy can recover from the mortgage mess.

This is not to say that it will be rational or feasible for investors to foreclose on all delinquent borrowers; in fact, this outcome would not be good for anyone. The right way to mitigate losses is through some combination of modifications (with principal and interest reductions), refinancing into government loan programs with possibly some sort of debt forgiveness, foreclosure while providing a renting option to the existing occupants, short sales, cash for keys, and temporary debt forbearance. No tool to resolve the mortgage problem should be considered off limits. The options should be considered by investors according to their economic interests, not due to political pressure to subsidize servicer banks clandestinely because they face financial losses in their second lien loan portfolios. Investors will resolve problem mortgages as quickly as possible while minimizing their losses, if given the chance.*

When the banks were faced with delinquent mortgage loans on their own balance sheets at the beginning of the mortgage crisis, they established a rational economic process to resolve these loans. The process was not foisted upon them by government coercion but rather created by the banks in their own self-interest. Contrary to popular belief, investors also want to resolve delinquent mortgages. Investors have no interest in having their money tied up in non-performing assets. They would prefer to work out the loans, minimize their losses, and redeploy the money into new investments. There is no reason to believe that the investors in securitizations would resolve a pool of loans any differently than the manner in which the banks resolved their own delinquent mortgages.

What should *not* happen is for the government to mandate how loans should be resolved. This will inevitably have the effect of radically increasing the losses to investors, and investors will resist all such programs as violations of their contracts. This is especially true if a program creates a loss for the investor and a corresponding gain for the servicer. As described in chapter 6, government programs enacted to fix the mortgage default problem have not worked and will never work as long as they cater to the economic interests of homeowners and banks while trampling the contractual rights of investors.

---

* It is worth emphasizing that the particular reasons for any individual borrower's credit problems are irrelevant to the investor, whether they include sloppy underwriting or homeowner fraud. The investor is only interested in fixing the problem. If homeowners misrepresented themselves on the loan application, it is of no relevance to the modification or foreclosure decision, except as it relates to the borrower's ability to continue making payments. An investor is not a prosecutor and should not be in the business of figuring out what the intentions of a defaulting homeowner were when the loan was originated. The investor's objective is to resolve the loan as quickly and efficiently as possible.

Dealing with investments that decline in value and suffering credit losses is part of being an investor. However, investors should tolerate neither losses that go beyond their contractual responsibilities nor parties that ignore their contracts in order to further economic or social goals. Programs mandated or promoted by the government to "help" homeowners create moral hazard problems that have economists worried; such programs are nothing more than invitations for homeowners to strategically default.

Government programs aimed at increasing bank capital or keeping people in homes they can't afford will extend the problem and do more harm than good. Furthermore, once Americans realize that their pension plans are being raided to bail out banks and pay for failed social policies, the political fallout will be substantial. Mortgage resolution has been delayed for over three years while efforts were made to further these policies, and private sector investments in mortgage assets have dried up as a result. "Successfully" solving today's crisis by coercion, intimidation, and retribution will result in a Pyrrhic victory if the most efficient vehicle ever devised for financing American homeownership is destroyed.

Resolving the Loss of Investor Confidence

The root cause of the loss of investor confidence has been the U.S. government's interference with and failure to enforce the contracts on which investors relied when they agreed to lend capital to the mortgage market. The politicians who intervened in an attempt to "solve" the mortgage problem may have sought to help their constituents avoid foreclosure and banks avert insolvencies. The role of government should instead be limited to making sure that the mortgage system is efficient, transparent, and as free from systemic risks as possible. If there is a social policy that the government wishes to encourage, it should provide economic incentives so that the parties can respond voluntarily to those incentives, not interfere with private contracts by fiat.

As discussed, contractual change by fiat is a strategy that will ensure that the MBS market will not survive as an efficient vehicle for the intermediation of credit in the long term. The United States has no exclusive monopoly on the securitization market; other countries will soon be able to compete for investor resources. In fact, abrogating contracts in the mortgage market will invariably affect the level of investment in other capital markets as well. The sole reason the United States has been successful in using the securitization market in the past is that investors demanded the securities created by those transactions.

Uncertainty regarding the laws of securitization will cause investors to demand investment protection through other legal systems, such as English courts, or to abandon the U.S. securitization system altogether. Should investors demand that English law govern a future U.S. securitization, it would mean that legal disputes surrounding American mortgage securitizations would be resolved in English courts. The benefits of this would include the fact that English courts are removed from U.S. political pressures and would be more likely to enforce the intended contracts between investors and servicers. English law is already the standard securitization law for non-U.S. transactions.

Neither of these options is particularly appealing to the American capital market, from either an economic or a reputational point of view. As discussed, the U.S. Treasury recently came out with a proposal that would have the private label market taking over from Fannie Mae and Freddie Mac.[123] It is unclear how this can work, when there is currently no private label market and the policies of the U.S. government are causing investors to take unwarranted credit losses and discouraging their participation in any future mortgage market.

With that in mind, I offer a few recommendations for restoring and rebuilding the investor confidence that has been shattered by government interference with private contracts. These suggestions should sound familiar but are worth reiterating:

1. The government should stop maligning investors for the problem. A quick assessment of the mortgage market will reveal that investor involvement is essential to providing affordable housing to millions of Americans. Investors bargained for their contractual rights with other securitization participants, all of which, with the possible exception of borrowers, entered into these agreements with their eyes wide open. Investors should not be vilified for seeking to enforce their contracts with servicers. Further, no rational objective is served by pushing the costs of social engineering and bank solvency onto investors, as this will discourage investor participation in any future mortgage market.

2. The government should encourage transparency in servicing activity to ensure that servicers are acting as per their contractual obligations. Servicers have the most control over the pace and ballooning costs of foreclosure, and they are the participants with the authority to effect a loan modification or other mortgage resolution. It is critical that these entities be monitored by the rest of the market to ensure that they are protecting investor interests rather than their own.

3. Lawmakers and regulators can and should be encouraging investors to band together to act as one group, which will greatly accelerate the resolution process.

The last two recommendations can be accomplished by efforts at increased transparency, namely, by requiring servicer reports to be audited and made available to investors. Publishing the ownership of MBS, or making investors' names available on a confidential basis, will also help investors to identify one another and amass sufficient standing in each deal to affect change.

If we do not take the right actions in the short term to resolve the existing problems with the mortgage market, there will be no efficient private mortgage market in the long term, as we will have alienated private investors. This is why politicians should not interfere with a market out of political expediency without considering all of the ramifications. Such interference has led and will in the future lead directly to the U.S. government—and thus, taxpayers—becoming the sole supplier of U.S. mortgage financing. Instead, government efforts should ensure that the ability to enforce contracts is never in question, thereby encouraging private investors to reinvest in the U.S. mortgage market and allowing the government to reduce its support. Homeowners and taxpayers alike can only benefit when the government is able to extract itself from the role of financing the entire mortgage market, and decisions regarding the structure of the market are left up to the experts: the private market.

"Risk comes from not knowing what you are doing."

—*Warren Buffet*

CHAPTER 8

Systemic Risk

The objective of a mortgage finance system is to facilitate the flow of capital from those with capital to invest (primarily pension funds, insurance companies, and endowments) to those in need of capital, primarily individuals seeking to own real estate. The goal is to do this as efficiently as possible while limiting systemic risk to the economy. Systemic risk is the risk of the collapse of the entire financial system or market, based on the interdependency or common risk of entities within that system or market. The United States has seen its economic system fall into crisis twice in the last thirty years due to problems with residential mortgages. It can no longer be disputed that our current mortgage finance system creates systemic risk and thus fails to meet these crucial objectives.

As we have discussed, the root cause of both the mortgage crisis and the S&L crisis was the same: sustained interest rate movements exacerbated by the prepayment option embedded in the conventional U.S. mortgage structure. Remember that a conventional mortgage loan can be prepaid by the borrower at any time without penalty. If a borrower has a financial option and chooses to exercise that option, it usually means that the lender, as the writer of that option, is in a loss position. Thus, a widespread penalty-free prepayment option has the tendency to create systemic losses for mortgage investors.

While a loss to an investor on an individual loan will not create an issue for the system, tens of millions of people doing the same thing at the same time (all prepaying or not prepaying) can result in a tidal wave of losses hitting the financial system whenever there is a large interest rate movement. This is a classic example of systemic risk. Financial firms have figured out how to "hedge" or offset mortgage risks when they are within limits, but it should be obvious that a system cannot give a large financial benefit to all homeowners and a corresponding loss to the financial sector and expect it to be absorbed all of the time without consequences.

Given the sheer amount of U.S. mortgage debt—over $11 trillion at the market's peak in 2007[124]—there will inevitably be a concentration of mortgage prepayment and credit risk in financial institutions. It is impossible to spread this risk around or hedge an exposure that is repeated tens of millions of times. The exposure of the investment community and the economy as a whole to systemic risk from mortgages is thus enormous. The failure of a financial institution will result in the government footing the bill for at least part of the loss. This exposure is not a product of the concept of "too big to fail." Systemic risk is not a function of the size of the financial firms; it stems from the systemwide creation and concentration of risk.

Simply put, if everyone has a similar thirty-year mortgage and decides to refinance at the same time, this will create a systemic event, regardless of the size of our financial institutions. Because all banks are exposed to interest rate risk, even if the large financial institutions were broken into smaller parts, a large interest rate movement would cause a larger number of smaller firms to experience the same problems. This was what happened in the 1980s when hundreds of S&L institutions failed around the same time from problems associated with interest rate exposure. Similarly, the failure of Freddie Mac and Fannie Mae would not have been any less devastating had the firms been broken up into smaller parts. The problem, therefore, is the unnecessary interest rate or option risk embedded in the conventional mortgage.

Because large financial institutions cannot effectively hedge this exposure to mortgage risk, they have found a way to implicitly manage it: dump the costs of extreme events onto U.S. taxpayers and investors. This might sound like hyperbole, but one need only examine the numerous bailouts of financial institutions over the last thirty years to realize that this is exactly what has happened. With few exceptions, each bailout had its origins in large, sustained interest rate movements that put the health of financial institutions in jeopardy, resulting in a hefty bill for others. In this chapter, we identify the various types of risk inherent in conventional mortgage lending and explore how each contributes systemic risk to our increasingly interdependent economy.

Prepayment Risk

Prepayment risk is the lender's risk of loss that stems from the right of homeowners to pay off their mortgage at any time without penalty. In finance terms, this right is called an interest rate option. While interest rate options are widely traded on a variety of contracts, home mortgages are a special case, because they are repeated millions of times, accounting for trillions of dollars of U.S. wealth. Embedding an interest rate option—a type of derivative contract—into the conventional mortgage structure by allowing homeowners to refinance without financial penalty creates the potential for devastating shocks to the financial system whenever interest rates move.

When rates decline, homeowners generally take advantage of the opportunity to obtain a lower rate, and mortgages are refinanced en masse. This creates a lot of business for the mortgage originators and lawyers involved in processing these new loans, but from a macro perspective, this does nothing but benefit the homeowner at the expense of the stability of the mortgage system. Similarly, when interest rates rise, homeowners again receive the bulk of the benefit because they have locked in a below-market interest rate. This apparent win-win situation for homeowners adds considerable risk to mortgage lending and inevitably results in homeowners paying the higher overall interest rates—termed "interest spreads" or "option premiums"—demanded by investors to compensate them for this risk.

However, these option premiums do nothing to protect the investors or the economy from the massive reallocations of wealth that can occur whenever interest rates rise or fall over a sustained period. Instead, the option premium is paid each month by the homeowner and increases the cost of homeownership. As Milton Friedman taught us, in life, as in economics, there is no free lunch. Each month that the homeowners do not elect to prepay, they pay the option premium in the form of higher interest payments. This option does not add to the economy's ability to intermediate credit or create wealth; it is as socially productive as a lottery ticket.

An example will show how this reallocation of wealth works in practice. When an investor lends money for mortgages with an 8 percent coupon rate and the rate drops to 5 percent after one year, the investor should experience a substantial economic gain, compared to investing that money at the new, lower market rate. That gain is limited dramatically, because the rational homeowner will simply prepay the loan by taking out a new loan (refinancing) at 5 percent, as per the homeowner's right under a conventional mortgage contract. If the investor calculates that the asset in which he or she is investing pays an 8 percent coupon rate and remains outstanding, on average, for 10 years, and it prepays after one year, the investor earns 8 percent for only one year and 5 percent for the remaining nine years (assuming rates don't rise or fall further). This equates to a loss of 3 percent for each of those nine years compared to what the investor initially expected to receive.

Looking at this same example from the homeowner's perspective shows that the homeowner will receive a windfall gain from the interest rate movement corresponding exactly to the investor's loss. The homeowner originally expects to pay 8 percent for at least 10 years but instead, after one year, must pay only 5 percent. This results in a gain of 3 percent for the homeowner for each year over the remaining years on the original mortgage. This is, plain and simple, a wealth transfer from the investor to the homeowner.

Let's examine the situation where interest rates are rising. In this example, the investor again lends money for mortgages at an 8 percent coupon rate with the expectation that the loan will remain outstanding for 10 years. If interest rates rise to 10 percent after one year, this means that the investor takes a loss of 2 percent for each of the remaining years in which interest rates remain at that level, compared to what the investor could be earning at the new market rate. This interest rate spike will also depress prepayment rates for homeowners below what had been expected. In turn, the investor will recoup his or her investment much later than expected, meaning that the investor is precluded from reinvesting that money at those higher market rates. Thus, in either scenario, the investor takes a loss on the investment.

Only when interest rates remain relatively stable does the investor "win" and the homeowner "lose," in that the homeowner is paying an interest rate spread or option premium for the right to prepay, but never exercising that right. This is the economic equivalent of buying a losing lottery ticket every month. However, as interest rates have become more volatile since the 1970s and homeowners have become more efficient at prepaying their mortgages in favorable interest rate environments, this last scenario has become less common.

Viewed in the context of a single loan, the interest rate option only impacts the investor and the homeowner and thus is of little interest to anyone other than the parties to the contract. However, when the exercising of such options becomes so pervasive that it creates a significant reallocation of wealth, it threatens the financial stability of major financial institutions and sectors of the economy. At that point, the problem is no longer limited to just a single homeowner and investor. As an analogy, consider the decision as to whether to vaccinate an individual against disease. If most people are vaccinated and only a few individuals are not, at the margin the decision to get vaccinated affects only those few individuals but not society overall. In fact, those few individuals are unlikely to contract the disease, because they are "free-riding" on the fact that others were vaccinated. If 90 percent of the population decides not to get vaccinated and there is an outbreak of disease, everyone suffers, because the disease and its costs will spread quickly.

This is precisely what happened in the United States with the failure of Fannie Mae and Freddie Mac. Each of these entities—and any other institution heavily invested in mortgage and MBS—was exposed to the "disease" of interest rate risk. When the interest rate disease hit these firms in the early 2000s, they responded by taking on additional credit risk in an attempt to "earn their way out" of the problem. This only exacerbated these institutions' interest rate risk. The disease proceeded to spread quickly across the financial sector, causing firms such as Bear Stearns, AIG, Wachovia, and Lehman Brothers to fail, and imposing massive costs upon society in the form of government bailouts.

In the terminology of finance and economics, there are externalities to mortgage transactions that create systemic risk. Public policy should encourage the removal of systemic shocks to the financial system, not insert more into the system simply because of tradition or a lack of understanding of these complex financial instruments. In short, if a new mortgage and MBS system is to be successful, prepayment risk must be better understood and more clearly managed in the origination of mortgages.

Credit Risk

The manner in which a mortgage note is structured will affect the creditworthiness of the recipient of that mortgage. For example, take a mortgage note structured with a variable rate, meaning that the rate adjusts contemporaneously with market rates of interest. If market interest rates increase, the homeowner will see his or her monthly mortgage payment increase (sometimes resulting in "payment shock"), making it more likely that the homeowner will default. In isolation, this might not be a particularly troubling fact, but when millions of homeowners are all hit with the same event at the same time, the impact to the overall economy is catastrophic. As we've seen in the years following the mortgage crisis of 2007, a flood of foreclosures on the market creates a drag on the economy and ends up costing taxpayers dearly.

Susceptibility to exogenous and systemic shocks should never be knowingly designed into a mortgage finance system, public or private. Thus, it would be wise to increase the reset periods for variable rate mortgages so that the impact of any interest rate increase on homeowner credit is spaced out or staggered, rather than manifested in a short period of time.

Institutional Risk

When an institutional investor or other lender is on the wrong side of a prepayment wave, and that prepayment wave is large enough, the firm may not survive. As discussed previously, this is one of the potential negative consequences of allowing the prepayment option to be embedded in conventional U.S. mortgage loans. However, before these institutions impose costs on taxpayers in the form of bailouts, they can exacerbate systemic risk by overleveraging and engaging in overly aggressive risk-taking activities.

When a firm is facing such large losses that failure is a material possibility, the firm often seeks out higher returns to "earn its way" out of the problem. This is especially true when that firm can fall back on government insurance for funding (e.g., deposit insurance). In that case, there is a strong incentive to take additional risk because the firm is betting with someone else's money and has enormous leverage. While this can work for some firms some of the time, in the aggregate, it will not. As detailed earlier, this type of double-or-nothing overreaching was the root cause of the S&L industry collapse in the late 1980s and a contributing factor to the collapse of Fannie Mae and Freddie Mac during the mortgage crisis.

The concept of "too big to fail" is at the heart of the institutional risk being thrust upon the American government and its citizens. The provision of a government safety net creates a classic moral hazard problem: executives will be tempted to take excessive risk in the hope of making outsized profits when they know they will not be allowed to fail. It would seem, therefore, that the logical solution would be to break up financial institutions into smaller firms, meaning that no one institution would be deemed too big to fail. However, in the case of home loans, this solution would not mitigate the institutional risk caused by the interest rate option. As discussed earlier, even if this risk were divided among dozens or even hundreds of smaller firms, a massive prepayment wave would result in many smaller firms all failing at the same time. This would have a similar overall effect on the economy as one or two large failures. The problem, once again, is the creation of unnecessary risk by including the interest rate option in conventional mortgages in the first place.

Investment Risk

In the years leading up to the mortgage crisis, there was outsized demand for deeply subordinated bonds. Historically, these junior bonds were sold at deeply discounted prices, so that when the prepayment wave of the early 2000s hit, the returns experienced by subordinate bondholders were extraordinary. Such outsized returns generated a massive number of investors willing to purchase MBS tranches with large amounts of credit risk. This meant that Wall Street was able to intermediate collateral that it could never have sold previously. Investor demand for credit risk encouraged the production of riskier mortgages, and eventually it resulted in the origination of mortgages that had virtually no expectation of being repaid. This problem can again be traced back to the prepay feature in the conventional U.S. mortgage.

The prepayment option essentially turns a mortgage into a lottery ticket, and while a few may benefit from this option, just as a few players will win the lottery, the overall losses far outweigh the gains.

Further, this embedded feature encourages investors to speculate on less-than-stellar mortgage credit in the hope of profiting when a prepayment wave hits. This, in turn, causes lenders to loan money to people who would otherwise not qualify to satisfy investor demand for credit risk. This engenders additional risk to the financial system in the form of investment risk. This problem, like the others mentioned in this chapter, would not exist but for the prepayment option of the conventional mortgage.

Why would any country intentionally inject such volatility into the instrument used by millions to purchase a home? More importantly, why would a country inject such a potentially catastrophic risk into its financial system? If informed and unbiased individuals were planning a country's mortgage system from the ground up, is there any chance that this risk could be viewed as acceptable? I think not. If we seek a mortgage finance system that minimizes systemic risk, it is essential to limit or eliminate the prepayment option in conventional mortgages.

A Brief Discussion of Conventional Loan Structures

Two categories of loan structures have been traditionally offered in the United States: fixed-rate and variable-rate mortgages. The conventional fixed-rate mortgage is generally a fifteen- or thirty-year amortizing loan that maintains a fixed rate of interest (and thus a fixed or "level" payment) over its full term. It also features a penalty-free prepayment option. Due to its stability and simplicity for the homeowner, this structure has been the preferred U.S. mortgage since the 1930s with the creation of the government backed mortgage market. It remains the dominant Fannie Mae and Freddie Mac mortgage structure and the "gold standard" for U.S. mortgages today. This structure has financed millions of homeowners for generations, and it worked well until the 1970s, when interest rates became significantly more volatile. Since that time, the conventional fixed-rate mortgage has engendered many of the prepayment problems and other risks discussed in this chapter, as interest rates have remained volatile while refinancing has become materially easier for homeowners.

Notably, the efficiency with which homeowners have been exercising the underlying option by choosing to refinance has increased over the last several decades, showing that homeowners understand the benefits of this option. As homeowners have become increasingly knowledgeable and mortgage credit has become more readily available over the last thirty years or so, the prepayment option has created a far more profound risk to the financial system.

The best way to understand the genesis and magnitude of prepayment waves is to see them graphically. The following chart shows the Mortgage Bankers Association Refinance Index compared to ten-year Treasury yields over the same period. Circled on the Refinance Index are several prepayment waves: the first in 1992-93, the second in 1997–1998, a large third wave in 2001–2003, and a fourth wave that began in late 2007 at the onset of the mortgage crisis and continued through 2009.[*] A review of the interest rates during these prepayment waves shows that prepayment rates and interest rates are inversely correlated, suggesting that homeowners tend to exercise their prepayment options in a rational manner. As the internet continues to make more information and options available to homeowners, thereby reducing the fixed costs of refinancing, the efficiency with which homeowners exercise their prepayment options should only increase.

---

[*] I note that while prepayments in the last few years have been large, they have been muted by the fact that homeowners have been constrained from prepaying due to declining home prices and their effect on homeowners' ability to qualify for new loans.

Mortgage Bankers Association Refi Index vs. Ten Year Treasury Yields

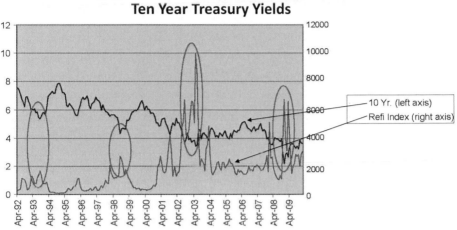

SOURCE: BLOOMBERG L.P., CUSTOM GRAPH, INDEXES: MBAVREFI AND GT10, GENERATED USING BLOOMBERG TERMINAL ON APRIL 15, 2011 (EMPHASIS ADDED).

The combination of painless refinancing and volatile interest rates is a dangerous one for the U.S. financial system and should be avoided, if possible. If ordinary homeowners can understand the mechanics and benefits of the prepayment option, lawmakers and lenders should also be able to understand this concept and should incorporate that understanding into an improved mortgage loan structure. Controlling interest rates is impractical if not impossible, so we must control the ease of refinancing through reforming the conventional fixed-rate mortgage structure. Not only would this reduce the systemic risk caused by the free prepayment option, but making refinancing more expensive or difficult would also discourage borrowers from taking out mortgages they could not afford with an eye toward refinancing within a few years if the rates drop. In sum, the beloved conventional fixed-rate mortgage has outlived its usefulness and should be consigned to the scrap heap of financial history. Increasingly, many others are beginning to recognize the significant costs embedded in this structure.[125]

This brings us to the other primary loan structure in the United States: the variable rate mortgage or ARM. The ARM features an interest rate that adjusts periodically based on an index. While there can be an infinite number of variations to this loan structure, the most common is one in which the interest rate is fixed for a period of time (usually one, three or five years) and adjusts or "floats" thereafter, usually on an annual basis. This ARM structure is sometimes called a hybrid ARM. ARMs in general have become more popular in recent years, because the initial payments are usually much lower than for fixed-rate loans, allowing borrowers to purchase larger homes than they could otherwise.

Earlier, I discussed the credit risk that could be injected into the financial system should a large percentage of borrowers choose an adjustable rate loan structure in which the loan rate adjusted concurrently with market rates (for clarity, we will call these "market-rate loans"). When interest rates suddenly rise, borrowers with market-rate loans see their monthly payments rise simultaneously, potentially causing widespread payment shock and a spike in foreclosures. The hybrid ARM represents a substantial improvement over both the fixed-rate and the market-rate loan. Compared to the fixed-rate loan, the hybrid ARM minimizes systemic prepayment risk and the corresponding risk of massive wealth reallocation, because it does not create long-term fixed-rate exposure for either the homeowner or the investor. Compared to the market-rate loan, the hybrid ARM diffuses potential credit risks because its interest rate resets on a longer fixed schedule (e.g., every five years rather than concurrently with market rates) during the variable rate period. Though ARMs do have more potential downside than fixed-rate loans in terms of causing systemic credit losses should interest rates spike, hybrid ARMs prevent these credit losses from hitting the market all at once, as would be the case with market-rate loans.

Part III:
Rising from the Ashes of Collapse: A Blueprint for Sustainable Mortgage Finance

> *"You can always count on Americans to do the right thing—after they have tried everything else."*
> —*Winston Churchill*

CHAPTER 9

A Model for the New American Mortgage

Having reviewed the structure of conventional U.S. mortgages and their tendency to infect the U.S. financial system with substantial systemic risk, it is time to discuss how we might be able to redesign the mortgage system in a way that would allow people to borrow for homeownership while insulating the economy from another financial crisis. The ultimate goal is to determine what types of mortgage loans make sense for our financial system, if we were designing one from the ground up. In doing so, we should not ignore the realities of the existing American system or the structures that other countries have created to address similar problems. In particular, we will focus on two interesting types of mortgage structures that have been developed abroad, both of which diverge significantly from the American model. By examining aspects of these mortgage structures that might help to reduce systemic risk, we can begin to understand how we might remodel the traditional American mortgage to return stability to the economy.

The Danish Fixed-Rate Loan Structure

The mortgage system in Denmark has survived for over two hundred years without a major financial or systemic problem. Though the country has experienced one sovereign default and numerous recessions and depressions during this period, the mortgage system has remained intact and fully functional. Similar to the treatment of mortgages in the American system prior to the mortgage crisis, individual mortgages in Denmark are sold into the public markets almost immediately upon issuance. Key attributes of Danish mortgages include the requirements that borrowers make a minimum down payment of 20 percent and retain personal liability for mortgage debts should they default. For our purposes, however, the most interesting aspect of the Danish system is its treatment of prepayments.

Prepayments are allowed in Denmark, but they are executed by having the borrower either prepay the loan at par or buy an amount of bonds equivalent to his or her indebtedness on the open market, at a discount. Those bonds are then retired in exchange for the release of the lien on the borrower's property. This allows the homeowner to repay the investor at a cost that reflects the current market value of his or her liability. This system is facilitated by the comparatively simple structure of Danish MBS, without the varying levels of subordination featured in most U.S. trusts, as will be discussed shortly.

For the homeowner, this structure creates the economic equivalent of a fixed-rate loan with the ability to participate in the depreciation of the market value of their note, which often occurs when interest rates rise. In that case, the homeowner would not end up with negative equity because the value of the mortgage note would also decrease. The main drawback to this system is that borrowers do not face a prepayment penalty that corresponds to the benefit of refinancing at a lower rate, meaning that borrowers' incentives still encourage them to refinance en masse when interest rates fall. This feature leaves systemic risk in the financial system that must be addressed in some manner.

Though this system does not remove the economic incentive to refinance in lower interest rate environments, it does remove much of the credit risk of the transaction because the value of the note declines when interest rates increase. The logic is that the value of the home is likely to decrease when interest rates increase; not having the homeowner shoulder this risk reduces the overall credit risk of the investment, meaning that there is less systemic credit risk in this bond structure. Consistent with these incentives, Denmark has not experienced any major turmoil to their financial system during the mortgage crisis of 2007. This is despite the fact that, going into the mortgage crisis, Denmark had a 101 percent ratio of mortgage principal outstanding to Gross Domestic Product (GDP)—far higher than the U.S. ratio of 80 percent.[126] Denmark has shown the world that there is a way to have a large and healthy mortgage finance system without the systemic shocks that are becoming all too common in the United States.

The Canadian Adjustable-Rate Loan Structure

The Canadian mortgage loan consists of a series of successive five-year loans that homeowners must refinance at the end of each five-year period. Homeowners must pay a variable prepayment penalty if they wish to refinance prior to the conclusion of any five-year period. This variable penalty is based on a present value calculation that effectively removes any incentive for homeowners to refinance in lower interest rate environments. As a rule, the principal is guaranteed by the Canadian government, thus mitigating the impact of homeowners unable to pay off or refinance their mortgages at the conclusion of five years. In essence, this system guarantees that homeowners' mortgage rates will remain at levels that are no more than five years removed from where the market stood at the time of origination and that homeowners will not refinance en masse. This creates an attractive asset for the banking system. However, it also means that homeowners are taking on much of the risk that rates will climb significantly higher during the five-year period.

This system would not be an ideal fit for the U.S. market because it is politically untenable at present to propose a government-backed mortgage system. Without government backing for this type of system, the country would face a massive systemic liquidity exposure should borrowers not be able to refinance their mortgages at the end of the five-year period. This would happen if there were a spike in interest rates and the borrowers could not make their increased debt payments. Pursuant to the Canadian structure, it would be possible for the borrower of 2011 to receive a five-year loan at 4 percent but have to roll that liability into a loan at 10 percent or higher should that be the market level at the end of five years. In this case, the borrower would not suffer from a liquidity event but from a solvency event. Thus, while this system has proven to provide a stable source of funds for the Canadian homeowner, the absolute level of government involvement and the systemic risk created by the potential for payment shock probably make this less attractive than the Danish model.

A Possible Loan Structure for the United States

While an infinite number of loan structures could be created that would enable the United States to finance homeownership, the Danish example, with its inherent stability, is the best place to start. To make it practical, we must adjust this model to the realities of the American system. First, to satisfy investor demand for different levels of risk and payment terms in the MBS marketplace (for example, short securities and long securities in the same transaction), arrangers seek to slice and dice securitized loans into a large number of pieces with varying risk characteristics. This feature makes it almost impossible for homeowners to repurchase the principal amount of their loan in the open market should they wish to refinance, as is possible in the Danish system. For instance, what amount of senior securities and what amount of subordinate securities would borrowers be required to purchase to satisfy their refinance obligations? If one investor were to own the entire class or the entire issue, how could a borrower purchase a proportional interest? Who would set the price? Given the realities of the divergent interests that have historically been brought together to finance U.S. mortgages, it is unrealistic to have homeowners go into the market and essentially repurchase their own loans.

Fortunately, other available structures have worked well to implement the same sorts of incentives, especially in the context of commercial mortgage loans. With a commercial fixed-rate mortgage loan, it is common to require the borrower to pay a prepayment penalty based on market interest rates at the time of prepayment. This eliminates the economic incentive for a rate and term refinance, the dominant source of systemic risk from well underwritten mortgages. If we took this model and added a small twist—that homeowners could prepay their loan at a discount when interest rates increased—we would then have a structure that featured the stability of the Danish system but still fit the American system. Further, if this prepayment penalty or discount was determined by calculating the present value of the remaining stream of cash flows and discounting those cash flows at the current mortgage rate, it would remove any economic incentive for homeowners to refinance.

There would thus be no economic reason for the homeowner to prepay or not prepay, as his or her liability could always be prepaid at a market level. At first, this structure may sound inflexible and unattractive, but the object of a mortgage system is to finance homes, not to introduce an interest rate side bet that destabilizes the financial system. Under this proposed system, the prepayment option price or interest rate spread that homeowners are paying for the right to prepay would disappear, meaning that borrowers would see a substantial drop in mortgage interest rates. The result would be a market that made homeownership accessible to more Americans while removing the systemic risks created by prepayment spikes and troughs. Moreover, the fact that this structure is symmetrical would preserve the logic and stability of the Danish system while removing the economic incentive to prepay when rates decrease. Mortgages would no longer act as interest rate lottery tickets.

The logic of the Danish system is that when interest rates increase, the value of the property likely drops. If the value of the property drops, the principal of the loan also drops, thereby reducing the credit risk of the loan and preventing homeowners from getting stuck in a negative equity position. If interest rates drop, homeowners should see the value of their home increase and will be able to compensate the investor should they wish to retire their note early.

Transportable Mortgage Loans

A logical problem with the structure I have proposed is that it makes it harder for homeowners to move if interest rates decrease and the property value does not increase proportionally. What happens if the homeowner wishes to move to a new home but faces a large prepayment penalty that would impair the homeowner's capital and make it difficult to qualify for a new loan? This is a legitimate question, but it is one that can be remedied by turning the loan into what I call a "transportable mortgage."

This structure addresses the situation in which a homeowner hopes to sell his or her existing residence and purchase another home, but interest rates have moved lower, meaning that the borrower would owe a large early prepayment penalty to the lender. A transportable mortgage would offer the borrower the option of continuing to pay his or her existing mortgage and put up the new home as collateral rather than paying that penalty. From the investor's perspective, it makes little difference which property is serving as the collateral for the loan so long as the value of the new property is greater than or equal to that of the old. From the homeowner's perspective, moving costs and the additional cost of the new home would be the only direct financial consequences of the move. If the new home turned out to be less expensive, the borrower could pay off a portion of the loan using the present value calculation described earlier.

This type of loan system would remove the impediment to labor market mobility that already exists in the current system when interest rates rise. Currently, homeowners who have locked in low interest rate loans under the existing system face the prospect of losing their good deals if they decide to move. This creates a deterrent for the work force to move to higher employment areas, where there might be greater demand for their labor. Under the transportable mortgage system I propose, borrowers may either retire their loan at a discount or continue making payments to the same lender and use the new home as collateral. This would preserve labor market mobility, a real competitive advantage of the U.S. economic system.

For homeowners wishing to trade up in the housing market, a second (additional) loan could be obtained. This additional lien should only be used for one purpose: to finance the direct purchase of a new home. Moreover, homeowners should be required to put in at least 20 percent of the incremental amount of the funds being borrowed. In essence, homeowners need to have saved up enough money to pay one-fifth of the incremental cost of their new home if they wish to trade up. Under this proposal, borrowers would not be able to use the equity they had built up in their home for the purposes of buying a new home, unless they chose to prepay the entire loan under the present value protocols discussed here. This also means that if the homeowner did not have real equity in their home, he or she would not be permitted to trade up for a more expensive home unless additional cash was put up for the purchase. This system would preserve the credit quality of the original loan and allow the new loan to be treated *pari passu* or "on equal footing" with the original loan. Ideally, both loans would be governed by a standard inter-creditor agreement that preserved the collateral of the first loan and allowed the homeowner to access additional funds to purchase a more expensive home.

While this structure may not strike many as a "win" for consumers, keep in mind that if the relationship between the increase and decrease in interest rates is symmetrical, it stamps the structure with the imprimatur of fairness. In addition, the mortgage treasury spread, or the rate the homeowner pays above the reference interest rate, will decrease because mortgage securities will become less risky based on the removal of the prepayment option. Finally, not subjecting the entire economy to massive prepayment waves will make the financial system more stable. This should be the primary goal of a country that is setting up a mortgage system.

*"You've got to be careful if you don't know where you
are going, because you might just get there."*

—*Yogi Berra*

CHAPTER 10

─■─

The Future Mortgage Finance System

To create a mortgage finance system that will endure and thrive,
I have argued that it is essential to understand first the problems
underlying the existing system, including flaws in the structure of
traditional mortgage loans, and why they caused that system to fail.
There is no point in replacing one flawed system with another that will
likely implode down the road.

The ultimate question remains: how should we build a successful
mortgage securitization system if we were forced to start over? Should
we provide homeowners with a free option to refinance at any time
or implement prepayment penalties? Should we permit lenders to sell
their entire economic interest in the loans they originate, or force
them to retain some of the risk? Should we allow servicers to service
first lien loans when they hold the second liens on their books? What
rights should we give to the trustee and by extension, investors, to take
action if the loans in the trust turn out to be defective? Who should
be independent and what does that mean?

These questions, and others, confronted me in Russia in the mid-
2000s. There, to complete a mortgage securitization, we needed to
design a mortgage finance system in a country where even the concept of homeownership was relatively new. It was necessary to design
the lending guidelines, the underwriting standards, the contractual

provisions of the trust agreements, the incentives created by the payout structure, and the relationships between the various parties. Drawing on my experience in mortgage finance, I constructed a system that not only worked—it thrived during one of most tumultuous periods for the world economy since the Great Depression. After witnessing the events of the past five or so years in the United States, I have learned even more about what should be incorporated into a new MBS system.

Of course, I could not merely apply the template from Russia to the American system and expect it to succeed. Each country poses its own unique set of challenges, based on a host of factors from the legal and regulatory framework in that country to cultural attitudes toward borrowing and homeownership. The role each government already plays in its country's mortgage market also has a huge impact on how its mortgage finance market can be constructed. Indeed, one can never build such a system entirely from scratch; one must take into account the systems and structures already in place.

In the United States, we have before us a unique opportunity. The private mortgage market is essentially non-existent, and the U.S. mortgage market has been *de facto* nationalized. Whether we like it or not, the reality is that the federal government is deeply involved in the vast majority of U.S. mortgage transactions, whether on behalf of Fannie Mae, Freddie Mac, or the FHA. At the same time, there is a push in Washington from both the White House and the legislature to wind down the GSEs and other aspects of government involvement, thereby providing private enterprise with an increased role in supporting and facilitating homeownership.[127] We are thus faced with an environment ripe for reform, and we have the chance to think hard about how the future of mortgage finance should look. In this chapter, I tackle two of the central questions of this book: how should we rebuild the U.S. mortgage securitization system, and who must take the initiative to implement these repairs?

I have spoken to few people in this industry who are happy with the current state of Fannie Mae and Freddie Mac. Even the formerly die-hard GSE proponents have been silenced by the monumental losses and mismanagement plaguing these institutions. If these GSEs are to be given a new lease on life, they should be deemed unambiguously public or private. The tap dance between government guarantees and private ownership is too confusing for investors and too easy for managers to exploit. This was a matter of debate five years ago, but at this point, the matter should be moot. The real remaining policy question is this: given that the GSEs are currently responsible for supporting virtually all new mortgage lending in the United States, how do we move forward without killing the entire housing market and economy?

Obviously, it would be impractical to shut down the GSEs overnight, but because the GSEs have loan limits or limits on the size of the loans that they will guarantee, it would be simple to slowly reduce that lending limit and allow the private label market to step into the void by offering larger loans. For example, the limit could be reduced by $5,000 per month. There is no magic in whatever number is chosen, but before this process can begin, there must be some changes in the private label MBS infrastructure. There is little point in slowly taking away financial support for the mortgage market when there is no ready alternative.

For the new private label market to succeed, a reformed legal structure must be put in place to protect investors and the entire U.S. economy from the key flaws that led to the current crisis. To date, there has been little discussion in political or business circles about how to design a securitization system free from the embedded conflicts of interest that led to the disintegration of the private mortgage market. Instead, certain politicians and financial institutions with vested interests in moving away from securitization have recently proposed various alternative mortgage finance systems. I discuss some of these and the reasons why they fail to fix the conflicts that engendered the mortgage crisis in appendix IV. I firmly believe that the only way to facilitate a privately-financed mortgage market is to work within the structure of securitization but impose market standards that will ensure that the parties' economic interests are aligned in all market conditions.

The market standards on which investors should insist, and which service providers should embrace in a new regime, follow. The reader should keep in mind a few overarching concepts. First, the purpose of these standards and increased transparency is to encourage the redevelopment of a private label market and the scaling back of government involvement. It would be terribly naïve to assume that investors will flock back to a market where neither the transaction structure nor the federal government protects their interests.

Second, financial transactions tend to go through an evolutionary process. When a type of transaction is novel, high transaction costs and time-consuming processes are involved in completing each step of the transaction. As the market matures, these processes become standardized and transaction costs decline. Market standards are soon developed, making the market more transparent and efficient for all participants. It is high time that securitization reaches this level of maturity.

The standardization of a complex financial market is not without precedent. My proposals for the mortgage market draw on examples from the International Swap Dealers Association (ISDA), which sets guidelines and provides market-acceptable standard documentation for swap contracts. I consider ISDA to be the paragon of how standardization can bring efficiency and reduced transaction costs to a financial market. Prior to the implementation of ISDA standards and paperwork, each interest rate swap, no matter how mundane, required lawyers on each side to draw up contracts and hammer out the terms. These processes are now much more standardized and well understood by the parties on all sides, reducing unnecessary expense and deception.

For the private label MBS market, I propose creating a new entity that serves, much like ISDA, as the standard-bearer for private label securitizations. This could take the form of an investor-controlled board that establishes guidelines for the issuance of generic pools of private label mortgages. It is logical that this entity also act as the trustee on future securitizations, as its role in both capacities would be the same: protecting investors against unnecessary expenses and loss associated with irresponsible lending and servicing practices. In addition, many other functions not considered essential prior to the mortgage crisis could be fulfilled by this new entity, now that the necessity of these functions has become obvious.

Third, my recommendations that the "market" adopt certain standards often constitute suggestions that governmental and quasi-governmental agencies adopt these standards. While I will be thrilled if the private market rises up and demands rationality and reform, a market controlled by the government has a low probability of spontaneous reform without explicit and intentional actions by certain key governmental entities. Even if the White House follows through on its proposal of winding down the GSEs, this process will take time, and I doubt that these entities (or their successors) will ever disappear from this market completely. In the meantime, these entities continue to define the standards to which the rest of the market will likely conform.

It is also important to highlight areas of reform over which the individual state legislatures have control. One such example is state recourse laws that allow lenders to pursue borrowers if the liquidation of the underlying property is inadequate to satisfy the mortgage note. The purpose of such a reform would be to ensure the uniform quality of mortgages in a mortgage pool and thereby encourage mortgage investment. Such a change would require individual states to change their laws so that better post-foreclosure enforcement is allowed. This would not be driven by a federal mandate, as each state has control over its recourse laws and would be free to do as it pleased. As a practical matter, individual states would have a powerful economic incentive to adopt and conform to new market standards for recourse and default resolution. If an individual state did not adjust its laws in a manner consistent with market standards, loans originated in that state would have to be placed privately, as they would not qualify for public securitizations. On the other hand, states that adopted these new standards would ensure that mortgage notes originated in those states were eligible for the public securitization markets, thus lowering the cost of homeownership for the residents of those states.

Finally, when looking to the future, the goal is to create a system where the economic interests of participants are properly aligned, and remain aligned throughout the life of the deal, whatever the market conditions. One major area of concern with the current model is the prevalence of conflicts between the servicers and the investors they are charged with protecting. Recent servicer performance has made it clear that servicers will not adhere to their contractual obligations from the PSAs when it is not in their immediate economic interests to do so. In this regard, we should consider restricting the firms that originate and sell loans from later servicing them. This would remove the primary conflicts of interest for the servicer, as that entity would have no other affiliation with the borrower other than maximizing the borrower's payments on the mortgage. However, this would not obviate all issues that a servicer faces within the securitization structure.

The relationship between the trustee of a securitization and the investors is another major area of concern from the perspective of conflicts of interest in future transactions. If investors were properly informed, no clear-thinking investor would allow a fully indemnified and passive trustee to be the fiduciary on any transaction in which it invests. Investors have control over this aspect of any deal; they do not have to purchase securities with passive trustees. In this capacity, they should demand that the trustee be unambiguously independent and provided with economic incentives to protect investor interests. To encourage this reform, rating agencies should refuse to rate a transaction that does not feature an active and independent trustee. Finally, investors should insist on abolishing the practice of allowing trustees to be indemnified by those they are responsible for monitoring. If investors fail in their demands for these changes, the federal government should intervene.

I recognize that these reforms will not be implemented overnight or all at once, but they could be adopted in phases, much like the phases of building a house. Accordingly, I lay out these proposals in three phases based on priority. A first phase consists of the essential changes that I believe *must* be made if a private securitization market is to return in the United States. Think of these items as forming the foundation of our securitization structure upon which our other reforms will be built. The second phase features the changes that *should* be implemented once essential reforms are made. These proposals are akin to the support beams, columns, storm windows, and roof that will make our structure strong and durable, allowing it to withstand the economic storms that the future will no doubt bring. The final phase includes the reforms that *can* be made, if our solid foundation and supports are in place. Think of these items as the paint, flooring, landscaping, artwork and other features that will add functionality and beauty to the house and allow the structure to reach its greatest potential. I believe the items in the *can* category should be implemented, but I am realistic as to how difficult some of these changes will be from a political and an embedded interest viewpoint.

I have further divided each phase into subcategories of *governmental* and *private sector* (or contractual) changes, based on the interested party that would likely be required to make these changes. As a practical matter, any of these changes could be implemented using private contracts or by government dictum. My preference is to have the market make as many of these changes as possible. From a political and economic viewpoint, however, it would be foolish to assume that the market can be reformed by contractual changes alone, as the contractual requirements present in the current MBS market were largely ignored by the biggest banks when they mattered most. It is impractical to think that banks will do what is best for the economy as a whole when faced with threats to their profitability, and given the history of government bailouts having been provided when those threats reached critical levels. Furthermore, we cannot assume that a traditionally passive investor base will suddenly become much more active in its investment activities and demand that the banks reform their contracts in any significant manner. In short, there will have to be a mix of government and private reforms if we are to rebuild our decimated private mortgage market. The three phases for reforming and resurrecting private label MBS follow.

What We Must Do: Changes Necessary to Rebuild the Private Securitization Market

Governmental Changes

1. **Ban short positions.**

Originators, underwriters, and trustees must be prohibited from having any short position in any transaction they oversee or help put together. (A "short position" is one in which the holder profits should the security fail or drop in price.) After the stock market crash and depression of the 1930s, a Senate commission called the Pecora Commission found that the CEOs of large companies were shorting their companies' stock. This provided an economic incentive for the CEOs to harm their own companies. Arising from the Pecora Commission's recommendation, it became illegal for employees or executives to short their companies' stock—the logic being that if you reward failure, you will have more of it. The same principle should apply to MBS. If an underwriter puts a deal together, the firm and all individuals employed by the underwriter should be banned from entering into any derivative contract that allows that entity to profit from the poor performance of the transaction. This may sound like common sense, but several SEC investigations into such conduct at major Wall Street underwriters, and the sizeable settlements that resulted, have shown that more needs to be done to eradicate this practice.

2. **Require skin in the game.**

All participants in mortgage securitization must have some form of "skin in the game"—that is, a direct stake in the success or failure of the transaction. Having skin in the game should apply to all levels of origination and intermediation of credit as well as to homeowners, who should be required to make a substantial down payment (around 20 percent) if the asset is going to be sold into the public capital markets.

Asking homeowners to save for a down payment may sound like a quaint idea, but it goes a long way in preventing foreclosures. As discussed earlier, positive home equity is the single most important factor in reducing the default rate.[128] Still, there will be political pressure to lower the down payment requirement for homeowners of modest means. That would be fine so long as these loans went into a government loan program for securitization as an agency security rather than as a private label security. Regardless, it would be reckless for a government program to permit borrowers to supply a down payment of less than 10 percent (and mortgage insurance should not qualify as a down payment). Otherwise, there is too great a risk of strategic default and a corresponding drag on the overall economy. If someone cannot accumulate a down payment of at least 10 percent, he or she simply cannot afford to buy that house. There is no shame in renting, and in some cases, it may be economically more sensible than buying.

For originators of mortgages and arrangers of securitizations, skin in the game for non-agency loans may take the form of a requirement that they hold on their books some portion of the credit risk for loans they originate or securitize. The theory goes that having to hold some of these loans for a minimum period would motivate these participants to ensure the quality of the loans with which they're dealing. The Dodd-Frank Wall Street Reform and Consumer Protection Act (the Dodd-Frank Act),[129] passed in 2010, included a requirement that securitizers retain no less than 5 percent of the credit risk associated with loans they securitize, so long as those loans are not considered Qualified Residential Mortgages (QRMs). This is a step in the right direction, but it does not go nearly far enough.

For one, the Act contains no similar requirement for originators, though it permits regulators to allow securitizers to lower the amount of risk retained if some portion of that 5 percent is retained by origina-tors. Second, 5 percent is a relatively small amount of risk to retain if it is the senior risk and a tremendous amount of risk to retain if it is the subordinate risk. Regulators have yet to determine exactly what type of risk this 5 percent should include. Finally, the exception for QRMs threatens to swallow the rule. As of the writing of this book, regulators are still hammering out the details of what qualifies as a QRM. Initial proposals provided a broad definition of QRMs, which would encourage originators and securitizers to deal simply in QRMs and bypass the risk retention requirement entirely. The consequences could be disastrous if originators and securitizers were not required to maintain some ownership in QRM assets.

Regulators should go even further, requiring originators and se-curitizers in *any* deal sold into the public markets to retain credit risk reflecting the performance of the underlying collateral. Remember that originators are the gatekeepers of mortgage credit, reviewing the documentation provided by the borrower to ensure that a particular loan is likely to be repaid. Similarly, securitizers are the gatekeepers of mortgage finance. As part of the process of putting a deal together, the securitizer performs due diligence or verifies that the information provided to the investor is correct. Hence, when a securitizer sells bonds backed by mortgage loans, it is attesting to investors that the deal is well structured and credible. Historically, the fact that this firm's reputation and future business flow were on the line kept the securitizer from selling "lemons" to investors. In the United States from 2003 to 2008, securitizers had insufficient reputational or economic incentives to put transactions together that were well structured and free from fraud. Why else would a reputable underwriter choose to put deals together with stated income loans, commonly referred to as "liar loans"?

This is why securitizers should instead be required to hold some amount of subordinate bonds on their balance sheets and to hold them for at least three years (when delinquency rates commonly peak and fraud has become obvious). Furthermore, the structure of those securities should be a Z-bond or an accrual structure (as explained in appendix VI). This structure would shorten the cash flows for the senior portion of the transaction by having the most junior bond be a Z-bond that grows over time and represents the absolute last cash flow in the deal. This structure would also concentrate the credit risk with the parties best able to control credit losses.

The only opportunity these firms should have to dispose of these securities prior to the expiration of this period is if they choose to transfer the bonds into a bonus pool that would be distributed to firm management and the individuals that put the deal together. This would tie banker and management compensation to the performance of the collateral and ensure that the people bringing the transactions to market have a profound and personal financial interest in getting the transactions right. Would anybody dispute that this would have made bankers and management more careful in putting these deals together? This would replicate the structure and personal responsibility of Wall Street that was common when senior members of a firm were partners and thus deployed their own funds when making financial decisions.

As with securitizers, originators should be subject to a "holdback," that is, some portion of their fees as deferred compensation. These funds should be held in a trust account until their release after a period of three years, which should be enough time for any fraud to appear. If fraud or poor underwriting were to emerge during that time, the funds would be forfeited. Furthermore, this account should be cross-collateralized (that is, collateralized by more than just the fees received by the originator for a specific loan) so that if a loan were to go bad, the loss to the originator would be greater than the fee it received for originating the loan. Cross-collateralization would ensure that the firm had enough capital to support its contingent liabilities and was discouraged from engaging in risky lending. This structure would provide the originator with skin in the game and remove any economic incentive to falsify information or documentation.

It is not important, or even desirable, that the losses absorbed by the originator be the full losses attributable to any particular defaulted loan. It is amazing what a holdback and a loss of several times an originator's commission will do to the firm's processes and actions when deciding whether to make a loan to a potential homeowner. That being said, the discovery of fraud should always engender 100 percent liability.

In Russia, I set up the transaction documents so that the originators would take the first loss in the pool through their ownership of the first loss security. Given that the issuer and the originator were the same, this correctly aligned the economic interests between the originator and the issuer on the one hand and the underwriter and securitizer (my firm) on the other. In this transaction, my firm took the second loss in the pool, and only after the issuers' securities and my firm's securities were wiped out would the senior investor experience any credit losses. This structure has performed flawlessly, and I attribute much of its success to this incentive structure.

"Skin in the game" for trustees, servicers, and other participants in securitizations would take different forms, depending on the role of each player and the outcomes that would be best for the trust as a whole. In all cases, the player's bottom line should be impacted positively when it achieves positive results for investors and negatively when it achieves negative results for investors. Aligning the players' contractual responsibilities with self-interest is the only way to ensure that they do not ignore the former in favor of the latter.

3. Eliminate subsequent second liens.

As discussed in chapter 9, regulators should consider barring homeowners from taking out home equity lines of credit or placing second or additional liens on their properties subsequent to their purchase. Servicing banks have shown with astounding consistency that they will use their position to their advantage, regardless of the contents of their contracts with investors. Even if servicers are barred from owning a second lien while servicing the first lien for another—creating an unmanageable conflict of interest—simply allowing borrowers to take out subsequent seconds adds unnecessary credit risk and instability to the mortgage system. We surely should not encourage homeowners to treat their homes as checking accounts.

Moreover, second liens are generally economically attractive only because they are subsidized by the federal government through the tax deduction for interest payments. If the government wishes to subsidize home ownership, it should focus that subsidy on home equity, not home debt. If the tax code were amended to treat home equity lines of credit and other second liens like credit card debts, it would remove any economic incentive for borrowers to take out second liens. At the same time, if borrowers wished to take equity out of their homes, they could still refinance at prevailing rates (plus or minus any prepayment penalty or bonus built into our new mortgage structure) into a larger loan. The one exception to this rule would be in the case of the transportable mortgage. In this case, borrowers could take out an additional lien to finance the direct purchase of a new home, but only if they were able to contribute 20 percent of the incremental amount of the funds being borrowed.* We want to ensure that borrowers maintain some skin in the game and minimize strategic defaults.

4. **Eliminate captive arrangements with servicer affiliates.**

Servicers are paid to maximize the value of loans for the ultimate investors. This means encouraging borrowers to make payments to the extent possible or liquidating the underlying property and maximizing the amount recovered in foreclosure. Given this role, servicers should not be in a position to extract profits from the foreclosure process when loans go into default. Specifically, servicers should be prohibited from using affiliated companies for servicing functions that are billed to the trusts. The reason for this is that there is an obvious conflict of

---

* The relationship between these two liens would be governed by an inter-creditor agreement, which ideally would provide that the second lien is *pari passu* with the first.

interest if the parent of the servicer is the firm being paid to perform a service, and the servicer has sole discretion to decide whether to use this service. The temptation is far too great for servicers to choose to do business with affiliated companies that may not be the best value for the trust or investors.

This might be clearer with an example: when a servicer is foreclosing on a loan and decides that a new appraisal is required, the servicer often chooses to hire an affiliated company to perform this task. The affiliated company charges a fee (say $2,000) that ends up in the pockets of the servicer's parent. The servicer has sole discretion to make that hiring decision. In essence, this constitutes a no-bid contract in which the buyers (the investors) have no say as to whether this service is necessary and the price is fair. This creates the opportunity for servicers to transfer money from the trusts to themselves, thereby driving up the costs of mortgage lending and investing, one appraisal and one bill at a time. The conflicts and the ability for abuse are obvious.

5. Enable investors to obtain investor lists.

The nature of the securitization market is that the investor base is fragmented. Because traditional PSAs require bondholders to band together to enforce their rights under these contracts, this fragmentation can be used to shield deal participants from the consequences of their malfeasance. Going forward, every investor should have the right to petition the trustee or the servicer for an investor list, should the investor be able to produce some sort of credible evidence of misconduct and agree to reasonable confidentiality provisions. Investors who did not wish to be identified should still be able to opt out of this notification process, but investors that affirmatively opt out of the process should still receive the notices of action issued on behalf of other investors.

Of course, investors should demand contracts that do not impose such high hurdles on investor action. If, for example, larger investors were not required to band together with other investors to take legal action, they would not need to take advantage of the right to obtain a list of the other investors. Alternatively, the PSAs could put the responsibility for investigating and policing the trust on the trustee, thereby making the trustee a real fiduciary of the investors and obviating the need for investor action. If the trustee was charged with these duties and was not indemnified by the servicer, the trustee would have an economic incentive to pursue the economic interests of the trust in court, should that become necessary.

However, to the extent that investor rights are not fully protected by a real fiduciary in the transaction and there remains some collective action hurdle to self-enforcement, a notification process and a process for investors to gain access to the names of the other investors in the transaction should exist. Many of these names are obscured due to the depository system that is used to streamline the payment of principal and interest to institutional investors. Instead, ownership transparency should be the norm. There should be a method for investors to find and communicate with one another so that investors can overcome procedural standing hurdles with relative ease. An accessible enforcement mechanism is the only way to ensure that deal participants honor their contracts.

Though investors could demand these sorts of provisions in future contracts, I believe that encouraging transparency is one of the primary roles that government should play in the securitization market. By adopting a political goal of increased transparency, the government would encourage investors to get together and resolve problems that crop up with a pool of loans. This country would never have experienced a foreclosure crisis like the one it is facing today if the loans at issue had not been trapped in securitization trusts that were not designed to deal with these sorts of problems. To the extent that lawmakers can enact laws or regulations that encourage transparency and communication between deal participants regarding solutions to problem loans, these acts would make the market stronger and more stable as a whole—not to mention send a message to investors that the U.S. government protects and upholds contract rights.

6. **Protect the right to audit.**

Another area in which lawmakers should encourage increased transparency is with respect to the flow of cash inside the MBS structure. Within any securitization, tremendous amounts of money constantly flow through a complex waterfall that determines who gets paid and when, but little to no accounting or reporting is required to verify that the cash flows are correct and that any losses are indeed legitimate. Investors essentially have no way to determine whether mortgage insurance claims are being pursued or collateral cash is being paid to the rightful owners.

When MBS transactions are performing well, there is little concern over whether the proper cash is being remitted, but when credit losses materialize, it creates a significant opportunity for the servicer to manipulate the cash flows being remitted to the trust. This can be detected only by having an independent accountant verify the numbers. Investors must be allowed to request such an independent audit from the trustee to determine whether cash is being allocated properly through the trust waterfall. This audit should generally be at the investors' expense. If the trustee does not comply with that request, or accounting irregularities are later proved, the trustee, as fiduciary, should be liable for any losses.

I pose this question: how long would a public company be allowed to maintain its public listing if it did not have its financial statements verified by an independent accounting firm? Such a company would not be publicly listed for long. It should be no different in the case of MBS. If there is no way for the investor to verify the accuracy of the accounting or financial information it is receiving, that security should not be allowed to be sold into the public markets. This MBS reform could be accomplished by contractual means. Nevertheless, if we seek to establish an audit standard that mirrors the one imposed on the public equity markets, this standard should be imposed by the government.

7. **Stop shielding homeowners from personal liability.**

In most cases, if a borrower takes out a loan and defaults, he or she is personally liable for the full amount of the debt, regardless of whether or not it is satisfied by the value of the underlying collateral. The creditor can come after the borrower's personal assets to collect any debt outstanding after the collateral is sold. There is one general exception to this rule in the United States: home mortgage debt. In most cases, when the borrower defaults on a mortgage loan and loses his or her home, the liability is extinguished, and the borrower gets to keep his remaining assets.

This feature, unique to the American mortgage system, has evolved over time and become incorporated in most states into law. When borrowers agree to borrow money for a home and later default, they face only a loss of that home, nothing more. This allows borrowers to be less serious when signing up for a mortgage loan and makes the loan more susceptible to strategic default when the value of the property decreases below the value of the home. Where is the logic in a system that allows a senior secured creditor (e.g., the mortgage holder) to suffer a loss when the unsecured creditor (e.g., a credit card lender) has the right to go after the assets of the debtor and get paid? This public policy makes little sense and only encourages overleveraging and strategic default.

Although this is the norm in the United States, it is the exception around the world. In most countries, when someone agrees to pay a loan secured by a piece of property, that person still owes on the loan even if the property is sold in foreclosure. The deficiency becomes a personal liability of the borrower and other assets can be, and are often, attached and sold. Some states in the United States allow enforcement of these deficiencies, but in practice, they are rarely enforced by servicers.

While this proposal may sound harsh, the fact is that the benefit of borrowing money comes at the cost of an agreement to pay it off. Enforcing this agreement ensures that prospective homeowners recognize that they are undertaking a major financial commitment that should not be taken lightly. Why should the borrower's largest and most secured liability not carry with it the threat of recourse to the borrower's other assets? Any other practice not only encourages reckless borrowing, it also encourages strategic default. Recall that England experienced a similar drop in property values as the United States after the mortgage crisis, but England's foreclosure and delinquency rates were far lower than those in the U.S.[130] This can be directly attributed to the fact that English law holds borrowers personally liable for paying off their mortgage debts even after they have defaulted on and vacated the property. In England, far more borrowers decided to continue paying their mortgages when prices fell than in America, mainly because they feared the loss of their remaining assets if they walked away. The English example demonstrates that it is possible to have a real estate problem and not suffer a collapse of the entire financial system.

8. **Avoid governmental interference.**

Once regulators and principals have set up the rules of the game, their only role should be enforcing those rules, not retroactively changing those rules and interfering with settled expectations. Clearly, regulators must now step in and make changes to the future mortgage finance system in several key areas, but this is different from stepping in after the fact and making changes to the way existing deals play out. In particular, MBS losses should be allocated as provided by law and contract, not dumped onto the shoulders of a convenient patsy based on political whim or expediency.

An initial step in the right direction would be for the U.S. Congress to pass a resolution saying that it recognizes that the rights of investors in securitizations are of paramount importance to the success of the securitization market and to the U.S. economy. This resolution should also explicitly state that the federal government has no direct economic interest in these pools of assets and has no intention of touching or interfering with the pools of collateral in any manner other than to enforce the rule of law. Such a small and largely symbolic act would go a long way toward restoring investor confidence and engendering the return of private investment in the U.S. mortgage market.

Private (Contractual) Changes

1. Eliminate trustee indemnification.

The Trust Indenture Act of 1939, passed to protect the interests of bond investors, requires that a trustee be appointed for any bond issue valued at over $5 million. The appointment of a trustee was intended to ensure that the rights of bondholders were not compromised. This comports with the traditional role of a trustee—to safeguard the trust and act as a fiduciary for its stakeholders. As with a corporate trustee, an MBS trustee must be active and responsible for the securitization trust.

However, it has become commonplace in residential mortgage securitization contracts for the trustee to be indemnified or protected by the servicers from lawsuits and judgments against the trustee. This removes any economic incentive for the trustee to act on behalf of bondholders—the stakeholders of the trust. MBS trustees have thus largely failed in their role as fiduciaries and champions of bondholder interests, because they face no real consequences for remaining passive and uninvolved. This is the epitome of "giving sop to Cerberus"—that is, allowing banks to pay off the watchdog for the freedom to ignore their contractual constraints. Like the other misaligned economic incentives in the structure of existing securitizations, this must be fixed going forward.

Further compounding this problem is the fact that to enforce their rights, bondholders must go through an intentionally cumbersome and opaque process just to figure out whether there has been misbehavior on the part of any participants in the securitization. Bondholders are not provided access to detailed information about the loans backing their investment, and they must petition the trustee to gain access to such information. Even if a bondholder is somehow provided with proof of misbehavior and turns it over to the trustee, the trustee is usually not required to do anything about it unless the bondholder can rally bondholders holding 25 percent of the voting rights to join the cause. This is not an easy task when one considers that bondholders tend to keep their holdings private and no registry exists containing the universe of bondholders that must be contacted.

When all of these hurdles are considered, it becomes obvious that the game is so rigged in favor of the trustee and the servicer that there is almost no oversight of the trust and the money flowing through it. This would never be tolerated in a union or corporate pension fund, yet it is tolerated, without a second thought, in the largest fixed-income market in the world: the U.S. MBS market. Ironically, these MBS assets are held by almost every pension fund in the country. Fortunately, investors have control over this aspect of any future deal. Given the profound public policy implications of trustee behavior, no sane investor should allow a fully indemnified and passive trustee to be the fiduciary on any transaction in which it invests.

2. Insist on trustee independence.

The MBS trustee should be 100% independent from the originator or servicer. This means that the trustee would not have any other business or economic relationships with any of the other parties in a securitization. While this may sound extreme, it is possible if a new independent trustee were formed. Total independence would remove any doubt as to a trustee's ability to objectively look at a situation, make an unbiased judgment and initiate an action that may be necessary against any participant in a transaction.

3. Facilitate investor standing to sue.

Limitations on investors' ability to sue deal participants are common in PSAs. These limitations usually take the form of "no action" or "collective action" clauses that require investors to amass a certain percentage of the trust and petition the trustee before they have standing to sue. Such clauses, while making it difficult for bondholders to enforce their contractual rights, have been interpreted by courts as setting forth the only permissible procedure for investors wishing to file suit. As discussed earlier, these limitations can be used as a shield, encouraging participants to behave badly and increasing credit losses on transactions. If servicers or originators have ignored their contractual responsibilities, why should all but the largest investors be precluded from pursuing them in court?

The historic logic for these contractual limitations was that it was in investors' interests not to have one rogue investor sue to gain an advantage over other investors in the trust. While this sounds reasonable, several banks (including Countrywide, in the case in which I was involved[131]) have successfully used this standing limitation to obtain protection against class action suits. By definition, in a class action suit, the investors have already banded together and the lead plaintiff is charged with representing the interests of all of the investors in the trust. Thus, the historic rationale for the collective action clause goes out the window in the case of class actions, and it is instead being manipulated to protect the banks from the consequences of poor performance.

Revising the traditional no action clause to enable class actions—or even require that suits be brought as class actions—would serve to both lower the bar to sue if investors find bad behavior and ensure that all investor rights are considered in any lawsuit, judgment, or settlement. Lest one worry that this reform would encourage more litigation in an already litigious society, it must be remembered that putting the class action weapon in the hands of investors would encourage the banks to honor their contracts more diligently. A credible threat to sue would also encourage the banks to deal reasonably with investors in settlement negotiations should malfeasance be discovered. Furthermore, we must keep in mind that if deal participants have skin in the game by owning a portion of the subordinate securities, there will be much less economic incentive to engage in malfeasance in the first place, as such practices will only hurt those participants' bottom lines.

Investors should demand that trust agreements provide them with greater access to the courts to protect their investments and rights. While it may continue to make sense for the trustee to be responsible for determining whether or not there has been a contractual violation with respect to claims brought by smaller investors, future PSAs should allow investors with large or small positions to pursue the servicer on a class action basis with the approval of the trustee but without the trust paying any of the litigation expenses. The investors with larger positions (say greater than 25 percent) should be free to pursue deal participants without the consent of the trustee, at the investors' expense. Keep in mind that in the new world of securitization, the trustee should be completely independent and no longer indemnified by the servicer or other participants. The trustee should thus be able to act in an impartial and proactive manner on behalf of the trust.

4. Implement variable default servicing fees.

The method for determining servicing costs needs a complete overhaul. Traditionally, servicers have been paid a fixed cost for servicing a pool of loans, regardless of the performance of that pool. The last five years have shown us that fixed-cost servicing does not work when a large percentage of that pool goes into default. The servicer should have the right or perhaps the obligation to hire a special servicer when there are problems in a transaction. A standard hurdle could be established in each transaction, but it should be based on the credit performance of the pool. The cost of special servicing should be paid by the trust, and the cost should be applied to the credit waterfall.

The fixed-rate servicing model forces servicers to make certain assumptions regarding the cost of servicing a pool of loans and price their services accordingly. When they acquire servicing, they have to make assumptions regarding future delinquency rates and the approximate costs to resolve those delinquencies, as defaults engender significant additional expenses for servicers. Should a pool of loans experience higher-than-expected delinquency rates, and the servicer is servicing those loans in compliance with the PSA and bondholder interests, the servicer will lose money. Thus, once the servicer has priced its services with a certain assumption regarding the delinquency rate and finds that the rate is much higher, the servicer has no economic incentive to comply with its contract. This is especially true given how difficult it is for investors to obtain legal standing to sue servicers that are not fulfilling their obligations.

On the flip side, it is usually in the investors' interests to pay for quality servicing when it is needed most: when borrowers become delinquent on payments. Under the current model, the only remedy for investors is to remove the servicer from its position and replace it with a new servicer. The costs of this are high, and the process is cumbersome. The current system creates economic inefficiencies that are in the interests of neither the investors nor the servicers.

This can be corrected by implementing a variable servicing fee that increases as delinquencies rise. This is also known as a default servicing fee and is currently being proposed in an effort by Freddie Mac, Fannie Mae, and other regulators to revamp the fee structure for mortgage servicing.[132] Nevertheless, revamping this fee structure could easily be accomplished by contract, as it would be in all parties' best interests.

A variable fee structure should work to realign incentives, if the funds are spent on resolving the credit problems within the pool. This can be accomplished by having the trustee, as the fiduciary of the bondholders, approve and allocate servicing fees on an as-needed basis, including having the power to hire a special servicer to resolve problem loans. The fees would essentially be added to the liquidation costs in the foreclosure process and come out of any recovery received by the trust on that loan. If a loan goes bad, it is better to have the owner pay to resolve the loan than to do nothing while the non-performing asset sits on the trust's balance sheet and the underlying property falls into disrepair.

5. Stop paying late fees to the servicer.

In a typical MBS transaction, when a borrower is late with on a payment, the servicer charges a late fee. The amount of this fee is generally regulated by state law, and it is typical for the servicer to keep these late fees if they are paid by the borrower or recoup them off of the top of any liquidation recovery. This can represent a substantial source of revenue for the servicers when there are widespread delinquencies in the pool. What is the economic incentive for the servicer receiving late fees on a mortgage loan to encourage the homeowner to bring their loan current? If the loan becomes current, the late fees cease. Furthermore, given that the late fees are added to the amount due at foreclosure, the late fees are ultimately paid for by the trust. That is to say, they are paid by the investor.

It is one thing for the servicer to lack the proper economic incentives to perform in the best interest of the bondholders, but it is a different matter entirely for the servicer to be motivated to act in the opposite manner and encourage borrowers to remain delinquent. This can be remedied by having late fees paid to the servicer only after the bondholders are made whole on any particular loan. This way, late fees are retained in the trust rather than paid off the top, and servicers are encouraged to maximize bondholders' recovery on the underlying collateral. Investors must demand that this incentive structure be overhauled if they are to return to the MBS fold.

What We Should Do: Secondary Changes Necessary to Bolster the Private Securitization Market

Governmental Changes

1. Bankruptcy "cramdowns" should be permitted.

Investors should not be afraid of bankruptcy judges. One of the most controversial topics in the debate surrounding solutions to the mortgage crisis has been whether or not mortgage "cramdowns" should be allowed. A cramdown is the informal name for the bankruptcy process in which a bankruptcy judge reviews and potentially restructures the principal balance and terms of a debtor's mortgage loan. Each state sets its own rules for bankruptcy proceedings and can decide whether or not cramdowns should be allowed.

Traditionally, it has been said that "investors" do not want mortgages to be subject to the oversight of bankruptcy judges. I believe that this is incorrect. The main parties that would not want mortgages to be subject to bankruptcy code are the servicer banks that would have their second lien loans wiped out in homeowner bankruptcies.

As of the writing of this book, cramdowns have been largely rejected by state legislatures because of misinformation spread by mortgage servicers. Investors would support this reform if lien priority was maintained and limits were imposed on how much the mortgage could be reduced relative to the investor's expected loss in foreclosure. Servicers object to cramdown provisions because their junior liens, primarily home equity loans held in their portfolios, would be extinguished. However, this process is good for the investment community and securitizations in general, and investors should not fear that the judge will wield this power irresponsibly. Judges got to where they are because of their reputation for acting in a fair and impartial manner. This is far better than having a conflicted servicer making difficult modification decisions with no incentive to protect the interests of investors.

To ensure consistent and predictable outcomes, limitations should be placed on how drastically the bankruptcy judge could reduce the principal balance of a mortgage loan relative to the value of the home. Furthermore, lien priority should be respected in bankruptcy, and senior liens should not be subordinated to junior liens. Under the current system, this would not make servicers happy, but in the brave new world of mortgage securitization, where servicers are provided with proper incentives to service a senior loan in the interest of the lienholder (and are perhaps restricted from holding a junior lien when they service the senior lien for someone else), they should support rational cramdowns.

2. Defaults should not generate tax subsidies.

Just as borrowers should not be shielded from personal liability when they default, borrowers should receive no special tax treatment for failing to pay their mortgage debts. Ordinarily, loan forgiveness is taxed as ordinary income. If the borrower defaults on a loan, the amount of the loan that is forgiven is treated as ordinary income subject to income tax. This can create a problem for a borrower who is already in financial straits. At the outset of the mortgage crisis, Congress passed legislation that removed this tax problem. Now, borrowers face no tax when a foreclosure on their principal residence results in their lender taking a loss and writing off that debt.[133] While this is a compassionate policy, it also essentially subsidizes defaults. This type of well-intentioned legislation creates precisely the wrong incentive: it encourages borrowers to walk away from their homes. In the midst of a foreclosure crisis, congressional compassion has exacerbated the mortgage crisis and helped turn "strategic default" into a familiar term in the mortgage lexicon. Lawmakers should overturn this legislation as soon as possible.

3. Revisit the mortgage interest deduction.

The current methods for subsidizing homeownership through the mortgage interest deduction should be reconsidered, as they encourage destructive social behavior. By way of background, the mortgage interest deduction was retained as part of a political compromise entered into in 1986 when the income tax system was overhauled.[134] Prior to the passage of this law, virtually all interest payments were tax deductible. In an effort to limit deductions for personal interest, Congress eliminated the deductibility of most interest payments but preserved a limited tax subsidy for home mortgage interest. This feature in the tax code had the distorting effect of subsidizing one type of loan over another and favoring homeowners over renters. This ongoing distortion causes a predictable and rational response from taxpayers—they overinvest in and overleverage their homes. It is unclear why we are encouraging borrowers to re-lever their homes by continuously removing equity, so they never build up any real ownership stake in their primary asset.

Though the list of what is wrong with this system is extensive, an illustration will suffice. According to a joint report of the Brooking Institution and the Urban Institution, 47 percent of U.S. taxpayers do not pay income taxes (this does not include payroll taxes and the like).[135] This means that the tax subsidy for mortgages is unavailable to the bottom half of all wage earners. In other words, ours is a system that subsidizes home ownership for the wealthy but not the poor. It seems doubtful that those on either side of the political spectrum would argue that this is good social policy.

The byproducts of this inducement to overleverage can be readily identified today. It has become commonplace to obtain 100 percent financing for the purchase of a home. Our citizenry has over $1 trillion in home equity loans outstanding.[136] This excessive debt load left our population far too thinly capitalized to weather a drop in home prices, which turned the bursting of a housing bubble into a financial calamity.

If politicians wish to subsidize homeownership, I propose a different mechanism for achieving this social objective without the distortions and inequities of the existing tax subsidy system. A government program could be created that subsidized homeowners' down payments and payments used to reduce their mortgage debt. This program would encourage borrowers to build equity in their homes rather than take out larger or additional mortgage loans. The program could work along the following lines: a first time homebuyer saves for a 20 percent down payment and uses it to purchase a home. The U.S. government then gives this homebuyer a tax credit of 10 percent (one-half of the 20 percent down payment), which is paid directly to the note holder to reduce the unpaid principal balance of the mortgage loan. Additional pay downs in each of the first three years (up to another 10 percent of the loan amount) generate tax credits of 45 percent, 30 percent, and 15 percent, respectively. These funds also go directly to the owner of the note and operate to reduce further the principal balance of the loan. This system both promotes home equity and assists homeowners in paying down their mortgage loan. After the initial period, the loan would no longer be subsidized with tax credits or interest deductibility. This tax subsidy would continue to create an economic incentive to pay off a mortgage loan and build wealth.

There are strong policy reasons to encourage homeowners to make a substantial down payment and to begin paying down their mortgage early. Aside from decreasing the incidence of strategic default during soft housing markets, this system would backstop the borrower during their first three years of homeownership, widely viewed as the most likely time for a loan to go into default. Requiring down payments and providing a one-time mortgage equity tax credit (or some finite dollar amount per homeowner) would go a long way toward mitigating this risk.

Obviously, some limits would need to be placed on the amount of, and frequency that homeowners could claim this tax subsidy. Furthermore, requirements would need to be set on how long the homeowner would have to own the home for the benefit to be fully vested. Finally, there would have to be a phase-in process to avoid harming the homeowners who purchased a home, believing that they were going to have an interest deduction, only to find that the tax code and the economic incentives had changed.

Nevertheless, if a decision is made to continue with a public policy subsidizing home mortgages, the subsidy should be implemented in a manner that is not regressive (that is, available to poor as well as the wealthy) and does not create the economic incentive for homeowners to take excessive risk with their personal balance sheets.

Private (Contractual) Changes

1. Eliminate servicer advances on delinquent loans.

Within a typical MBS trust agreement, clauses often exist that provide that the servicer will "advance," or lend, a missing mortgage payment to the trust when a loan is delinquent. This prevents the interruption of cash flows to investors and ensures that the MBS perform in a predictable manner. When a servicer advances principal and interest to the trust, the transaction appears to be performing as intended. While this keeps the cash flowing to the subordinate holders, it increases the conflicts of interest within a transaction. Consider that when the loan is finally resolved through foreclosure and the trust takes a loss, the advances that the servicer paid are added to the loss. This is because the servicer recoups these advances off of the top of the disposition proceeds. This seems reasonable, but the reality is that subordinate investors have been receiving cash flows that are the byproduct of delays in the resolution of loans. This has the effect of shifting losses to the senior bonds while allowing the subordinate bonds to avoid losses they would have taken had the loan stopped paying when it went delinquent. This is the root cause of tranche warfare between senior and subordinate bondholders, as discussed earlier.

An alternative method is to create a liquidity waterfall in the trust rather than to have servicers advance principal and interest. The subordinate securities would effectively be reduced immediately when a loan is delinquent (rather than upon resolution) and the credit loss would be more concentrated in the subordinate securities. Remember that in the new securitization regime, the subordinate securities would largely be held by the originators, servicers, and underwriters/arrangers of the MBS securities, the parties who helped create the securities and/or the parties best able to control the losses experienced by the trust.

2. Standardize underwriting guidelines.

I am a firm believer that the private label market should and could create standard underwriting guidelines for public issuance of MBS. This process could be overseen by an organization similar to ISDA or by a group of investors dedicated to encouraging market transparency. At the very least, it should not be overseen by the originators. While this action would greatly inhibit loan product innovation, innovation in this space is often another way to describe masking credit risk and making it more difficult for the homeowner to understand his or her loan. If originators wish to create low- or no-documentation programs, they are free to place those loans or a securitization backed by those loans in the private placement markets. If the standard back-end DTI ratio for the agency markets is 32 percent, loans with back-end DTIs of 50 percent should be placed in the private placement markets. If a pool does not meet established underwriting standards, the SEC should not allow the transaction to be sold in the public markets. Investors in the public markets should be able to rely on some uniform standard of credit. Though this will inhibit innovation in the public markets, this may, in fact, be a desirable outcome. Rather than encouraging innovations that act to shift risk to less sophisticated parties, the goal of securitization reform should be to make this process as transparent as possible, thereby allowing investors to accurately assess and manage risk.

Prior to the mortgage crisis, it was assumed that the rating agencies were doing much of this work, but evidence has shown that this assumption was largely inaccurate. The issuer-funded rating agencies were unable or unwilling to "look under the hood" of MBS transactions and attempt to understand the likely default rates of the loans. Their interest was in maintaining their business relationships with the issuers and ensuring that their competitors did not steal their business by being more lenient in their ratings. This created a classic "race to the bottom." Later, we discuss some reforms that could be made to the existing rating system if we wanted it to perform more like the "due diligence cop" it was assumed to be, but it is obvious that we can rely on these agencies, as they exist currently, to do little but wield large rubber stamps.

This is another reason that market standards that are simple and easy to verify must be established for underwriting. This country has a long history of reasoned mortgage lending: we know how to make loans that will succeed or at least fail at a predictable and manageable rate. If there is some compelling reason down the road to diverge from these established standards, investors will demand changes and initiate a slow process of modifying the guidelines. It is hoped that this process would be overseen by a group dominated by the investors, similar to ISDA. However, allowing issuers to change the underwriting standards at will and on a deal-by-deal basis, and then assuming that investors or rating agencies will be able to understand these guidelines and assess the risk in each particular case, is a recipe for another disaster.

3. Standardize deal documents.

Just as underwriting guidelines should be standardized, deal documents should conform to a set of accepted standards. Part of the problem in resolving the mortgage crisis of 2007 is that the documentation surrounding the securitizations is heterogeneous, making it difficult to determine the content of the relevant trust documents. This may sound trivial, but when there are over six thousand unique trusts, with PSAs often containing over a thousand pages, reading each one individually to determine the participants' rights is a daunting task. There is no good reason for the legal creativity exhibited in the PSA documents underlying existing private label transactions.

In the case of interest rate swaps, ISDA created a standard set of documents that forms the backbone of virtually all swap agreements. If one looks at the interest rate swap market of twenty-five years ago, each transaction required a detailed negotiation and unique documentation. When ISDA agreed on standardized swap documentation, the market became more generic and efficient. Transaction costs were minimized, and the market grew dramatically. The mortgage market is about the same age as the swap market, and while standard documentation has been created for Ginnie Mae, Fannie Mae and Freddie Mac deals, there has been little attempt to standardize the documentation in private label mortgage securitizations. It has proven to be virtually impossible to have any sort of comprehensive legislative response to the failures in private label deals or respond rationally to the challenges facing the loans trapped in these securitizations. If these deal documents are standardized going forward, it will make it far easier to resolve any future problems without having to come up with one thousand different solutions.

4. Minimize systemic risk at all levels.

Systemic risk should be minimized by each party in the system wherever possible. This includes investors, homeowners, insurers, lenders, bankers, and government agencies. By systemic risk, I mean a risk or event that, should it materialize, would create losses across a large number of securitization trusts and endanger the economy as a whole. Some systemic risks associated with private label securitizations cannot be avoided, such as a sharp decline in property values. However, several structural innovations seem to have little purpose other than to generate larger fees for Wall Street and obscure the nature of a transaction. These would include the following:

Embedded interest rate swaps

An embedded interest rate swap is a type of derivative contract that is commonly included in the PSA of a securitization. The most common type of interest rate swap is one in which the trust pays a fixed coupon rate of interest in return for the receipt of a floating coupon rate of interest. The trust would be obligated to pay this fixed rate on the outstanding balance of the pool of collateral. These financial derivatives are often embedded in mortgage deals so that the investor can convert the underlying fixed-rate mortgage note into a more manageable, floating-rate bond, while relieving the investor from the work of having to arrange the swap itself. While embedding an interest rate swap accomplishes this objective, it does so at the expense of multiplying a risk across a large number of securitization trusts. Namely, if the swap counterparty fails and the trust is faced with a bankruptcy claim under an ISDA contract (the standard agreement for swaps), the trust becomes a party to the bankruptcy, creating uncertainty within the trust.

A better way to turn the fixed rate flows into floating rate flows is the use of a structural technique called an inverse interest-only strip. While this may sound complex, it is simple for investors in practice. The structure converts the fixed-rate bond into a floating-rate bond using an interest-only bond—representing the difference between the two coupons—that floats in the opposite direction as the floating rate index. The only difference for the investor would be that the bond would have a cap (this is a necessity for structural reasons that need not be detailed here). The investor could always choose to lift the cap on the floating-rate bond by entering into an interest rate cap agreement. However, this agreement would be outside of the trust and, should the swap counterparty fail, the trust would not be affected. The trust could also issue fixed-rate bonds, and the investor could swap that bond's fixed-rate interest payments for a floating-rate cash flow.

Because the inverse interest-only bond would be economically identical to an interest rate swap with a cap, Wall Street arrangers would be left with only one reason to embed an interest rate swap in a securitization: generating fees on the swap and obscuring the true economics of the transaction.

Embedded currency swaps

Embedded currency swaps are similar to embedded interest rate swaps except that the currency swap converts one currency into another. As with interest-rate swaps, Wall Street sometimes seeks to include currency swaps in securitization transactions. The ostensible purpose of this is to be able to use collateral denominated in a local currency but market "hard" currency securities—that is, securities denominated in a currency that is not likely to depreciate suddenly or to fluctuate greatly in value. While this may sound like a good idea, there is one logical flaw: if the swap market or a major participant were to fail, the implications for the transaction and the market could be profound. Why would a country link a key part of its financial system to the health of the swap market, especially when there is no economic reason for that link? I suspect that this decision is again motivated by a desire on behalf of the arranger to earn a fee for booking the swap.

There is another way to arrange the same economics and benefits of the embedded currency swap without creating systemic risk: create a class of security that can be easily swapped by the investor. Historically, if there were a ruble denominated class in a Russian MBS, but investors instead sought securities denominated in another currency, the arranger could turn that class into a floating-rate U.S. dollar bond by embedding a currency swap into the transaction. That swap would be a "pay ruble and receive U.S. dollar" swap. The issued bonds would thus be U.S. dollar-denominated bonds. However, if the bonds were issued instead as ruble bonds, the investor could arrange the same swap and achieve the same economic position. This would put the investor in the same position as embedding a swap into the transaction, yet there would be no systemic risk to the deal or the mortgage market in the host country. The key difference is that in the first instance, the deal would fail if the swap counterparty were to fail. In the second instance, if the swap counterparty were to fail and the swap was outside of the transaction, the MBS deal would not fail or be downgraded.

In the past, this issue has arisen only in non-U.S. dollar transactions and then only in countries with a currency that was not considered one of the hard currencies. Given the unprecedented turmoil in the financial markets over the last few years, currency swaps may become more common in securitization systems around the globe. This is unfortunate and should be avoided if possible.

External liquidity facility

Under the current system, when a loan is delinquent, the servicer lends the trust the missing payment so that the bonds can be paid. This is done to create bonds that feature a high probability of making their full coupon and principal payments at the appropriate times. If the servicer no longer advances delinquent mortgage payments into the trust (as advocated earlier), a liquidity facility will need to be created to make up for shortfalls in the transaction due to missed payments. This liquidity facility could be provided by the arranger of the trust and would handle the advancement of interest and principal that was previously provided by the servicer.

The other option would be to have the trust create its own liquidity through a liquidity waterfall within the trust. Under this system, the lowest-rated bonds would take the full brunt of any liquidity shortfall, and the more senior bonds would absorb any shortfalls only after the more junior bonds had suffered losses amounting to their entire cash flow. While this has been implemented only in non-U.S. deals because of the custom of the servicer advancing such payments, if servicer advancement were abolished in the United States, such liquidity facilities would become highly useful. In the past, Wall Street has dealt with similar problems by creating an external liquidity facility that advanced cash for a fee. However, it is not necessary to rely on an external facility and the external risk that this type of instrument creates, as the liquidity facility can readily be engineered into the trust.

As a point of interest, the Russian deals that I completed had internal liquidity facilities that were designed into the transactions. These were necessary because we did not have servicer advances in Russia. This structure results in any credit losses being concentrated in the most subordinate portion of the transaction. It also avoids the traditional fee charged by arrangers for this service.

The systemic risk created by embedded swaps and liquidity facilities is not merely hypothetical. On a recent trip to Russia, I was flattered when one government official thanked me for having previously explained to him why external risks should not be injected into transactions. While I had spoken at conferences numerous times on this exact topic, I did not specifically recall the conversation to which he was referring. The Russian official reminded me that I had been discussing a Gazprombank deal that had unnecessary structural weaknesses, and had told the Russian officials that if the parties on whom the deal depended ultimately failed, the deal would fail too.

It turned out that a subsidiary of Lehman Brothers had been the deal's swap counterparty, the liquidity facility provider, and the swap and liquidity guarantor. When Lehman went down, the deal collapsed with it. If Russia had had dozens or hundreds of such transactions outstanding, their mortgage finance system would also have collapsed, all because some arranger wanted to earn clandestine fees for unnecessary services. The Russian official told me that while he had not fully understood my points at the time of our original conversation, he now understood them. He assured me that the Russians would not make the same mistake in the future.

Poolwide mortgage insurance and wraps

Poolwide mortgage insurance—also known as guaranty insurance or a "wrap"—is a product through which an insurance company guarantees the performance of a particular class of security or a pool of collateral. The companies that issued this type of insurance for private label transactions were MBIA, Ambac, FGIC, and the other monoline bond insurance companies. AIG also took on much of this exposure in the form of credit default swaps. This concentrated exposure pushed a number of insurance companies close to or into bankruptcy.

If a class or pool of collateral is not well understood or generic enough to stand on its own, it should not be sold into the public markets. That is, if a pool of collateral or class of security needs third-party credit enhancement to be viable or marketable, it should only be eligible for private sale. This product creates a systemic risk by concentrating a large amount of mortgage risk into a small number of systemically important institutions, which, as we saw with AIG, must be bailed out by the government if the housing market sours. Furthermore, many of the bond insurers also guaranteed municipal bonds, and the losses in the mortgage arena have jeopardized the credit quality of those municipal bonds. The bottom line is that we must avoid placing too much reliance on any one securitization participant.

5. Redesign the subordination structure.

The subordination structure of an MBS deal should be redesigned to reduce conflicts between and better align the economic interests of the different classes of bondholders in a securitization. The premise underlying this reconstruction is that subordinate bondholders should not be receiving payouts while the transaction is taking credit losses. The structure I propose, called a "shifting Z-bond," would result in the subordinate classes receiving little or no cash flow until the more senior bonds in the bond capital structure were paid off. The subordinate bonds would thus have little or no value in a transaction that experienced high credit losses. This structure would result in the subordinate securities having a much longer exposure to the transaction relative to the common subordination structures the market was accepting when it was last operational.

If the loans serving as collateral deteriorate, the control over the trust decisions should travel up the credit waterfall. The responsibility for determining how losses should be mitigated would then fall on the investors most affected by such losses. Accordingly, the subordinate structure within a private label transaction should become more of a Z-structure for the lowest-rated securities. As the losses wipe out the lowest securities, the most junior securities that are still paying should convert into a Z-structure, and investors holding those bonds would become part of the "Servicer Control Party," with certain rights in the PSA to mitigate losses. These investors would get a cash flow only if they were able to prevent credit losses from wiping out their securities. If bond losses extinguish the subordinate securities, the investors closer to the top of the credit waterfall should then become the Servicer Control Party, inheriting control over the transaction.

This new structure should be coupled with the servicer being afforded increased flexibility to determine how to deal with deteriorating collateral. Investors in securitizations should have access to the same modification techniques that are available to bank investors. The Servicer Control Party would be endowed with the legal standing to instruct the trustee to take action and the responsibility for making the difficult judgment calls regarding the best resolution for a particular problem loan. Trustees would thus be taking orders from the investors most affected by problem loans and would be charged with ensuring that the servicer follows investor instructions, provided they are within the constraints of the PSA.

If mortgage modifications are to be allowed in a securitization, the deciding party should not be the servicer but a designee of the Servicer Control Party and the independent trustee. Such a system would align economic incentives with contractual responsibilities. For those curious about how the shifting Z-structure and other alternative structures would work, details may be found in appendices V and VI.

While my Russian transactions did not have the complete shifting Z-structure advocated here, I did use a Z-bond structure and required the servicer to retain the Z-bond. This had approximately the same effect as the shifting Z-structure. I have to admit that I did not anticipate the scenario in which the complete shifting Z-structure structure would be necessary. Future Russian transactions that I put together will feature a more sophisticated structure, as should future deals in the United States.

What We Can Do: Long Term Changes that Will Allow Private Securitization to Flourish

Governmental Changes

1. Minimize economic incentives to refinance.

As discussed earlier, the current conventional loan creates a systemic risk when you consider the aggregate exposure it creates for of the economy. This exposure can be mitigated by having a prepayment penalty that compensates the investor for the economic impact of the change in interest rates. These types of penalties would minimize the incentives for rate and term refinancing and put an end to the prepayment waves that occur when current mortgage rates drop below outstanding note rates.

The largest beneficiaries of this change will be American taxpayers and prospective American homeowners. The taxpayer will benefit, in that the propensity for financial institutions to become insolvent and drag down the economy or require a bailout with taxpayer money will be radically reduced. Prospective homeowners benefit because long-term mortgages will become more affordable. A mortgage loan without free prepayment options would feature a more affordable note rate, reflecting the decreased risk to the investor associated with owning that loan. Depending on the interest rate cycle, this could reduce the rate the homeowner pays by as much as 1 percent. This would extend the possibility of home ownership to large numbers of people who would not have been able to afford a conventional fixed-rate loan with a prepayment option.

The main objection to this proposal will probably come from Wall Street and mortgage originators. They will object because originating new mortgages in a refinancing wave is a profitable business. Eliminating refinancing waves curtails this periodic source of revenue for the banks, but it is difficult to argue that the repeated refinancing of mortgage loans is a socially productive use of resources. Instead, this line of business should go the way of the Betamax.

While this change could be implemented privately through modified trust contracts, I have included this proposal in the governmental section, because it would be more effectively implemented by regulatory bodies. The GSEs could alter the market in one fell swoop by guaranteeing only loans that do not contain a traditional prepayment option. Furthermore, the SEC could approve only certain types of collateral for securitization in the public markets. This would be the fastest and most efficient manner of modifying this deeply ingrained feature of traditional mortgage lending.

2. Overhaul deed recording system.

An adequate title recording system is essential to building a stable mortgage market. The title system in the United States runs through county recording offices and has thus evolved over time on a local basis, based on a patchwork of small municipalities charged with the responsibility of recording deeds for over one hundred years. Generally these municipalities have not updated their systems in many years. Moreover, many municipalities levy a sizable tax (often about 1 percent) on each owner wishing to record a deed or lien transfer. These localities often tax the transfer and the recording of mortgage liens on a per-transaction basis. Accordingly, if a lien were to be transferred several times, a tax might be levied for each transfer. This cost structure clearly hampers the development of any mortgage market.

The mortgage industry attempted to make this process more efficient for securitization and more readily allow for the rapid sale of loans, with the creation of the uniform Mortgage Electronic Registration Systems (MERS). MERS was designed to augment the existing deed-recording system by allowing those trading mortgages to do so without specifically updating the lien at the local municipality or (more importantly) paying the tax. MERS also effectively created an electronic link between the local deed-recording offices, which was a step in the right direction. However, this system lacked transparency and allowed the banks to cut corners with documentation, meaning that the proper documentation showing ownership and chain of title was unavailable when foreclosure was necessary. This in turn led to scandals over allegations that fraudulent documents and robosigners were used in foreclosure proceedings to "paper over" these deficiencies. While this is a sideshow to the underlying mortgage problem, it is a serious matter when systemic fraud is being perpetuated on the courts.

A simple way to handle this problem would be to require, when loans are originated with an eye toward selling them into securitization, that each loan be originated in the name of the trust that is intended to be the ultimate recipient of that loan. This would avoid one of the primary sources of deed-recording problems: the desire to get around the tax at the municipal level whenever the loan changes hands. Though this tax should probably be paid when the loan is initially recorded, it is silly to think that a 1 percent tax should be assessed each time the underlying note is transferred. Putting the note in the name of the trust or a nominee name avoids this recording tax, but it does not add to the document accuracy and transparency needs of the mortgage market. This issue can be addressed by investors demanding that documents be held by an independent, third-party custodian.

3. Overhaul how rating agencies are compensated and selected.

In the United States, the Nationally Recognized Statistical Rating Organizations (NRSROs) have a unique legal status: up until recently, they were the only organizations approved to determine which non-governmental assets were suitable for investment in money market funds. These organizations also exert a much broader influence, in that the rating of a transaction greatly affects that transaction's marketability.

The federal government has outsourced much of the regulatory process to conflicted rating agencies by attaching different capital charges to securities with different credit ratings. The original rating agency business model consisted of an independent agency that was paid by the investors and was not dependent on the originators for its revenue stream. Over time, rating agencies determined that they could earn more money by charging issuers for their ratings. This turned out to be like a person on trial putting his or her friends on the jury. Somewhat predictably, this market devolved to the point where rating agencies were effectively willing to rate anything for a fee. Clearly, this model must be overhauled.

To illustrate the flaws embedded in the current rating system, let's examine how that system works, including the components that are included—and not included—in the evaluation of MBS. When rating a particular MBS deal, a rating agency looks at a number of factors including the following:

1. The servicing rating or quality of the servicer.

2. The quality of the collateral and originator.

3. The structure of the transaction.

Before any rating agency will rate a transaction, the servicer must have been reviewed and given an acceptable servicer rating. The servicer rating is based on specific servicing metrics. If the rating agency determines that the servicer is acceptable, it will be approved to service collateral for a rated transaction.

Next, the rating agency will review the data on the loan tapes, which provide the basic characteristics of the loans in the transaction and well as the reps and warranties that have been provided by the loan sellers and sponsors. The rating agency estimates credit losses under a variety of stress scenarios, under the assumption that the data in the loan tapes and the reps and warranties in the PSA are accurate. The stress scenarios are used to establish the amount and nature of the overall subordination that will be required for the deal, as well as the manner in which subordination will be split among the various tranches to achieve various credit ratings. If there are accounts that provide credit or liquidity support, these factors will be evaluated as well. The rating agency may also take into account the quality of the legal opinions supporting the transaction and the strength of the contractual support for the transaction from the servicer, trustee, or other deal service provider. These all amount to checks on whether this deal is contractually sound.

What is missing from this analysis is any consideration of the actual credit quality of the underlying loans. In particular, rating agencies rarely, if ever, reviewed any due diligence that had been conducted by the issuer as to the collateral loan pool. This was despite the fact that these due diligence reports might have revealed important deficiencies in loan underwriting, incorrect information in the loan data tapes, or untrue reps and warranties, all of which would have markedly increased the risk of default. Keith Johnson, the former president and COO of due diligence provider Clayton Holdings, testified before the Financial Crisis Inquiry Commission that his firm offered such reports to the ratings agencies prior to the mortgage crisis, but the agencies were not interested.[137] The explanation was that if any agency had possession of such reports and was forced to consider them, it would no longer be able to offer ratings as high as its competitors and would thus lose market share. This is the perfect illustration of why the issuer-pay ratings model is dysfunctional.

Down the road, the U.S. government could require that the rating agencies revert to the original, investor-pay model, but this is unlikely to work given the ease with which information moves in the current market—once the information is released to a paying investor, it is likely to leak into the public domain where it would be freely available. Moreover, it is unlikely that much worthwhile information will be developed if the rating agencies cannot be adequately compensated for providing it. This poses a massive problem: the ratings agencies are permanently conflicted unless an entirely different revenue and business model can be developed for the industry.

A possible solution would be to have a committee of investors or the independent trustee pay for and select the rating agency or agencies that would rate the security they were considering. This would remove the financial incentive for these ratings agencies to cater to the investment banks. Individuals at these agencies will still be tempted to provide overly rosy ratings when they hope to someday work at a particular investment bank, but the rating agency's management will be likely to keep a watchful eye over such conduct. Further, if an individual ends up moving from a rating agency to an investment bank, it should trigger an automatic review of the ratings on prior deals involving that individual and his or her new employer. Of course, this system might create an incentive for the ratings agencies to be overly conservative in their ratings, recommending that investors buy only the least risky products. In any event, such a system would be far more objective than one in which the security salesman is paying the bills.

Another possibility would be to have the rating agencies paid from a common fund supplied from a fee on the underlying transaction, with the investors making the ultimate decision over whether or not to hire a particular rating agency. No matter what payment system is implemented, there should be a decoupling of the financial link between the party creating the security and the party rating the security. The government could revise its NRSRO selection and approval process to sanction only ratings agencies that employ payment models that encourage objectivity. Otherwise, in a process that was initiated by the Dodd-Frank Act, the government could simply remove all references to ratings in legislation and regulation, leaving it up to the market whether to obtain or trust the ratings from any given company. One rating agency has already adopted a model of collecting fees only from investors. That firm, Egan-Jones Ratings Co., markets itself as non-conflicted and better able to offer unbiased ratings than the firms that are hired and paid by the large issuers.

Recently, Joseph A. Grundfest and Evgenia Petrova[138] of Stanford Law School proposed that there be an investor owned and controlled system that would fund the rating agencies. These so-called Investor-Owned and Controlled Rating Agencies (IOCRA) would be delinked from the investment bankers hiring them and would be hired and compensated by an investor-run organization. These agencies could either be for profit or not for profit, but the essence of the proposal is that a banker should not hire its own judge. Furthermore, it would be likely that the rating agencies would end up less involved in the structuring of the transaction. The bankers would have to do their own structuring with their lawyers rather than asking the rating agencies what they thought was an acceptable structure and subordination level.

This proposal would be a significant step in the direction of having objective ratings that the bankers could control only by responsible structuring, not by economic or political influence.

There are many options available to solve this problem, but what is clear is that bankers should not be allowed to hire rating agencies, as this creates a conflict of interest. At the very least, this conflict harms investor confidence by creating a perception that the rating agency is not entirely objective, a perception that appears accurate based on recent history.

Private (Contractual) Changes

1. Encourage transparency and clarity wherever possible.

Investors should demand increased transparency from issuing banks. Prior to issuance, the securitizer should make all loan files and a summary of the collateral available to any investor that requests this information. The loan files should consist of the underwriting details of each loan with non-public borrower information removed. This information would allow investors to analyze the loan files should they choose to do so. The summary should follow the traditional format, with the loans broken down into categories so that the investor could start to understand the distribution of risk in this pool of collateral.

Investors should also demand more standard and transparent remittance reports. Remittance reports are the monthly reports produced by servicers at the time the bonds are purchased, and each month thereafter, detailing the activity of the pool for the month. Failure to provide this report or the data—thereby preventing the paying agent from preparing a servicer or remittance report in an accurate and timely manner—should be considered a servicer default and the trustee should be required to replace the servicer. That is, if the investors do not and cannot get the information needed to understand what the servicer is doing in a timely manner, the servicer should be fired.

Another problem is that these remittance reports have not been standardized, audited, or verified to ensure that they provide accurate or consistent information. Accordingly, these reports often contain inaccuracies and inconsistencies. Some trustees have their analysts release reports in entirely different formats across similar transactions. Drawing comparisons across reports when they do not have consistent information or terminology makes finding errors and malfeasance much more difficult.

As part of the standardization of the PSA and the securitization process, specifications should be developed regarding what is to be reported within a remittance report and the definition of terms within that report. There should also be independent verification of the accuracy of the reporting or at least the ability of the investors and/or trustee to verify readily the accuracy of the reported numbers should they suspect foul play by the trustee or servicer. Updated remittance reports should be made available each month on the website of the trustee along with ongoing access to loan files. The remittance report should include detailed information on the resolution of each loan.

The new securitization regime can and should be investor controlled and align the economic interests of servicers and investors for the duration of the deal, whatever market conditions may occur. In the event that the servicer still fails to act in investors' best interests, the servicer should lose its servicing rights. Recent servicer performance has made it clear that contractual provisions alone are insufficient to dictate servicer behavior when they conflict with a servicer's economic interests.

2. Create a separate custodian to hold deal documents.

Investors should demand that the physical documents that make up the legal claim on the underlying properties be kept with an independent document custodian, not the servicer or trustee, as they are currently. The logic of this is clear: improve document accuracy and transparency while eliminating the reliance on the servicer to turn over documents that may ultimately prove damaging to the bank. Under the current system, an investor must rely first on the trustee to request the documents from the servicer and then on the servicer to provide those documents in a timely manner. This system has proven to be far too cumbersome and time consuming to be practical or effective. Moreover, given the incentives at play, the servicers are reluctant to cooperate in this exercise when the result could be the forced repurchase of thousands or possibly millions of loans incorrectly underwritten by those same servicers.

This obvious conflict of interest can be remedied easily if investors get together and decide that they will invest only in deals where the loan documentation is held by an independent third party. Besides having sole responsibility for holding the underlying documents in a securitization, this custodian would have to certify that the proper documents were in hand before the securitization could close. It would be the trustee's responsibility, as the fiduciary to the investors, to oversee this process and the custodian's work. Full and complete documentation should be required by the independent trustee for a loan to be placed in a securitization and sold to the public. For the record, my Russian transactions all featured an independent custodian that held the original mortgage loan documents.

3. Public mortgage transactions should have a standby servicer.

Creating a standby servicer would allow the trustee to replace the servicer easily should the trustee determine that the servicer has not fulfilled its contractual responsibilities. This standby servicer would receive periodic updates of the computer files of the primary servicer as they pertain to the loans in the transaction. If the primary servicer refused to turn over deal documents even after removal, the standby servicer would have access to all of the servicing activities for the pool of collateral. This would mean that the primary servicer could be removed by the trustee without fear that access to the relevant loan documents or computer files would be lost. The rating agencies, independent trustee, and investors should insist on this as a feature of any future mortgage transaction, as I did in my Russian transactions.

4. Require Servicer Independence

Servicers and originators should be separate from each other. Corporate independence between the servicer and originator would provide an additional check and balance between the production of the loan and the public marketplace. This is one additional check for fraud. Under the current mortgage finance system, servicers must advance funds when a mortgage note is delinquent. Given that servicers would no longer be called on to provide these funds, the role of servicer would not be a capital intensive business, but rather a data processing business. This would open this function to a number of different market participants.

* * *

The goal of these proposals is to make the MBS market both transparent for investors and regulators and more efficient at connecting the providers and consumers of mortgage credit. Transparency and standardization will reduce transaction costs and lead to more affordable loans for prospective homeowners. Meanwhile, updated mortgage loan and securitization structures will reduce the systemic risk imposed by securitization on the U.S. economy.

Though I estimate that the reforms proposed herein may reduce MBS cash flows and increase costs by three to four basis points, the resulting gains from lower transaction costs, lower credit risk, and improved stability for the financial system will far outweigh these costs, and reduce the overall cost of homeownership.

The following chart is a quick reference guide to the changes discussed in this chapter.

SUMMARY OF PROPOSED REFORMS NECESSARY TO REOPEN THE PUBLIC MORTGAGE SECURITIZATION MARKET

	Must	*Should*	*Can*
Governmental Changes	• Ban Short Positions • Require Skin in the Game • Eliminate Subsequent Second Liens • Ban Captive Servicing Arrangements • Make Investor Lists Available • Allow Investor Audits • Ensure Homeowner Responsibility • Avoid Governmental Interference	• Allow Bankruptcy Cramdowns • Avoid Subsidizing Defaults • Eliminate or Redesign Interest Tax Deduction • Make GSEs Unambiguously Either Public or Private	• Minimize Incentives to Refinance • Overhaul Deed Recording System • Overhaul Ratings Agency Selection and Fee Structure
Private (Contractual) Changes	• Ban Trustee Indemnification • Insist on Independent Trustee • Strengthen Investor Standing to Sue • Implement Variable Default Servicing Fees • Have Trust Retain Late Fees	• Eliminate Servicer Adva • Require Uniform Underw • Standardize Deal Docum • Minimize Systemic Risk • Redesign Subordination Structure	

217

"All that is valuable in human society depends upon the opportunity for development accorded the individual."
—*Albert Einstein*

CHAPTER 11

How Does Mortgage Finance Fit into a Developing Market?

We have discussed what the United States can do to rebuild its mortgage system so that it continues to attract international capital and provide affordable mortgages for its citizens. The lessons of this book, however, are not directed solely at the American system; they are applicable to emerging nations looking to develop mortgage finance systems as stabilizing forces for their economies.

There is no fundamental difference between a mortgage transaction in a developing country and one undertaken in the United States. The goal should be to provide capital as efficiently as possible without putting the economy at risk from systemic shocks. In fact, nations such as Saudi Arabia,[139] Mexico,[140] and Chile[141] are already turning to mortgage finance to promote economic growth and to reduce the possibility of economic and political turmoil. Leaders of these nations understand that economic stability fundamentally stems from such factors as consumer confidence, hope, and opportunity. By providing prospective homeowners with access to capital, mortgage finance systems help to promote all three of these factors.

A leading emerging market economist, Hernando DeSoto, has written extensively about the important role that access to capital plays in the economic growth of developing countries. In particular, DeSoto has focused on how less-developed countries can allow their poor to access the capital embedded in their homes when the necessary infrastructure is in place, including deed-recording systems and the ability to pledge title to a property. Active mortgage markets will provide such access to a wider segment of the populations of developing countries, allowing those individuals and the nations at large the opportunity for much broader economic growth and development than would otherwise be available.

Furthermore, as shown on the following chart, mortgage debt is already a large source of funding for many developed countries and is becoming a larger source of funding for many developing countries as well. Once the basic requirements for completing an MBS transaction are fulfilled, including an adequate title recording system, courts that enforce contracts and "true sales," and a system for securing collateral, a mortgage finance system can flourish. Nations that have these essential building blocks in place, as a large number do, possess the resources to attract capital, encourage the growth of small business, and provide housing to many who previously would not have dreamed of such opportunity. A properly structured MBS system provides originators that do not have enormous balance sheet capacity with the ability to originate loans and investors that do not have origination capacity with the ability to commit capital and expertise to a new mortgage market. Furthermore, the exercise of having to negotiate and sell a pool of collateral in the open market, with the concomitant need to provide transparency to potential investors, is a sobering reality check for the developing nation and a welcome development for the investment community.

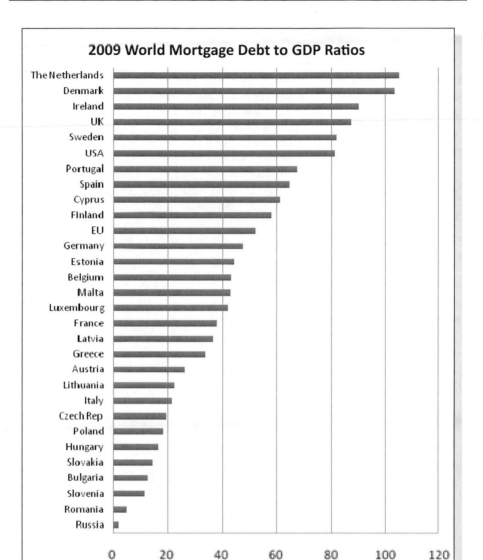

SOURCE: EUROPEAN MORTGAGE FEDERATION, "HYPOSTAT 2009: A REVIEW OF EUROPE'S MORTGAGE AND HOUSING MARKETS," NOVEMBER 2010, 70, WWW.HYPO. ORG/OBJECTS/6/FILES/HYPOSTAT%202008%20-%20LIGHT%20VERSION.PDF

In addition to the benefits to the emerging nations of establishing a mortgage finance system, the United States would benefit directly from the increased economic stability such mechanisms provide. People who have hope and opportunity are more likely to become productive, contributing members of society. Further, economic growth and stability in emerging nations would provide the United States with reliable trading partners, additional investment opportunities and more durable allies. Most importantly, the competition for international investment capital engendered by additional mortgage finance markets would motivate the United States to improve its own, so that it can avoid future problems and remain competitive for that same pool of capital. Investment money is a global commodity; to compete for it, one must have the necessary financial infrastructure. It is therefore a worthwhile endeavor for the United States to concentrate on building sound mortgage systems, both at home and abroad.

To put the need for investment capital in developing countries in perspective, consider the current mortgage situation in Russia. As of 2010, The Russian economy consisted of approximately $1.47 trillion of GDP.[142] By one measure, the top five banks (all government banks) had the equivalent of just under $600 billion in assets, while the next twenty-five banks (all private banks) had the equivalent of $250 billion in assets.[143] This meant that the top thirty banks accounted for approximately 57 percent of Russian GDP.

The Russian banking system is characterized by a plethora of small private banks. Only the top one hundred banks have more than $1 million in assets.[144] Moreover, the estimated need for mortgages to finance housing over the next five years is generally viewed to be in excess of $300 billion. This amounts to 35 percent of the current banking assets of the top 30 banks in the country. Where is the banking system going to get the balance sheet capacity for this type of growth, especially when there are other demands on the banking system's existing balance sheet capacity? The reality is that, in absolute terms and relative to other developed countries, Russia lacks sufficient capital to generate the volume of mortgages required to finance the country's housing needs.

From the perspective of those in the United States who would like to see a successful, stable, and prosperous Russia, this is not a good thing. A strong and stable capitalist Russia is not a threat to the United States but a friend. Political and economic stability stem from a population provided with opportunity and hope, not one that lacks the necessary capital to fund its growth. Russia, like many other emerging nations, needs a private MBS market. Properly structured securitizations have the potential to act as a stabilizing force, by providing a country with the means to finance housing demands and other opportunities for its population. This is in addition to the fact that private securitization generates productive and profitable investments for the world's available capital. Successful securitization is not just an economic asset; it is a diplomatic and political asset as well.

For any country wishing to have an active mortgage market financed by MBS, the minimum legal and economic requirements are as follows.

Legal Requirements

1. Laws that allow the free flow of capital into and out of the country. This includes the absence of overly restrictive taxes or tariffs.

2. A deed-recording system that removes ambiguity surrounding the ownership of a given piece of property and the ability to place a lien on that property.

3. Laws that allow the transfer of ownership of mortgages to a new owner and allow that transfer to be recorded, recognized, and enforced by the courts. The transfer must be able to survive a bankruptcy challenge and not be subject to the risk that a bankruptcy judge might reverse or "claw-back" the transfer. Instead, the transfer must be deemed a "true sale."

4. Laws that allow investors to perfect their interest in the pool of collateral. These would enable investors to prove their ownership

in and right to foreclose on the properties underlying their investments, if necessary.

5. Laws that allow investors to seize and liquidate the collateral in an expedient manner. These would allow foreclosure to proceed efficiently and without unnecessary delay.

6. A court system that provides for the equitable and reasonably swift resolution of contractual disputes.

7. A track record of government respecting private property rights and not nationalizing private property.

Economic Requirements

1. An investment grade rating for the host country and investor confidence that this rating will persist.

2. A reasonably stable currency that third parties will be willing to denominate as one side of currency swaps.

3. Sufficient population and GDP to produce enough MBS collateral to attract international investment capital and justify due diligence efforts.

In my experience, the following are *not* essential for an emerging securitization market to succeed:

1. A well-capitalized banking system.

2. A history of complex financial transactions.

3. A minimum per capita income.

4. A democratic government.

5. Explicit government financial or housing subsidies.

6. A well-developed domestic investor base.

7. A legal system capable of dealing with securitizations, so long as transactions are permitted to be governed by another country's law (preferably English law).

While it is beyond the scope of this book to delve into each of these issues in depth, I touch on a few of the most interesting problems in this chapter.

Public Markets May Not Be Available to Smaller Countries

Countries that cannot produce enough collateral to support a market for institutional-sized transactions will be unable to access the public markets. Investors that purchase MBS will want to have a substantial position in each country in which they invest. If a fund is managing $25 billion, it is unreasonable for them to participate in a market that can produce only $250 million worth of bonds per year. If that investor can expect an allocation of approximately 10 percent from each transaction in which it participates, its total annual purchases for that market would only be $25 million. When you consider that the investor will have to complete a substantial amount of due diligence on the proposed MBS structure and the particular laws of each host country, $25 million per year is far too little to attract institutional investment. Countries would need to produce the equivalent of a few billion U.S. dollars' worth of private label MBS to be able to access the international capital markets. However, smaller countries could still access the securitization market on a private basis. Such transactions would likely be negotiated with a single investor, like a large international bank, and not offered to the public.

Securitizations with Non-hard Currency Host Countries

As mentioned earlier, it is preferable to use a widely traded and relatively stable currency for the underlying mortgage note in any securitization system. However, it is tempting to originate underlying loans in a hard currency (for example, U.S. dollars) and structure the MBS transaction as a U.S. dollar-denominated bond transaction (a "dollar/dollar" transaction) in a country that does not use the U.S. dollar as its national currency. While feasible, structuring a dollar/dollar transaction or a transaction using the currency of any other non-host country opens up the transaction to a number of systemic risks:

1. **Currency fluctuation risk**. If there is a currency fluctuation, the monthly payment in terms of the local currency can change substantially. This creates a risk of payment shock for the homeowner and a credit risk for the investor.

2. **Currency control risk**. There is always a risk that the host country will impose currency controls with respect to the currency underlying the transaction. These would be implemented by the host country's government to reduce the hard currency exiting the country to pay foreign debts. This creates a risk that the MBS investor must evaluate and price when it purchases the host country's securities. It is important for the host country to enable the free flow of capital into and out of their market. If it does not, no capital will flow into the country as no one will be willing to take on the long-term risk of mortgages when significant currency control risk is present.

While currency risks will never disappear completely from within the MBS structure, they can be mitigated for the senior bondholders by including some additional features. When mortgages and MBS are issued in a non-local currency, the credit risk due to currency exposure can be mollified by having larger subordinate classes and creating subordinate classes that do not pay any cash to the subordinate holders (see appendices V and VI). However, while this additional subordination can help to fix this problem, it is a poor fix at best. Cross-currency structures also inject systemic risks into the securitization process.

A better solution for this problem would be for mortgage notes to be issued in a local currency and for the investor to purchase a currency swap to convert the MBS payment stream into hard currency. For example, a Russian MBS deal could produce bonds denominated in rubles and be collateralized by mortgages denominated in rubles.

This ruble/ruble transaction would remove the currency risk from the homeowner and place it with the investor. The investor could handle this currency risk in any manner it deemed reasonable, including purchasing a currency swap. While this may seem cumbersome, it removes a systemic currency risk from the entire MBS transaction. This also assumes that the investor can obtain a currency swap for the host country currency. If the currency is the Russian ruble, this will not be a problem, as the ruble is a stable and traded currency. On the other hand, if the reference currency is the Zimbabwe dollar, a currency swap will be all but impossible to obtain.

In the event that there is not a defined market for the specific currency, a final option would be to have the trust itself enter into the currency swap. This option should only be used if it is necessary to complete a transaction and should not be needed for currencies with any substantial currency swap market. Securitization is a "garbage-in, garbage-out" vehicle; it can only reallocate the risk of an underlying pool of collateral, not reduce or remove that risk. Securitization cannot start with a risky currency that is not generally accepted or swappable and turn it into a less risky security that is generally accepted.

Thus, a mortgage system that is based on a non-local currency is an economic nightmare waiting to happen. If that system comes to dominate the local mortgage market, currency devaluation would lead to wholesale payment shocks and a series of systemic defaults. It is for this reason that non-local currency transactions should be used only as a last resort and then only as a method of introducing the country's mortgage product to the international capital markets. As a practical matter, sometimes arrangers must make compromises in order to create an asset that is attractive to investors, especially for a new market. In such cases, currency is usually the first compromise. However, once a mortgage product has been established, the country should transition as quickly as possible to a system that is based on its own currency.

Removing Points of Failure from the Underlying MBS

Ratings agencies view securitizations from a "weakest link" perspective. This means that the entire securitization cannot be rated any higher than its weakest or lowest-rated participant. This is a simplistic methodology that does not take into account the deal's potential exposure to an adverse credit event. As an example, assume two different securitizations: Securitization X has six participants, two rated 'A' and four rated 'BBB'. Securitization Y has two participants, one rated 'A' and one rated 'BBB'. Using the 'weakest link' methodology, each deal would be rated 'BBB.' However, these two securitizations do not have equal exposure to an adverse credit event. Securitization X has three times the participants (6 vs. 2) and four times the lowest-rated participants (4 vs. 1) compared to Securitization Y. Logic dictates that the securitization with the most opportunities to fail will fail more frequently, and thus a logical rating system would rate Securitization X lower than Securitization Y..

Accordingly, if we wish to minimize the actual risk of failure in a transaction, we should reduce the number of participants—and thus opportunities to fail—to a minimum. Issuers and countries that wish to have a stable securitization market should insist that unnecessary features, such as currency swaps, are removed from securitizations if the investors can easily replicate those features in the open market. This way, if a swap provider fails, as did Lehman Brothers, securitizations are unaffected and free from unnecessary risk of failure.

As with many of the risks discussed in this book, these additional and unnecessary embedded risks do not become a major problem until they become popular and are replicated throughout the mortgage system, at which point they become systemic problems. What would have happened to a country's mortgage system if the majority of its MBS were swapped into dollars using a Lehman Brothers currency swap? With Lehman Brothers in bankruptcy, the MBS investors would have no way of valuing their assets or knowing whether the trust was on the hook for paying the swap counterparty until the swap turned around. Whenever there is a chance that a large number of transactions will encounter the same problem at the same time, thereby interrupting the capital flow into the country funding the underlying mortgage notes, it sows the seeds of a financial crisis.

This is not only an argument for removing unnecessary embedded risks; it is also an argument for diversifying the participants in the MBS trusts within any host country. For example, if investors held a MBS bond structure that was easily swappable from the local currency to a hard currency but which did not feature an embedded currency swap, each investor would be free to choose its own swap counterparty, thus spreading the risk around rather than concentrating it in a smaller number of hands. Each investor would also be free to move its swaps to a new counterparty when it perceived that a problem might exist with the current provider. International investors that would logically invest in emerging market MBS transactions would have the financial expertise to enter into and manage currency swaps.[*] If there were problems with the swap market, investors would deal with the problem outside of securitization transactions, and the securitizations themselves would not be directly affected by the problem.

The Proper Role of a Host Government

Ideally, the role of a host government is to allow the free market unconstrained access to its MBS markets. In practice, the areas in which the host government should get involved are as follows:

1. There are clear, negative social consequences to embedding unstable mortgage structures into the host country's financial system. As we have seen in the United States, the underlying structure of the mortgage loans can have implications that go well beyond what

---

[*] Keep in mind that the goal for the host country of an emerging mortgage market should be to reach the point that the capital markets are willing to accept its currency on a stand-alone basis without the need for swaps, guarantees, or unnecessary weak links.

anyone could reasonably expect when the initial loans were originated. If the dominant or conventional mortgage in a particular country has structural deficiencies, as does the thirty-year fixed loan in the United States, these deficiencies could wreak havoc on a financial system. Making matters worse, the negative effects of such deficiencies may not be felt for a generation or longer, giving the defective loan structure time to become ingrained in a growing mortgage market and replicated in dangerous quantities. To be successful, the host mortgage system must have as close to a zero systemic fail rate as possible and must outlive every banker and politician that touches any part of the system. Thus, host governments should restrict the types of mortgages eligible for securitization and sale in the public markets.

2. The creation of an efficient MBS market has tremendous value for a country, and governmental encouragement will speed the establishment of this system. Encouragement may take the form of government assistance in creating the underlying infrastructure for the securitization market (e.g., the deed-recording system and the proper legal framework), but if systemic risk is to be contained, governments should avoid the temptation to relieve the securitization participants from the consequences of deficient conduct. Each participant must have the proper incentives to ensure that these transactions have the highest possible chance of success.

3. Host governments may also wish to provide concrete financial assistance to the transactions, as this will speed the development of the market. This may include but is not limited to the following:

   a. Providing credit support to the transactions in the form of a partial guarantee or the purchase of some form of subordinate interest in the securitizations.

   b. Providing liquidity to the market by allowing the resulting senior securities to be eligible for financing from the host country's central bank.

Many emerging nations meet the criteria for creating MBS transactions and tapping into the capital available in the public markets. Encouraging these nations to build the infrastructure for these transactions will lead to great economic and political benefits for those nations, as well as for the United States. Given that these structures will be built from the ground up, we are faced with both the opportunity and the imperative to ensure that these structures feature as little systemic risk as possible and that the structural mistakes that led to the collapse of the U.S. market are not repeated abroad.

*"Most economic fallacies derive from the tendency
to assume that there is a fixed pie, that one party
can gain only at the expense of another."*

—*Milton Friedman*

CHAPTER 12

Conclusion

When cave dwellers discovered fire, their lives improved. They were able to cook their food and more easily stay warm. They also, no doubt, occasionally burned themselves as they learned to harness this new tool. When societies developed language, their lives improved. They were able to communicate feelings, warnings, and ideas more efficiently, as well as pass on information to future generations. They were also able to use language to harm one another with insults and lies. When planes began to fly, they sometimes crashed. However, aviation technology developed, and today people fly through the air without a second thought.

Similarly, the advancements of finance and economics have brought prosperity but also their fair share of mistakes. The Great Depression of the 1930s is generally considered a colossal failure of monetary policy, and we anticipate that we will never again make the mistake of tightening our money supply during a severe recession.

Growth and technological development always come with their share of missteps and growing pains. New tools can be abused if not properly applied. Innovators can make mistakes. We must be careful not to vilify the new tools that have the potential to engender tremendous improvements to our society, but instead learn how to use them properly. Though mistakes have been made in the application of structured finance to mortgages, securitization has the potential to be a powerful tool for economic growth by making homeownership more affordable and accessible.

I know this first hand, as I have had the privilege of working with my firm to complete the first securitizations in Russia. This technology now enables the typical Russian family to purchase a home and gives its members a reason to go to work to pay for that home. Many of these families could not have dreamed of owning their own home a decade ago. Our government, and our people, should benefit enormously from having a stable and economically prosperous Russia.

Bringing this financial technology to emerging economies has the potential to benefit not only foreign financial institutions but also entire populations. It is incumbent upon us to lead by example. The United States has long been the global leader in financial transparency, and its securitization system has long been viewed with awe and envy around the world. This system has allowed the United States to outcompete other countries for international capital in the past, but the poor decisions made in structuring those deals during the Boom Years, and the subsequent U.S. governmental response, call into question whether this competitive advantage will persist. If the problems with the U.S. securitization system are allowed to fester, it will leave a massive stain on the reputation of the United States, and this country will no longer be venerated as a place where honesty and fair dealing are the norm. This will open the door for other countries to step in and provide a viable alternative for investors. As investors are provided more options for mortgage market investments, they will be tempted to direct funds toward countries that have decided not to inject politics into the capital markets. As we have seen in the United States, the politicization of finance happens all too easily and is difficult to reverse.

We are at an important crossroads and must decide what role the tool of securitization should play in rebuilding our decimated housing market. We have seen the massive destruction of wealth that can take place when ignorance and misaligned economic incentives are allowed to permeate the process of securitization. Should such ignorance again characterize the actions of lawmakers, banks, and investors, another meltdown and further problems are not far off. Continued failures and torpor in the U.S. MBS markets will send a signal to the rest of the world that this type of investment is risky and politically damaging, thereby impairing the ability of both the United States and emerging markets to house their populations. This will have profound implications for the stability of those countries and the security of the United States. However, it is my firm belief that with a relatively small amount of understanding about the incentives of the players and the nature of the mortgage instruments involved, these problems can be averted.

I have offered suggestions for how the mortgage market should be structured going forward and how the type of profit-maximizing behavior that the theories of capitalism tell us to expect can be channeled to promote the success of a new mortgage system. The onus for fixing this system should rest on the shoulders of the investment community, by which I mean the investors, not the banking professionals that put deals together. Bankers will not bother with drafting the intricate details of a liquidity facility or any of the other features I recommend unless investors demand them. The investors are the ones with the cash; if they do not purchase the instruments that bankers seek to create, bankers will have no incentive to create them. Investing is difficult work, and investors need to make more of an effort to understand the instruments into which they are investing trillions of dollars of other people's money. If they do not, those whose money they manage should remove them from their positions and possibly even sue them for violating their fiduciary duties. As Thomas Tusser famously said, "A fool and his money are soon parted." Institutional investors must not be fools and they must work for their clients' interests, not their own.

I have been asked by a number of people why I wrote this book. It is not because I harbored much hope that it would wind up on *The New York Times* bestseller list. As readers that have made it this far have no doubt realized, this material is unlikely to win them any friends at a cocktail party. I hope that my readers consist of people that really wish to understand the current mortgage problems in the United States and abroad and who care about resolving these problems in the most efficient manner possible. This includes laypersons as well as professionals involved in structured finance or investing in the products created by those professionals. I realize that my ideas could be used by my competitors to create U.S. securitizations as well as securitizations in a yet-to-be-determined emerging country. If the ideas in this book can be used to compete with me at my own business, it will mean that I have pushed the boundaries of thought in this space and encouraged the creation of more efficient solutions to the problems of mortgage finance. Nothing would make me happier.

I also wrote this book with the hope that political and regulatory leaders would take the time to learn how structured finance can be used to make the capital markets more efficient and funnel capital to the sectors that need it most. I have had the pleasure of dealing with a large number of staff members of elected and appointed officials. Prior to these meetings, I harbored skepticism about many of our representatives, based on their misguided actions undertaken in the name of "dealing" with the mortgage crisis. However, every individual I met in the U.S. government expressed a desire to better understand these problems and learn how to fix them. These meetings persuaded me that our lawmakers simply lacked the expertise to handle these issues and did not know to whom they could turn for help or advice. For these individuals, I have provided an introduction to securitization and the developments that led us away from rational lending practices, as well as a road map for returning to a logical system. If lawmakers have further questions or are interested in implementing some of the reforms I have suggested, my door is always open.

In addition, I wanted to address how emerging nations could develop nascent mortgage markets to avoid the problems the United States has experienced since 2007. The securitization of mortgage notes can not only fund a country's housing sector, it can also create financial assets that will provide better returns to investors than are otherwise available. As countries become wealthier, they need to invest their surplus capital, just as the Eastern portion of the United States needed the Western portion to absorb capital. Providing access to the capital markets is not charity. A provider of capital is doing so entirely in its own self-interest, with the goal of earning a return on that capital. Consumers of capital want the cheapest and best terms for that capital. It is the role of the banks to bring these two parties together. In the case of mortgages, bankers are responsible for ensuring that these instruments do not create so much systemic risk that the country's financial system is put in jeopardy, as it was in the United States.

Providing open and equal access to the world's capital markets will benefit everyone, even those who already had access to affordable capital. The free flow of capital will tend to achieve a better allocation of capital to the sectors that can use it most productively. Consider what the world would be like if capital was not shifted from supporting horse stables and buggy whip manufacturers to financing the manufacture of automobiles. Without access to capital and the free movement of capital, the vast majority of people would have had a materially poorer life. It seems self-evident that the people most discontented with their political and economic systems are those people without access to capital and thus opportunity. Reducing the number of discontented individuals in foreign countries can only improve the security and stability of those countries, their neighbors, and their allies. If it is possible to devise a system that allows more people to compete to obtain this capital, it would be unconscionable to prevent them from accessing this capital. Such competition would allow homeownership to be financed in the countries with the greatest demand, without the need for government or taxpayer support. In short, governments, including that of the United States, should be establishing sound securitization systems, rather than directly guaranteeing or subsidizing homeownership.

What the U.S. government certainly should not be focusing on is propping up the banks and making the problems of the mortgage crisis appear less severe than they are. In particular, it should not continue to pursue mortgage strategies by any of the following methods:

1. **Promoting regulatory forbearance of bank capital requirements.** By this I mean not properly accounting for the true nature of the economic impact of the crisis on the banks' balance sheets. These policies allow banks to operate based on fictional capital and accounting items rather than based on firm economic value or equity. This only decreases transparency and encourages investor deception. This same strategy had disastrous effects during the S&L crisis and led to the collapses of Fannie Mae and Freddie Mac.

2. **Driving interest rates through the floor.** This has the effect of lowering the cost of a bank's raw material: money. Dropping the cost of federal funds and then lending money to the banks at that new, lower rate constitutes a wealth transfer from the savers (workers and retirees via their pension funds and IRA accounts) to some of the wealthiest private institutions and banks in the country. We are on the verge of having one pension fund after another collapse due to persistently low interest rates and underfunding.[145]

3. **Making it politically or economically impractical for investors to pursue their contract rights.** United States political leaders must conclude that the large banks cannot be given a pass to dump underwriting errors on investors. Such a pass will make it more difficult to move on from this crisis because investors will not be willing to invest in new U.S. MBS due to the perception of political risk. We need a government that insists that firms honor

contracts and provides aggrieved parties access to the court system. These aggrieved parties should not suffer harassment or intimidation because they seek to exercise those rights and enforce their agreements.

4. **Implementing programs designed to prop up the banks at the expense of other sectors of the economy.** This economic strategy is the same as the one that the Japanese undertook in an attempt to fix their banking crisis of the early 1990s. The Japanese refer to the banking crisis as "The Lost Decade." The Japanese are in the twenty-first year of their lost decade. As of 2011, the United States is in the fifth year of its own.

However we choose to characterize the causes of this crisis, one thing is clear: we must not be indifferent to the actions of our professionals and lawmakers in addressing these problems. When we look back in a generation at the events surrounding the mortgage crisis, these actions will be seen either as another step toward a financial Armageddon or as the first step in rebuilding our essential financial machinery. Given my belief in mankind and its ability to solve its problems, and with the help of the ideas proposed in this book, I believe that it will be the latter. When I reflect on why I have bothered to push so hard for a transparent and contractually viable solution to the current financial mess, it boils down to the fact that I have three kids for whom I, like any other parent, want the best. I do not want my children or their children to ask me in twenty or thirty years why I didn't do more to stop "The Disaster Called the Twenty-First Century."

APPENDIX I

William Frey Letter to Secretary Paulson and Chairman Bernanke (3/22/08)

Greenwich Financial Services, LLC

Seven Greenwich Office Park
599 West Putnam Avenue
Greenwich, CT 06830

———

Phone: (203) 862-3600 Fax: (203) 862-3601

March 22, 2008

Mr. Henry M. Paulson
Secretary of the Treasury of the United States of America
Department of Treasury
1500 Pennsylvania Ave NW
Washington, DC 20220

Mr. Ben S. Bernanke
Chairman-Board of Governors Federal Reserve System
21st & Constitution Ave NW
Washington, DC 20551

Dear Sirs,

I am a believer that Milton Friedman did more to improve the life of people around the world than any other economist in the past century. So, I will start this letter off with a profound apology. For those who believe markets should operate freely and unimpeded, this will sound like nails scratching on a blackboard.

The US mortgage market and liquidity crisis is a problem that cannot be solved in a manner that is acceptable to the American public without the direct intervention of the US Government. The problems of home foreclosure and capital market disruption are related, but the latter is a symptom of the former. The root cause is that the guy on Main Street is not paying his mortgage. When that problem is addressed, there is no rational reason to believe that the mortgage market will not function in an efficient manner.

How to Get the US Population Current on Their Mortgages?

People who are delinquent on their mortgages are, for the most part, good people that have gotten into an untenable situation with either a loan that put them in harm's way or a home that has decreased in value. The secret to getting them current on their loans is to make it economically beneficial.

Both of you have repeatedly made the point that the proper way to deal with the problem is to have the banks and borrowers work out solutions mortgage by mortgage. While you are on the right track, this idea does not meet with the reality of the US mortgage market: most mortgages in the US have been turned into Mortgage Backed Securities (MBS) that are traded in the capital markets. The MBS system pools groups of mortgages and then divides the risks into different classes of assets and sells them to different types of investors. This has expanded opportunities for both investors and homeowners. The level of sophistication of this market is the envy of the world and, in spite of the current problems, is a national asset. However, it means that the banking system no longer operates as Jimmy Stewart's bank did in "It's a Wonderful Life", where a banker can sit down with a borrower and work out a problem.

Today, the local bank does not own the mortgage. The bank is now a "servicer". It is not possible for a servicer to negotiate with each borrower and put losses or reduced interest rates through to the investors. Let me explain why. The loan that was sold is now subject to rules that are embodied in a securitization contract. If interest rates on a securitization are reduced, the holders of the senior classes of assets are hurt to the benefit of the subordinate class holders. If the principal is reduced, subordinate bond holders are hurt to the benefit of the senior classes. There are many dozens of investors in a typical mortgage securitization. It is not possible or practical to get them to agree on changes that benefit just one class of bond holder. Some securitization contracts, mainly with subprime collateral, allow for some flexibility regarding the reduction of interest rates for a limited number of loans; however, I know of no Alt-A or Prime loan securitization that allows for such flexibility.

Meanwhile, interest rates are coming down, but mortgage rates have barely budged. Yes, the mortgage/treasury spread dropped by 30 bp or so in the last week with the announcement that FNMA and FHLMC would be allowed to purchase large amounts of securities. However, there is little capital available for mortgages today so the mortgage/treasury spreads remain at historically wide levels. If the yield spread between treasury and mortgages returned to more "normal" levels, US mortgages would be 100 to 150 bp cheaper. A 5.0% 30 year mortgage would be the norm.

So, What Should US Policy Be?

If the US Government wants to have borrowers stay in their homes, which is generally considered to be the loss mitigating strategy, then the existing loans must be prepaid and removed from the mortgage securitization pools. How can this be done? Who wins and who loses?

Well, the answer lies in two organizations that are already dependent on the support of the US government: FNMA and FHLMC. First, we must face the reality that these organizations are likely to require some sort of US Government bailout. They have accepted credit risk on $6 Trillion dollars of US mortgages by guaranteeing pools of loans, many of which will require large losses to be taken when they are not paid back. They also hold $2 Trillion of assets directly on their balance sheets, but their combined equity is only about $70 billion and they are reporting record losses. We must face the reality that these organizations are very likely technically insolvent and already pose a massive liability to the US Treasury. If FNMA and FHLMC were "nationalized" or declared "insolvent" the obvious would be recognized. After FNMA/FHLMC were taken over by the Government they would be backed directly by the Government and spreads between FNMA and FHLMC securities and US Treasuries would decrease substantially.

Homeowners able to refinance could then benefit from lower interest rates. However, this does nothing for homeowners unable to refinance due to low market values relative to their loans or other restrictions on their access to historic FNMA/FHLMC financing..A program that I will call the Refinance Assistance Program, described below would help these homeowners and reduce foreclosures. The benefits of a refinancing wave would help all obligors that choose to take advantage of such an opportunity. I have not addressed whether the shareholders of FNMA and FHLMC, with a current market capitalization of $50 billion, should be compensated, but in a crisis of the magnitude the US is currently facing, I am sorry to say, the $50 billion is chump change.

How Would The Refinance Assistance Program Actually Work?

Homeowners would be allowed to refinance their existing loans under a program where the Government owned and restructured FNMA/FHLMC would make a 100% LTV loan to the homeowner. Furthermore, the part of the existing loan in excess of 100% LTV would be segregated into a separate obligation; we will call this a "wart" and will deal with this later. The precedent for reducing a loan amount happens in corporate reorganizations and bankruptcy on a regular basis and is called a "cram down". The appropriate size of the new loan should be set based on market values in the area. While this would create a potential problem of manipulation, it is no different a problem than the Government faces when it steps in to help victims of a natural disaster in which homes are destroyed.

With the repayment of the original loans, and a new 100% LTV loan at lower interest rates, the borrower would have lower monthly payments and a loan no greater than the value of the house. The borrower would then have an economic incentive to keep the house. This is substantially better than having the homes stand vacant and be vandalized, or having them dumped on the real estate market at prices that drag down other homeowners. Losses in the credit markets would be reduced, helping banks and other investors shore up their balance sheets. Furthermore, the capital markets would know that the new loans, coming through the New FNMA/FHLMC, were backed by the US Government. These instruments should trade actively, bringing liquidity back to the markets.

The prepayments (which would be very high) on the old MBS securities would go first to the senior most investors and then would retire those that provided the credit support (this is the general way that the cashflows work in a FNMA/FHLMC MBS deal, the ones currently causing losses and liquidity problems for investors). This would get cash to the senior investors and they would presumably put it to work. Furthermore, non-primary residence loans would be excluded from the New FNMA/FHLMC program. They would go through the normal loss procedure and investors that took credit risk will have substantial losses.

Chances are that the most senior investors (the AAA investors) would have their losses greatly reduced. In any case, highly illiquid and assets of uncertain value would be cleared out, solving the valuation issues with the balance sheets of financial institutions.

What should happen to the wart? This is really a public policy issue. If borrowers are stuck with that liability, then they may rationally choose to walk from their existing loan and this new program would not be effective. If borrowers are allowed to walk away from the wart then the cost of the bailout bill will rise. It may make sense for the obligor to repay the wart from the increase in the value of their property when they sell the house. So, the wart would become an out of money option that the US Government may collect at some future date. However, the exact structure of this is really a public policy debate that is best decided in that forum. But the loss mitigation strategy of keeping people in their homes is intact.

How Much Would The Refinance Assistance Program Cost the Taxpayer?

A reasonable estimate would be about $500 billion. This may be sticker shock, but the number should be looked at in the context of the size of the US GDP. The current US GDP is $12 Trillion. The cost of the bailout would be about 4-5% of US GDP. This is a very manageable level when the alternatives are considered. How much would it cost the US to slide into a substantial recession? How much would it cost the US if the banking system suffers more damage or collapse? How much lower will US GDP be for the next handful of years without a resolution to this economic crisis? Finally, how much is it going to cost the taxpayers when FNMA and FHLMC collapse? FHLBs? A major bank?

The taxpayer will have questions, of course. Would this solution provide a subsidy to the financial institutions? Yes. Would it provide a subsidy to the homeowner? Yes. Would it bail out those that made stupid investment decisions? Yes. Would it bail out the US economy? ABSOLUTELY. Does the US Government have a practical alternative? To date, the answer appears to be NO.

Does this Create a Moral Hazard?

Without question this plan risks setting a terrible precedent in which the Government bails out the poor decisions made by loan originators, homeowners and investors. However, this is merely a reflection of reality. It is beyond comprehension that the Government would let FNMA or FHLMC fail and not step in to support their obligations. It is beyond comprehension for the Government not to step in to support a major financial institution whose failure could set off a chain of failures due to interlocking contracts, as with Bear Stearns. Future regulation of banks and brokers should reflect this de facto support and the massive contingent liability taken by the Government for poor decision making by the banks and broker dealers. Furthermore, there should be a serious discussion on whether the securitization markets became too good at the intermediation of mortgage credit risk and whether some overall limits should be placed on the minimum LTV that should be acceptable for securitization. Once again, this is a public policy matter that should be decided at a point in the near future, but the US Government needs to act quickly to provide relief to homeowners and the capital markets.

Why Should the US Government Pay for All of This?

The US Government has a contingent liability from this mess and already is likely to have a very large bill. Last week the Federal Reserve had to bail out Bear Stearns (and with it the capital markets) and is likely to have to make accommodations or take over positions from other broker dealers or banks. The Rubicon was crossed last weekend and we cannot go back.

If you believe in free markets, the Refinance Assistance Program is a terrible idea; the only ones worse are all others. So, let's deal with the situation and get on with the obvious job at hand. People can keep their homes and the existing financial infrastructure of the US banking system will not be permanently broken or destroyed.

William Frey

President
Greenwich Financial Services, LLC
Russian American Mortgage Company, LLC

APPENDIX II

---■---

House Financial Services Committee Letter to William Frey (10/23/08)

United States House of Representatives
Committee on Financial Services
2129 Rayburn House Office Building
Washington, DC 20515

October 24, 2008

Mr. William Frey
President
Greenwich Financial Services, LLC
599 West Putnam Avenue
Greenwich, CT 06831

Dear Mr. Frey:

We were outraged to read in today's *New York Times* that you are actively opposing our efforts to achieve a diminution in foreclosures by voluntary efforts. Your decision is a serious threat to our efforts to respond to the current economic crisis, and we strongly urge you to reverse it. Given the importance of this to the economy and to what it means for future regulatory efforts, we have set a hearing for November 12, and we invite you now to testify. We believe it is essential for our policymaking function for you to appear at such a hearing, and if this cannot be arranged on a voluntary basis, then we will pursue further steps.

For the hedge fund industry, which has flourished for much of the past decade, to take steps so actively in opposition to what is currently in the national economic interest is deeply troubling and will clearly have serious implications for the rules by which we operate in the future if this posture of obstruction of our efforts is maintained.

We very much hope you will be able to tell us very soon that you have reversed your position of trying to obstruct the operation of the bill that was overwhelmingly passed by Congress and signed by the President this summer, and we hope that you will also affirm your presence at the hearing on November 12.

BARNEY FRANK

MAXINE WATERS

LUIS V. GUTIERREZ

PAUL E. KANJORSKI

CAROLYN MALONEY

MELVIN L. WATT

APPENDIX III

William Frey Letter to House Financial Services Committee (11/12/08)

Greenwich Financial Services, L.L.C.
Seven Greenwich Office Park
599 West Putnam Ave.
Greenwich, CT 06830

Phone: (203) 599-4475

November 12, 2008

Chairman Barney Frank and Ranking Member Spencer Bachus
House Financial Services Committee
2129 Rayburn House Office Building

Dear Chairman Frank and Ranking Member Bachus:

My name is William Frey and I am Principal and CEO of Greenwich Financial Services (GFS). My firm is a broker dealer that specializes in the structuring and distribution of Mortgage Backed Securities (MBS). I ask that this letter be made a part of the record of the hearing of the House Committee on Financial Services entitled, "Private Sector Cooperation with Mortgage Modifications-Ensuring That Investors, Servicers and Lenders Provide Real Help for Troubled Homeowners," on Wednesday, November 12, 2008, at 10:00 a.m., in room 2128 of the Rayburn House Office Building.

Because this Committee is interested in MBS, it is important to note that I have worked in the securitization industry since the industry's infancy in 1981. My experience encompasses virtually every aspect of securitization, from structuring and trading MBS to researching and analyzing the securitization market. After nearly 15 years with major firms including Morgan Stanley, Smith Barney, and Bear Stearns, I founded GFS in 1995. I received my B.S. from Cornell University in 1979 and my MBA from Carnegie Mellon University in 1981. At my present firm, I have structured and sold billions of dollars of MBS securities with various types of collateral. I also acted as a financial advisor to GNMA for more than 5 years, ending in 2004. In that capacity I was responsible for working with GNMA to select new product and program offerings as well as assessing various types of market and credit risks. GFS was awarded this contract with KPMG as its partner.

As mentioned above, I own a broker dealer, GFS, which puts together MBS transactions. I have never put together a transaction using subprime collateral, and the last alternative-A (alt-A) transaction I structured was over five years ago. I chose to not structure deals backed by subprime and alt-A mortgages because I believed that they were of low quality and I did not want my business to be associated with them.

1

I am submitting this statement for the record because on October 24th, six members of this Committee issued a letter in response to my comments in a *New York Times* article regarding investors' objections to the restructuring of mortgage loans (Tab 1). The letter requested that I appear at this hearing. Early this week I was told that my testimony was no longer needed but that a written statement could be submitted for the record. My written statement consists of two parts. The first part seeks to clarify the record regarding what I believe are inaccurate characterizations of my work. The second part seeks to offer specific recommendations on how to improve the American mortgage-backed securitization process in an effort to prevent similar crises in the future.

For the record, I would like to clarify that I do not manage a hedge fund, as erroneously assumed in the letter to me dated October 24. I hasten to add that there is nothing wrong with hedge funds, given that they invest the retirement and education funds of millions of average Americans. I am an individual investor and I manage a family fund. What this means is that I invest my own money in the U.S. and international capital markets, and I do so judiciously and carefully after much research and analysis.

All of the credit support securities I own were originated before 2004 and are not based on subprime or alt-A collateral. The loans backing the securities I own have low loan-to-value ratios (meaning high levels of equity) and are performing well. The borrowers were not tricked by teaser rates or encouraged to misrepresent their incomes. These are securities backed by mortgages secured by the homes of thousands of ordinary hard working Americans who are making their payments as agreed, honoring their contractual commitments.

The reason I have no exposure to subprime is that I simply did not believe that the credit risk of those securities and collateral was justified. Being involved in making loans to people that cannot repay those loans has never made business sense to me. Contrary to popular opinion, there were some investors in this market that elected not to participate in the unsound securities that triggered to the current economic crisis.

Before proceeding, I would like to applaud Congress and this Committee for their expressed desire to provide relief to homeowners, many of whom are holding mortgages that are now 'underwater.' Eight months ago – before Fannie Mae and Freddie Mac failed – I proposed a solution to this critical issue with a similar goal. Indeed, in March of this year, I sent a letter to Secretary Paulson and Chairman Bernanke (Tab 2) suggesting a sensible, balanced and economically viable course of action. In that letter I explained an unfortunate fact of life: if a homeowner's loan is included in a mortgage security, he will have a more difficult time receiving the necessary relief than if his loan is owned directly by a bank. This is why FDIC Chairman Sheila Bair has been having more success modifying loans on Indy Mac's balance sheet than modifying loans in securitizations.

2

Proposed Solutions

Mortgage securitizations are managed by a contract called a "Pooling and Servicing Agreement" (PSA). A PSA is the basis for the securitization and binds investors, as the providers of capital, with the issuers, as the consumers of capital. This is not the contract of the homeowner with either the bank or the firm that originated the loan. Instead, a PSA may cover thousands of loans and is the contract that specifies a Servicer's obligations to bondholders and spells out a Servicer's authority and ability to restructure mortgages. The contract that I was, and am still, seeking to ensure that Congress remains focused on is the PSA. Let me offer some recommendations of how the Hope for Homeowners (HHO) program may be improved, given the existence of these contracts.

The HHO program allows Servicers to renegotiate loans to the lesser of 90% of market value or 31% of the homeowner's income as a loan payment in cases where such renegotiation is a better outcome than foreclosure. The question, though, is who determines what is the better outcome? Renegotiations are in the hands of the Servicers, who have financial incentives to avoid foreclosure, regardless of the outcome. Keeping someone in their home is cheaper than foreclosure for the Servicer, even if it creates greater losses for the mortgage investor. Furthermore, there may be other financial benefits to Servicers for each loan that is renegotiated. Finally, all participants in the mortgage market are under political pressure to have homeowners stay in their houses. One need look no further than the letter I received from this Committee on October 24th to see evidence of the intensity of this political pressure (Tab 1).

In the current form of the HHO program, there is effectively no oversight for objectively determining the better outcome. Servicers that have much to gain from the renegotiation of mortgages have an incentive to pass unjustifiable losses onto investors. Supposedly, investors' interests are protected by the Trustee of the mortgage securitization. However, in all PSAs with which I am familiar, the Trustee is indemnified for servicing errors. There is no party watching out for the bondholders' interests and decisions are left in the hands of the Servicers, which often created these problems in the first place through fraudulent loan originations.

If the HHO program is seen as encouraging Servicers to restructure mortgages beyond the limits in the PSA contracts, the program could create serious new liabilities for the Servicers. These Servicers, which are largely banks looking for ways to increase fee income and reduce expenses, have strong incentives to engage in mortgage restructuring at the expense of bondholders.

In the context of our current housing crisis, it is essential to be clear about who are the investors in residential MBS. These investors are not only investment banks, college endowment funds, and sovereign wealth funds, but ordinary Americans in significant numbers. Investors in private label MBS include pension funds, public retirement systems, private sector retirement funds, and individual investors from all walks of life. To hold MBS does not automatically make one a "hedge fund" investor, but more likely an everyday, investor investing in the fabric of American life.

3

There are some PSA agreements that contemplate restructuring of loans, but many do not. If a Servicer were to restructure a loan covered by a PSA that did not allow for the restructuring of loans, the Servicer exposes itself to a lawsuit. In aggregate, such legal liabilities are likely to be so large that most Servicers would not accept them. Even if a Servicer is on reasonably solid ground, it is difficult to believe that many would risk the legal exposure that could result.

Larger Issues

The hazards to bondholders and Servicers point to the even larger issue at stake; whether the HHO program will be viewed as conferring the ability to alter legally binding agreements, often years after they are made, without the consent of all the affected parties. The ability to summarily alter binding legal agreements flies in the face of protecting contracts, which is a concept the Founding Fathers felt was important enough to reference in the Constitution. Despite recent rhetoric, I emphasize that the primary issue is not about a few rich guys get hurt when mortgages are restructured, but rather the US Government can tamper with their investments contracts. As any US lawyer will tell you, contract rights are an integral part of the US economy. Investors from around the world are watching and asking: if they buy US securities, will they need to factor in a risk they never before anticipated that the US Government will alter the contracts supporting their investments without compensation? If this is the case, investors may start to demand political risk insurance, as is common for securities from developing countries.

Further, without a solution that protects existing US contracts, there is little chance that any material amount of loans will be restructured under the HHO program. I am not the only one with these doubts; Edward Murphy of the Congressional Research Service concluded in an October 22, 2007 report that "Further clarifications may be required to assure Servicers and trusts that they will not be subject to investor lawsuits if they provide workouts to troubled borrowers." (Tab 3) What policymakers must do is to remove the legal uncertainties for the Servicer. I think that this can be accomplished in one of two ways:

- The Government has the ability to indemnify, either partially or totally, the Servicer and Trustees for potential lawsuits that will result from the loan modifications.

- The Government could step up and purchase the loans directly from the MBS trusts. Given the contractual realities, public policymakers may wish to consider this option as an alternative to the inevitable foreclosure for pools of collateral that cannot be restructured within the MBS trust.

4

Both of these options will shift much of the loss from investors and homeowners (who would normally bear this loss) to the US Treasury. While this would be unfortunate, the Government appears to have few other options if it wishes to avoid many of the foreclosures that are in process. Moreover, the liquidity and credit crises experienced in the last year are overshadowed by a crisis in confidence today. These crises can only be exacerbated if there is also uncertainty about whether or not legal contracts are honored in the United States.

Suggestions for the Future
In addition to the suggestions above regarding the HHO, I also submit that this committee should take new steps to create a more stable mortgage securitization system for the United States in the future. In order to prevent a recurrence of today's problems in the US mortgage market, a number of changes must be made to the mortgage origination and securitization process. These changes include:

1. **The current 30 year fixed rate prepayable loan must be reconsidered.** This type of loan places great risk on the shoulders of the mortgage investor. Prepayments can devastate a portfolio regardless of whether the portfolio is prudently hedged or not. Investors cannot manage the option value in these investments without great residual risk. This is the risk that ultimately led to the financial problems with the Savings and Loans in the 1980's and was a root cause of the "accounting scandals" with FNMA and FHLMC. This risk is somewhat channeled to appropriate investors with the MBS "slicing and dicing" of cashflows, but the creation of this systemic risk is very real and not possible to hedge for the economy as a whole.

   Possible solutions include issuing five year loans with 30-year amortization schedules that are renegotiated at the end of the term. These types of loans are common in Canada and other countries. Also, prepayment penalties based on the then-current interest rates would also mitigate the risk to the investors. Ultimately, risk reduction to investors will bring investors back to this market in the volumes needed to properly fund America's housing needs. Furthermore, because the loan would be less risky for the investor, the interest rates homeowners would pay on their loans would decrease.

5

2. **Minimum credit underwriting standards must be applied to loans that are securitized and sold in the public capital markets.** Since investors and rating agencies seem to have difficulty making judgments on the appropriateness of loans in public offerings, a minimum loan-to-value (LTV) underwriting standard for public transactions would insure that massive amounts of inappropriate collateral would not be originated and placed in the public markets. This standard LTV, while subjective, should probably be 80%. Loans originated above this threshold should have to remain in unsecuritized form and would likely stay on the originator's balance sheet. This would force more careful credit review by originators of such loans. Loans originated for the GSE's (currently FNMA and FHLMC) should have similar stringent LTV standards with some accommodations for first time homebuyers. This could link to suggestion number 3 detailed below.

3. **The Government should stop subsidizing home mortgage debt by ending, or phasing out, the home mortgage deduction.** A tax subsidy encourages homeowners to take on too much leverage, thereby placing a large risk on society in general. Equity could be subsidized by having homeowners receive some sort of tax credit for the first home purchase. This credit would be applied to the down payment. This credit would obviously need limits, but the concept of subsidizing equity, as opposed to the debt, would remove some of the systemic risk placed on society by high LTV mortgages. Furthermore, additional periodic principal paydowns could trigger some sort of partial tax credit in the first few years of a loan's existence. This period has historically been the time in which defaults have occurred.

4. **The Government must limit the use of home equity loans.** The logical limit for the use of home equity loans would be to forbid their use in the purchase of a home. Instead of using home equity loans as down payments, prospective homeowners would have to actually save and place their savings into a house as a down payment. While this concept may seem logical, it was forgotten over the last several years. Furthermore, post-purchase limits based on home purchase price or current market value should also be in place. Large scale use of homes as piggy banks places the financial system at an unacceptable level of risk.

6

5. **The SEC should remove conflicts of interest in MBS transactions by requiring Servicers own portions of their securities.** Currently there is an accounting disincentive to retain the first loss bond in a securitization by the originator or Servicer. This leads to inordinate amounts of risk being passed to the capital markets as the Servicer does not retain "skin in the game". This is a simple aspect of securitization to fix. The minimum percentage a Servicer should own should be 1% of the transaction in a subordinated position. The number need not be huge, but ownership is important. The Servicer should be required to hold this position for no less than three years. This would insure that any underwriting errors would be taken as a loss by the party that is best able to avoid the bad loan decision.

6. **MBS issuers should remove, or limit, the Trustee indemnification that is common in virtually all securitizations.** Legally, the Trustee for a securitization is responsible for enforcing the contract rules as a fiduciary of the bondholders. However, in most PSAs Trustees are indemnified by Servicers for any bondholder lawsuits that result from improper servicing or other servicing errors. This has the effect of the fox buying off the guard of the hen house. Speaking bluntly, there is no one guarding the interests of the bondholders.

7. **Laws must prevent borrowers from avoiding personal liability in the event of foreclosure.** Such laws would encourage homebuyers that run into trouble to not abandon their homes. Post foreclosure liabilities are common in England and discourage homeowners from walking away from their obligations. Such liabilities could, of course, be dismissed in the event of bankruptcy.

While these changes may sound radical, they are essential to reducing the probability of a systemic housing meltdown and in mitigating that downturn, should this type of housing problem recur in the future.

7

Conclusions

The major point in the letter I received from six members of this Committee on October 24, 2008 was the fact that I sent letters to mortgage Servicers instructing them to make sure that their actions were in absolute conformity with the contract in which the Servicer and I are both a party. The precedents for honoring contracts, and the Government insistence on the enforcement of contracts through the courts, is deeply ingrained in American business and American life, and it is enormously respected abroad. I will therefore continue to make absolutely certain that parties with whom I contract will fulfill their contractual responsibilities, just as I will fulfill mine under extant US law.

In conclusion, I intend no disrespect to this Committee in its discharge of business. Because of my respect and admiration for this body, I think it is important to be a voice for contractual rights. It is not in the interest of the United States, either now or in the future, for there to be any suggestion to its citizens and the world at large, that US contract rights are in any way insecure.

Sincerely,

William Frey

8

APPENDIX IV

Alternative Private Sector Mortgage Finance Structures

The following two mortgage finance structures have been proposed as alternatives to MBS. For the reasons that follow, neither is capable of financing the U.S. housing market as efficiently and with as little risk to the financial system as securitization.

Covered Bonds

Covered bonds have come up repeatedly in conversations as a potential solution for the beleaguered mortgage market, because they are thought to do a better job of incentivizing issuers to securitize only properly-originated mortgages.[146] A covered bond is a security issued by a bank (or some other financial institution) that is backed by a specific pool of mortgages. The full credit risk and prepayment risk of the mortgages is retained by the issuer. If the issuer fails to repurchase a defaulted loan or does not maintain predetermined ratios of collateral to bonds outstanding, the transaction is terminated and the bond investors are made whole by the issuer. If the issuer becomes insolvent, covered bond investors have exclusive claims on the mortgages backing the covered bonds. The basic benefit of this transaction for an investor is that it concentrates the full risk of the mortgage loans on the balance sheet of the issuer. Theoretically, this encourages the issuer to exercise good judgment when originating the underlying collateral.

While covered bonds feature some desirable characteristics, the fact that the mortgages remain on the balance sheet of the issuing institution creates a couple of problems. First, this feature limits the covered bond market to those issuers with the balance sheet capacity sufficient to retain all of the collateral. This could pose a barrier to entry in the mortgage origination market, limiting competition and potentially raising mortgage rates. Secondly, these types of securities pose a potential systemic risk to the economy, as the risk of these bonds is likely to be concentrated on the balance sheets of the handful of issuers with the balance sheet capacity to originate covered bonds. Whenever a significant amount of risk is concentrated in a handful of institutions, it puts the entire financial system at risk. This concentration of risk was at the heart of the S&L crisis of the 1980s and the Fannie Mae/Freddie Mac problems of today.

Covered bonds were widely used in the United States in the early 1980s (then called "builder bonds") and in other countries with less-developed mortgage markets, but they have never been a large component of any financial institution's balance sheet. Outside of the United States, these structures have become more popular in recent years. However, the volume of covered bonds issued in these countries has not expanded to the extent that the solvency of the financial system would be threatened should the price level in the real estate market decline. Though these bonds are attractive to investors because they are simple and do not require the investor to consider or understand the underlying credit and prepayment risk of the underlying mortgages, they are not the panacea that policymakers have made them out to be. The goal should be to promote securitization structures that minimize risk to the financial system, and covered bonds fail this standard and create an additional layer of systemic risk.

Real Estate Investment Trusts

Recently, at least two large money managers that have substantial interests in U.S. MBS have filed to establish Real Estate Investment Trusts (REITs).[147] The major requirement of a REIT is that it hold real estate assets and distribute 90% of its income in the form of dividends every year. The REIT does not pay tax and thus avoids the "double taxation" of a traditional corporation.

A REIT could be the next generation of security that finances U.S. mortgage production. A mortgage would be considered to be a real estate asset pursuant to REIT regulations. The REIT could thus purchase unsecuritized mortgages and thereby provide capital to the mortgage market. The owners of the REIT would become the economic owners of those mortgage loans. The key advantage of this structure as compared to the historical securitization model in the U.S. is that the REIT would have a single person or entity that would be responsible for the direction given to loan servicers. The manager of the REIT would act as the owner of the mortgage notes in the REIT and direct the servicer to act pursuant to the best interests of the REIT. This would remove the potential for problems with the servicing entity not being responsive to the owners of the assets. There would no longer be the need to amass a 25 percent ownership stake to take action with respect to the mortgages, as there would be no trustee and the manager of the REIT would have complete control over the assets.

The downside of this structure is that it is essentially a concentration of prepayment risk and credit risk, similar to how Fannie Mae and Freddie Mac were acting as aggregators of prepayment and credit risk. With the REITs holding large amounts of the same exposure, this creates a concentration of risk. With banks likely being the primary financiers for these entities, a type of systemic risk to the banking system would be created. If prepayment speeds were faster or slower than expected, these REITs would suffer losses. If the REITs were sufficiently levered and the prepayment speed difference was great enough, REITs could begin to fail. If a large credit event was to occur, this concentration of mortgage risk would prove problematic.

REITs thus have the potential to be the next version of Fannie Mae and Freddie Mac and the next bailout candidate for the U.S. government. They would end up placing the government at risk, either by becoming too big to fail or by owing so much money to the banks that the banking system would end up failing should there be a large prepayment or credit event. This is the identical risk that Fannie Mae and Freddie Mac inflicted on the financial system.

Furthermore, if Fannie Mae and Freddie Mac are to be phased out over time in the name of eliminating the risk that was being dumped on the government, and REITs were tapped to take their place, these entities would become very large very fast. With $12 trillion of mortgages outstanding in the United States these REITs would quickly become the largest financial institutions it the country, or close to it. I suspect that there would be a small handful of large REITS, but even if there were many REIT participants in the market, they would all have the identical exposure and would logically suffer credit problems at the same time. Failure would be as systemic as it was with the S&Ls and Fannie and Freddie.

APPENDIX V

—■—

Types of Subordination

There are multiple types of subordination used currently in MBS structures. In addition to the structures detailed below, there can be combinations and modifications that cover the entire subordination spectrum.

Pari Passu Structure

Pari passu is a Latin phrase meaning "with an equal step" or "on equal footing." In the context of subordination structures, it means that the senior and the subordinate bond pay down at the same rate. This is a relatively weak form of subordination. As cash flows into the trust, it is allocated to senior and subordinate bonds according to the portion of the entire trust comprised by each class. Consider a pool of collateral valued at $100 million with a 10 percent subordinate bond, meaning that it features senior bonds valued at $90 million and subordinate bonds valued at $10 million. In a *pari passu* structure, for each dollar of principal flowing into this hypothetical trust, $0.90 would be distributed to the seniors and $0.10 would go to the subordinates. In the event of a credit loss, the subordinate bonds would cease receiving distributions of principal and absorb the entire loss. A resumption of principal flows to the subordinate classes is generally possible under several circumstances depending on the structure, the most common of which is that payments would resume only when the seniors were paid down to the point that the original ratio of senior to subordinate bonds was restored.

This structure maintains the agreed-upon ratio of senior to subordinate bonds but leaves a serious "tail risk" with the senior bonds. By tail risk, I refer to the possibility that the collateral remaining after a prepayment will absorb a credit loss. In conditions conducive to a pre-payment wave (usually lower interest rates), homeowners that are able to refinance will generally do so, creating an adverse selection. Poorer credit collateral will remain in the pool as better quality collateral, which can most readily qualify for refinancing, prepays. As the pool "renders down," the overall credit quality of the remaining collateral worsens. Should a credit loss occur after a substantial prepayment event, most of the subordination will have already paid off. The senior bonds would thus be exposed to credit losses, losses that would not have happened but for this prepay-driven adverse selection problem.

Sequential Structure

Under this structure, the subordinate bonds receive only interest payments until all of the senior securities are paid in full, at which point they receive interest and principal payments. Unlike the *pari passu* structure, the proportion of subordination in a sequential structure increases over time if no credit losses are taken, as the senior bonds render down while the subordinate bonds do not.

Shifting Interest Structure

This is the most common subordination structure in U.S. RMBS. It features a series of triggers that release ever-increasing proportions of principal cash flows to the subordinate holders. It is common in a fixed rate transaction for the subordinate holders to receive only scheduled principal amortization and none of the unscheduled principal cash flow until the end of the fifth year. After the fifth year, the subordinates' percentage participation in the unscheduled principal cash flow would increase each year until the eleventh year, when the participation would proceed *pari passu* with senior bonds. This has the effect of releasing unscheduled principal to the subordinate investors only after the deal seasons and proves its creditworthiness.

Within U.S. RMBS structures, the triggers determining payments of principal to the subordinate bondholders vary based on the specifics of the collateral. In ARM deals, it is common to have the trigger be a specified percentage of collateral paying down—typically 50 percent—rather than basing the trigger on a certain period of time having elapsed. Under this common structure, the subordinates would not receive any unscheduled cash flow until the collateral outstanding hits 50 percent of the original balance. When that occurs, the subordinate bonds would share principal cash flows *pari passu* with the seniors, provided the pool performance was acceptable. In deals with fixed rate mortgages serving as collateral, time triggers are more common.

Net Interest Margin Structure

The Net Interest Margin (NIM) structure comes in many forms, but the overarching feature is that some of the excess interest in the transaction, or interest-only strips, are "saved" in an account, or directed to a bond or fund, that holds those proceeds as additional subordination. Assume collateral with a 9 percent coupon rate underlies bonds that pay a 6 percent coupon rate. That 3 percent difference, or interest margin, can be used to provide the transaction with additional credit enhancement (to provide a buffer against credit losses). If that 3 percent were placed in an account that held those funds as a reserve to cover any credit losses, the structure would become more secure over time, as that 3 percent continues to accumulate over time, generating additional collateral. As long as credit losses do not exceed cash inflow, the collateral backing the NIM bonds continues to grow. While the rules vary with different bonds, the PSAs for NIM bonds often establish that excess interest be released at specified dates, if the credit of the transaction meets certain hurdles.

Z-Bond or Accrual Structure

This is the strongest form of subordination, because the Z-bond in this subordination structure receives no cash flow at all until the senior bonds are paid in full. Unlike the sequential structure, which pays interest, the Z-bond accrues interest by adding unpaid interest to the principal balance of the bond. This type of subordination thus increases the proportion of the subordinate class (as would a sequential structure) as well as the absolute size of the subordinate class relative to the senior bonds. Again, this result is predicated on credit losses being less than the increase in the Z-bond due to accretions. I believe that this should be the structure of choice for private label RMBS arrangers going forward, as it enables the proper alignment of incentives for deal participants.

Additional Observations

There are endless variations on the above themes. When evaluating subordination, it is important to look at the actual terms of the subordination and understand the circumstances in which the subordination cash flow may be released from the deal and paid to investors. Furthermore, it should be remembered that the owner of the subordinate securities, including the NIM bond, may often be the same entity that is controlling the servicing for the transaction. If this is the case, a conflict potentially arises, as it is possible to manipulate servicing to effect release of the NIM bond or to bring about other trigger events in the deal structure. Such ownership by servicers is not a rare event and represents a flaw in the securitization process. The subordination structure suggested in appendix VI would greatly reduce the economic opportunity for improper servicing when the servicer and the subordinate holder are the same.

APPENDIX VI

Learning from the Commercial Mortgage Market to Create More Stable Subordination Structures

I have discussed several problems with the deal structure used in most residential mortgage securitizations. While there are many possible deal structures, as detailed earlier, they are all variations on the same central theme: subordination. As we have learned more about the causes of the mortgage crisis, it has become clear that changes are required in the basic subordinate structure and servicing of RMBS. The main questions we should ask in creating a more successful deal structure for RMBS are these:

1. Who should control the servicing?

2. What constraints should be placed on those servicers?

3. How should those constraints change with changing market conditions?

To answer these questions, we can draw from commercial mortgage securitization, which has not experienced nearly the same level of market dysfunction as its residential cousin. In the commercial mortgage backed securities (CMBS) market, the subordinate holders generally make decisions regarding the management of the property and have a role in servicing the mortgage. Having the governing contracts specify that subordinate bondholders—effectively the equity holders in the deal—have the responsibility to make key servicing decisions has led to much more rational servicing decisions and improved loss mitigation. This would be a logical improvement for the RMBS market. In the proposal for an improved subordination and servicing responsibility structure that follows, I take features from the CMBS market and combine it with the Z-bond or accrual subordination structure discussed in appendix V to create a more flexible and efficient subordination structure.

Replacing the Existing Subordinate Structure in MBS Transactions

The following terms need to be defined:

Abdication

When a Servicer Control Party decides to abdicate its servicer control responsibilities. This would have the effect of transferring such responsibilities to the next more senior class of ownership.

Change of Control

Occurs when the Collateral Losses and Expected Losses hit the Threshold Level.

Collateral Losses

Realized Losses plus Expected Losses on the collateral pool. This is a proxy to determine the threshold point at which a Servicer Control Party no longer has a true economic interest in the pool of collateral over which it has servicing control.

Expected Losses

Fifty percent of the collateral that is sixty or more days delinquent. This is designed to estimate future losses on the collateral. The purpose of using Expected Losses instead of actual or Realized Losses is that anticipating losses will allow for the removal of a Servicer Control Party whose economic interest is so damaged due to the performance of the collateral that it can no longer be expected to serve as an active Servicer Control Party.

Realized Losses	The actual losses that have been realized on the collateral pool.
Shifting Z-structure	A subordinate structure in which the first loss bond starts as a Z- or accrual bond as discussed in appendix V. As losses reach the agreed upon threshold, the accrual nature of the subordinate bonds moves up the credit waterfall (to the next most subordinate bond) and with this the control of servicing policies.
Servicer Control Party	The individual or firm designated by the investors as having control over the servicer and servicing protocols for an RMBS transaction.
Threshold Level	The point at which Collateral Losses exceed the ownership interest of the Servicer Control Party.

One goal of a new subordinate structure should be to align servicer decision making responsibility with the losses that will result from improper decisions. To express this in another way, those who stand to lose the most should be in charge of determining loss mitigation and servicing policies. Under the current MBS structure, servicer control and servicing policy does not reside with an entity that has an economic interest in ensuring that rational loss mitigation decisions are made. A new way of determining servicing protocols and who controls the servicer is needed. Consider the following example:

A deal is comprised of one senior class and three subordinate classes. The most junior bond, or the "first loss bond," would be a shifting Z-bond. This Z-bond would be retained by the issuer and would receive no cash flow but would accrue interest at a predetermined rate. The issuer, being the owner and servicer of the first loss bond, would be designated the Servicer Control Party, responsible for controlling the servicing and servicing the loan in accordance with certain protocols specified in the PSA. Thus, the deal participant most at risk of credit and fraud losses would also be the deal participant most able to discover and prevent these abuses. This party would receive a cash flow if and only if all bonds senior to that party's bond were retired.

Under this arrangement, the second loss bond would receive an interest cash flow but no principal repayment until all of the more senior bonds were retired. The third loss bond would have the same structure as the second loss bond but would be treated as senior to that bond. The senior bond would receive all of the principal and interest that the trust received, unless and until losses reached the senior bond. If everything goes well with the deal, the servicer does its job properly and the deal pays as expected.

What happens when things do not go well with the transaction and a significant number of borrowers stop making monthly mortgage payments? When the deal experiences Collateral Losses that reach the Threshold Level, the Servicer Control Party shifts to the next-most junior class of bondholders. This results in the transferring of control over servicing practices and policies to the party most at risk of economic loss. When a class of bondholders becomes the Servicer Control Party, the bonds held by those investors become Z-bonds, meaning that they accrue interest but do not pay out unless the Servicer Control Party is successful in mitigating losses. If the Servicer Control Party does not mitigate losses to the point that the next-most junior bonds are fully protected, it receives no cash flow from its bonds, and its investment is wiped out completely. The control of the servicing thus moves up the capital structure, starting with the most junior (at-risk) bonds in the structure.

If the Collateral Losses and Expected Losses reached the Threshold Level and wipe out the first loss bond, the Servicer Control Party would shift from the current servicer (and owner of the first loss) to the owner of the second loss bond. This second loss investor would have wider latitude and control over servicer policies than the first loss entity. This new Servicer Control Party would be empowered with the legal authority to make servicer policy changes, within the limits prescribed in the PSA. For example, this investor could order a portion of the collateral to be sent out for special servicing and authorize loan modifications under certain circumstances. The purpose of these policy changes would be to provide a party with the economic incentives to mitigate credit losses when the deal develops difficulties. This would likely result in higher servicer fees for the trust, but the decisions on this would be made by the party that is the most affected economically: the investor that currently faces the greatest risk of loss.

If the losses or Expected Losses increase further, the third loss bond would assume control over the transaction and have even greater discretion regarding servicing. The PSA would have to provide limits on this decision-making authority, but this party should have wider latitude than the second loss party. Should losses wipe out those bondholders, the senior bondholders would become the Servicer Control Party. At that point, the trustee would send a notice to the owners of these securities for those investors to elect a party to resolve the problems in the trust. This would constitute a *de facto* creditors committee. This level of control bestowed upon this committee should be essentially absolute and include the following:

a. Full authority to replace the servicer without cause.

b. Unlimited ability to place servicing with special servicers.

c. Unlimited ability to reduce borrower interest rates.

d. Unlimited ability to reduce borrower principal.

This ownership group should have the contractual rights to act as owners of the collateral.

When a bondholder is designated the Servicer Control Party, it would also have the option of abdicating its responsibilities. If the collateral supporting the deal is too impaired for the bondholder to have a material economic interest, it is in the best interest of the trust as a whole that the decision-making authority move up the credit waterfall as quickly as possible. For example, if the second loss investor realizes that it cannot possibly change servicer policies enough to recover any economic value from its bonds, it should abdicate its Servicer Control Party responsibilities and allow the more-senior bondholders in the credit waterfall to take control of the transaction. In order to provide that bondholder with an economic incentive to step aside, Abdication should prevent the bondholder's bond from converting into a Z-bond, meaning that the bondholder would continue to receive interest unless and until the credit losses wipe out its bond. In the unlikely event that every class of bondholders elected to abdicate, the original servicer would retain that role and continue to service the loans according to the much more lenient servicing protocols specified in the PSA.

Finally, there should be a periodic review of the Servicer Control Party. This would allow investors to change the servicing policies, should the ownership of the transaction be transferred through the secondary market. Selling one's securities would be considered an Abdication for purposes of being the Servicing Control Party.

What does this form of senior-subordinate structure accomplish?

First, the shifting Z-structure would ensure that the party making the servicing decisions is the party with the economic incentive to act rationally. This eliminates the possibility of the servicer making decisions contrary to the interest of the bondholders, or more accurately, putting its interests before those of the bondholders it is contractually obligated to protect.

Second, this structure provides more latitude, or flexibility, for the servicer when the deal starts to have credit problems. This avoids the difficult situation in which the servicer is obligated to mitigate losses, but is restricted by the PSA and cannot easily adjust the PSA to deal with unforeseen problems. The shifting Z-structure allows the affected bondholders the discretion to increase the servicer's latitude to mitigate losses, while providing the servicer with a single point of contact and authority from which to take direction.

Third, this structure eliminates the possibility of subordinate bondholders bleeding cash out of the deal when a stalemate emerges in servicing policies. If the subordinate investor decides that losses will destroy its bond, it notifies the trustee, and the Servicer Control Party moves up the credit waterfall to the next-most senior class of bonds. Currently, subordinate bonds have an economic interest in not having credit problems resolved expeditiously, because they receive a cash flow until such time that their bonds take credit losses and are extinguished. By implementing the shifting Z-structure and pairing Servicer Control Party responsibility with a shifting Z-bond, the subordinate bondholder would have an economic incentive to either resolve the problem or get out of the way.

Finally, this structure creates a unified group of senior bondholders empowered with the authority to act as owners of the collateral, if they are threatened with losses. If credit losses impacted the senior bonds, absolute control of the transaction would be conferred upon the senior bondholders, who could take the aggressive steps needed to mitigate losses. The entire bond structuring in the senior classes would disappear, and both losses and principal would be shared pro rata. This feature would eliminate the differing economic incentives between the front and the back of a senior structure, thereby preventing the tranche warfare that tends to arise when a deal begins suffering losses.

APPENDIX VII

Sample Representations and Warranties Typically Given by Countrywide Regarding the Mortgage Loans in Private Label Transactions

- The information set forth on Schedule I to the Pooling and Servicing Agreement with respect to each Mortgage Loan is true and correct in all material respects as of the Closing Date.

- No Mortgage Loan had a Loan-to-Value Ratio at origination in excess of 100.00%.

- Each Mortgage Loan at origination complied in all material respects with applicable local, state and federal laws, including, without limitation, usury, equal credit opportunity, predatory and abusive lending laws, real estate settlement procedures, truth-in-lending and disclosure laws, and consummation of the transactions contemplated hereby will not involve the violation of any such laws.

- Each Mortgage Note and the related Mortgage are genuine, and each is the legal, valid and binding obligation of the maker thereof, enforceable in accordance with its terms and under applicable law. To the best of Countrywide's knowledge, all parties to the Mortgage Note and the Mortgage had legal capacity to execute the Mortgage Note and the Mortgage and each Mortgage Note and Mortgage have been duly and properly executed by such parties.

- The origination, underwriting and collection practices used by Countrywide with respect to each Mortgage Loan have been in all respects legal, prudent and customary in the mortgage lending and servicing business.

- Each Mortgage Loan that had a Loan-to-Value Ratio at origination in excess of 80% is the subject of a Primary Insurance Policy that insures that portion of the principal balance equal to a specified percentage times the sum of the remaining principal balance of the related Mortgage Loan, the accrued interest thereon and the related foreclosure expenses... All provisions of any such Primary Insurance Policy have been and are being complied with, any such policy is in full force and effect, and all premiums due thereunder have been paid...

- There is no material monetary default existing under any Mortgage or the related Mortgage Note and, to the best of Countrywide's knowledge, there is no material event which, with the passage of time or with notice and the expiration of any grace or cure period, would constitute a default, breach, violation or event of acceleration under the Mortgage or the related Mortgage Note...

- Each Mortgage Loan was underwritten in all material respects in accordance with the underwriting guidelines described in the Prospectus Supplement.

- The Mortgage Loans, individually and in the aggregate, conform in all material respects to the descriptions thereof in the Prospectus Supplement.

Glossary

AAA	The highest bond rating conferred by Standard and Poor's and Fitch.
Aaa	The highest bond rating conferred by Moody's.
Accrual bond	A CMO tranche that does not pay interest monthly; interest due is accrued, capitalized, and added to the principal amount of the tranche.
Adjustable-rate mortgage	A first lien mortgage with an interest rate that is determined periodically by reference to a publically available index, such as LIBOR or the one-year Treasury rate.
Advance	See "servicer advance."
Agency	In the mortgage context, generally refers to Ginnie Mae, Fannie Mae, or Freddie Mac. See also *GSE*.
Alt-A Loan	This subprime loan is generally characterized by reduced documentation requirements. Unlike conventional mortgage applications, these so-called "stated income" or "no doc" loans did not require the borrower to produce a W-2, income tax return, or any other form of income verification.
Amortize	To pay or schedule the payment of principal in installments.
ARM	See *adjustable-rate mortgage*.
Bondholder	The owner of a bond. In the context of this book, we refer to the owner of a mortgage backed security or a REMIC interest.
Cash for keys	An informal name for the arrangement between a defaulting borrower and a lender, in which the lender agrees to make a payment to the borrower in exchange for the title of the mortgaged property (i.e., turning in the keys).

CDO   See *collateralized debt obligation.*

Certificate holder   See *bondholder.*

Claw-back   See *true sale.*

CMBS   See *commercial mortgage backed security.*

CMO   See *collateralized mortgage obligation.*

Collateral   The assets backing a debt, which may be seized to satisfy that debt in the event that the debtor does not repay. In the context of this book, collateral consists generally of the mortgages in an MBS securitization trust.

Collateralized debt obligation   A debt security collateralized by a variety of debt obligations including bonds and loans of different maturities and credit qualities.

Collateralized mortgage obligation   An MBS security that features structured cash flows. These cash flows are paid to various bondholders based on the credit waterfall, as stated in the PSA.

Commercial mortgage backed security   Any security collateralized by commercial mortgages.

Conventional fixed-rate mortgage   A mortgage that conforms to Fannie Mae and Freddie Mac guidelines. This mortgage is generally a fifteen- or a thirty-year fixed-rate loan.

Coupon rate   The interest rate to be paid to investors in MBS, CMOs, and other bonds and debt-related securities.

Cramdown   An informal name for the transaction in which a bankruptcy court reduces the principal balance of a residential mortgage.

Credit default swap   A financial transaction that ties the investor's return to the credit performance of another transaction.

Credit enhancement   An insurance policy, subordination, or other structuring tool that improves the performance of an MBS or tranche of an MBS.

Credit rating agency	A private firm that issues ratings on securities. The three major rating agencies are Moody's, S & P, and Fitch.
Credit waterfall	The payment priorities that are prescribed by the PSA of a CMO.
Debt-to-income ratio (back end)	The ratio of a borrower's total monthly debt payments (mortgage, credit cards, etc.) to his or her total monthly income.
Debt-to-income ratio (front end)	The ratio of a borrower's monthly mortgage payment (taxes and insurance included) to his or her total monthly income.
Default, homeowner	When a mortgagor fails to make timely payments on his or her home loan.
Default, servicer	When the servicing bank does not comply with the servicing requirements in the PSA.
Derivative	A financial instrument whose price and/or return is tied to the performance of another financial instrument.
Depository Trust Company	A subsidiary of the Depository Trust and Clearing Corporation, DTC was created to provide clearing and settlement efficiencies by immobilizing securities and making "book-entry" changes to ownership of the securities, thus allowing securities to be held in electronic form or "street name," rather than the name of individual investors. This keeps the investors' holdings private and makes it easier to trade the securities.
DTC	See *Depository Trust Company.*
DTI	See *debt-to-income ratio.*
Embedded interest rate swap	A derivative contract included in the PSA of some CDO transactions that is part of the credit waterfall.
Employee Retirement Income Security Act	A federal law that sets minimum standards for most voluntarily established pension and health plans in private

industry to provide protection for individuals in these plans.

ERISA See *Employee Retirement Income Security Act.*

Externality A positive or negative effect from an economic transaction that is not included in the price of that economic decision.

Fannie Mae The Federal National Mortgage Association (FNMA). In 1997, Fannie Mae announced that it would refer to itself as "Fannie Mae" in official documents and encourages others to refer to the company as "Fannie Mae" rather than "Federal National Mortgage Association" or "FNMA."

FDIC See *Federal Deposit Insurance Corp.*

Federal Deposit Insurance Corp. A U.S. government corporation that guarantees the safety of deposits in member banks, currently up to $250,000 per depositor per bank. The FDIC also oversees the safety and soundness of member banks and has the power to place and manage banks in receivership.

Federal Home Loan Bank A "bank's bank." The twelve FHLBs are owned by their bank members and provided with certain tax advantages by the U.S. government. They are responsible for providing liquidity and low-cost funding to the banking system.

Federal Housing Administration A U.S. government agency that promotes homeownership. This agency is part U.S. Department of Housing and Urban Development.

Federal Housing Finance Agency The primary regulator of Fannie Mae, Freddie Mac, and the FHLBs.

Federal Savings and Loan Insurance Corporation The now-defunct entity that insured savings and loan deposits prior to the S&L crisis.

FHA See *Federal Housing Administration.*

FHFA See *Federal Housing Finance Agency.*

FHLB	See *Federal Home Loan Bank*.
Fiduciary	An entity that has an obligation to act for the benefit of a third party.
First lien	A mortgage that, according to the title, is the most senior loan on a mortgaged property.
Fitch	A credit rating agency and a National Recognized Statistical Rating Organization.
Fixed rate	A mortgage interest rate that, according to the loan documents, does not change for the life of the loan.
Flip	To buy a property with the intention of quickly selling it.
Foreclosure	The process by which a servicer takes possession of a home to satisfy a defaulted loan.
Freddie Mac	Federal Home Loan Mortgage Corporation (FHLMC). In 1987, Freddie Mac's board resolved to operate as "Freddie Mac" and encouraged others to refer to the company as "Freddie Mac" rather than "Federal Home Loan Mortgage Corporation" or "FHLMC."
Ginnie Mae	The informal name for the Government National Mortgage Association (GNMA), a government-owned corporation. Ginnie Mae is part of the U.S. Department of Housing and Urban Development and is not a GSE. Its securities carry the explicit full faith and credit of the U.S. government.
Government Sponsored Entity	The major GSEs are Fannie Mae, Freddie Mac, and the Federal Home Loan Banks. Securities issued by the GSEs do not carry the explicit full faith and credit of the U.S. government.
GSE	See *Government-Sponsored Entity*.
H4H	See *Hope For Homeowners Act*.
HAMP	See *Home Affordable Modification Program*.

Hard Currency	A widely traded and accepted currency. A hard currency can be easily used as the reference currency in a currency or interest-rate swap.
Hedge	A transaction that reduces the risk of adverse price movements on an existing investment position. Although hedges reduce potential losses, they also tend to reduce potential profits.
Holdback	Deferred compensation that is forfeited if a certain event occurs. For example, an origination fee that is deferred and not paid if the loans in an MBS transaction were to default or fraud is discovered.
Home Affordable Modification Program	Established by the Helping Families Save Their Homes Act in 2009, the goal of this program was to improve the foreclosure environment.
Hope for Homeowners	Title IV of Division A of the Housing andEconomic Recovery Act, Public Law 119-289, 122 Stat. 2654 (2008). The goal of this law was to improve the foreclosure environment.
Hybrid ARM	An ARM with an initial interest rate that is fixed for a number of months and which then adjusts based on predefined terms.
Interest rate option	A security or part of a security which, under its terms, features changes in its cash flow based on changes in interest rates.
Interest rate swap	A derivative contract that effectively takes a fixed-rate class of MBS or other fixed-rate security and converts it into a floating class of MBS or other floating-rate security for a fee.
Intermediate	To act as a mediator between two different markets.
International Swaps and Derivatives Association	A trade organization of participants in the market for over-the-counter derivatives that has created standardized derivative deal documents.

Inverse interest-only strip	A tranche in an MBS transaction that is a mortgage derivative with no principal and which floats in an inverse direction to a reference interest rate.
Investment grade	A security rated Baa and above by Moody's or BBB and above by S & P or Fitch.
Investor	See *bondholder.*
ISDA	See *International Swaps and Derivatives Association.*
Lien priority	Establishes the order in which lien holders are entitled to payment when a property is foreclosed upon.
Lien shifting	Changing the *de facto* seniority of a lien on a property.
Loan-to-value ratio	The amount of a mortgage vs. the value of the property.
Low-doc loan	An informal name for a mortgage loan originated using underwriting standards that did not include extensive documentation of income or assets. Sometimes referred to as a "stated income loan."
LTV	See *loan to-value ratio.*
MBS	See *mortgage backed security.*
Moody's	A credit rating agency and a nationally recognized statistical rating organization.
Moral hazard	A policy or characteristic of the environment that encourages excessive risk-taking behavior, often by bringing about the very harm it was designed to prevent. The most common example is that people will generally take more risk when they have insurance to protect them from the negative consequences of their behavior, thereby engendering additional negative consequences.
Mortgage	A lien on property.
Mortgage backed security	Any security collateralized by mortgages.

Nationally Recognized Statistical Rating Organization	A company that provides credit rating services that the U.S. Securities and Exchange Commission (SEC) permits other financial firms to use for certain regulatory purposes.
Negative equity amortizing loan	Occurs when the value of the property is less than the total value of liens against the property.
Negatively amortizing loan	A mortgage with a scheduled monthly payment that is less than the interest due each month. To cover the shortfall, the principal amount of the loan increases by the amount of the shortfall. Also referred to as a "neg am" loan.
No-doc loan	An informal name for a mortgage loan originated using underwriting standards that did not include the documentation of income or assets. Sometimes referred to as a "stated income loan."
Non-investment grade	Rated below Baa by Moody's or below BBB by S & P and Fitch.
Note	A legal document that supports a loan.
NRSRO	See *Nationally Recognized Statistical Rating Organization*.
Option	The right, but not the obligation, to buy, sell, or take some other action, usually at a predetermined price during a limited time period. Options in mortgages usually refer to the right to make prepayments on a mortgage.
Origination	The issuance of a mortgage loan.
Par	One hundred percent of the stated principal amount of a loan.
Pari passu	A legal term meaning that two legal claims have equal priority.
Paying agent	An entity that makes dividend payments to stockholders or principal and interest payments to bondholders on behalf of the issuer.

Payment shock	The problem created when a homeowner's adjustable rate loan resets and the monthly payment increases substantially.
Pecora Commission	This commission initiated the Pecora Investigation on March 4, 1932, under the authority of the United States Senate Committee on Banking and Currency, which was charged with investigating the causes of the Wall Street Crash of 1929.
Piggyback loan	A second lien that closes at the same time as the first lien.
PMI	See *Private mortgage insurance.*
Private mortgage insurance	Loan-level insurance purchased by the loan originator that provides partial protection against loss resulting from foreclosure. The benefits of PMI policies usually transfer to the trust when loans are sold into securitization.
Pool	As used with loans, a group of mortgages.
Pooling and Servicing Agreement	The contract or legal agreement that governs a CMO.
Prepayment	The payment of principal before it is scheduled by the mortgage amortization schedule.
Prepayment risk	The risk that is incurred by MBS investors that borrowers will pay off their mortgage before the scheduled maturity of the mortgage collateral.
PSA	See *Pooling and Servicing Agreement.*
Put-back	An option to sell (put) something—usually a loan—back to the seller, or the act of selling that item back to the seller. From the seller's perspective, this is also referred to as a repurchase obligation.
Real Estate Mortgage Investment Trust	Often referred to as a CMO. The REMIC Regulations refer to a section of the IRS code that provides favorable

tax treatment for trusts that contain mortgages and meet certain other requirements.

Real estate owned
A property that has been foreclosed upon and is now owned by the lender.

Regulation Q
A federal regulation that limited the amount of interest a bank could pay on demand and time deposits.

REMIC
See *Real Estate Mortgage Investment Trust.*

Remittance report
A monthly report produced by the securitization trustee that specifies all receipts and disbursements related to a CMO.

REO
See *Real estate owned.*

Representations and warranties
Contractual statements by which one party gives certain assurances to the other, and on which the other party may rely.

Residential mortgage backed security
Any security collateralized by residential mortgages.

RMBS
See *Residential mortgage backed security.*

Robosigner
A term popularized in 2010 that refers to a range of poor servicing practices such as hiring contractors and others to sign loan documents as if they were bank employees. These signers often attested to matters of which they had no personal knowledge.

S&L
A savings and loan association.

S & P
Standard and Poor's, a credit rating agency and a nationally recognized statistical rating organization.

Safe harbor
Legal protection.

Second lien
A mortgage that, according to the title, is the second-most senior loan on a mortgaged property after the first lien.

Securitization	The act of pooling assets into a trust and selling the economic interest to investors.
Securitization trust	The legal vehicle that houses a securitization.
Senior bond	A CMO tranche that is the last bond to take credit losses in the REMIC credit waterfall.
Servicer	The bank that collects and remits homeowner's monthly payments to investors. In the case of the private label market, payments are made to the REMIC trust. The servicer receives a fee for this activity.
Servicer advance	A payment of principal and/or interest to the REMIC trust or other investor by a Servicer in the absence of a payment by the borrower.
Servicing report	See *Remittance report*.
Short sale	The sale of property at less than the unpaid principal balance of the mortgage that is made to avoid foreclosure. A short sale results in the lender taking a loss on the property and therefore must be approved by the servicer or Trustee.
Strategic default	A mortgage default that occurs when a borrower has the financial ability to make the payments but chooses not to.
Street name	The registration of a security in a name that is common to all investors. This device allows the DTC to keep records on the actual owners to accommodate efficient trading and payment of principal and interest. Holding a security in "street name" also provides anonymity to the investor.
Subordinate bond	A CMO tranche that takes credit losses before the senior bond in the credit waterfall.
Subprime	A mortgage that is of a lower credit quality, with a higher likelihood of non-payment, than a prime loan.
Systemic risk	The risk of the large scale collapse of a financial market.

TILA	See *Truth in Lending Act.*
Tranche	A class of securities in a CMO.
Tranche warfare	The situation in which one class or tranche of a REMIC has opposing or conflicting interests with other classes in the same REMIC transaction.
True sale	When a seller of collateral transfers ownership of the collateral and there is no possibility of the sale being rescinded (i.e., subject to a claw-back) in the event of seller insolvency.
Trustee	In the case of a securitization, the bank that is charged with overseeing the transaction.
Truth in Lending Act	A U.S. federal law designed to protect consumers by requiring the key terms of the lending arrangement and all costs to be made clear to the borrower.
Underwater	See *negative equity.*
Underwriter (of a bond)	The Wall Street firm that brings a securitization to market.
Underwriter (of a mortgage)	The analyst that reviews the financial condition of a borrower and the property that is being mortgaged, and determines whether the loan should be made to that borrower.
Unsecured credit	A loan that is not collateralized by any tangible property.
Variable rate mortgage	See *Adjustable rate mortgage.*
Wrap	A guarantee of a CMO trust or tranche provided by a third party.
Z-bond	See *Accrual bond.*

INDEX

A

Agency for Housing Mortgage Lending xxxiii, xxiv

AIG 152, 204

Alt-A xxxvvii, 48, 58, 132

Ambac 204

B

Bank of America viii, xl, xlii, 51-53, 96-101, 125, 132-133, 152

Bear Stearns xxvii, xl-xli, 51-52, 59-60, 152

Bernanke, Ben ix, xxvii-xxviii, 241

C

Calyon lii

Canadian MBS xxi, 8, 163-164

cash for keys 41, 141

CDO 27, 55

Chilean mortgage market 219

Citibank xl, 51, 54

Clayton Holdings 211

Countrywide viii, ix, xxi, xxv, xxxii-xxxv, xlii, 42, 51-53, 84, 95-101, 109, 125- 126, 189

Countrywide Settlements....

Attorneys General viii, xxxii-xxxiii, 12, 53, 84, 95-97, 98-100, 111, 126

FTC 102-103

cramdown 192-193

credit waterfall 37, 40, 123-124, 190, 205, 269, 272-372

D

Danish mortgage market 161-163

Depfa Bank xlii

Deutsche Bank xlii, xliii

Dexia xlii

Dodd-Frank Act 177, 212

E

English housing market 76, 186

F

Fannie Mae xxiii, xliii, 5, 7-8, 16-17, 20, 28, 35, 62-64, 89, 108, 144, 148, 152-153, 155, 170, 191, 199, 238, 260-262

Federal Housing Finance Agency xliii, 28

FGIC 204

Federal Housing Administration xliii, 8, 15-16, 103, 108, 170

ABOUT THE AUTHOR AND EDITOR

William A. Frey began his career on Wall Street in 1981 in the then nascent field of securitization. After nearly fifteen years in major firms including Morgan Stanley, Smith Barney, and Bear Stearns, Bill founded Greenwich Financial Services (GFS) in 1995, where he serves as principal and CEO today. Under Bill's leadership, GFS has structured and sold billions of dollars of mortgage backed securities. In 2003, recognizing that the U.S. MBS market was fueled by loans that were unlikely to be repaid, Bill decided to look for opportunities in other countries. GFS completed the first Russian securitization transaction with auto loans in 2005 and followed in 2006 with the first MBS for Russian mortgage certificates. Each of these deals won a "Deal of the Year" award from industry groups. More importantly, neither has suffered any credit losses during the recent worldwide financial turmoil.

Recently Bill has emerged as the most vocal advocate for bondholder rights in the wake of the Mortgage Crisis. The central theme of Bill's advocacy is that the solutions proposed by federal and state governments will do more harm than good. The proposed changes usually ignore the contracts that govern mortgage securities, massively increasing losses to bondholders who are typically pension and retirement funds. Furthermore, the U.S. forced abrogation of trillions of dollars of investor contracts will stop the flow of private capital to the United States, thereby choking off the eventual recovery of the housing market and, indeed, the entire U.S. economy. Bill's advaocacy for contract integrity and his visionary solutions that work for all market participants are recognized as key components in the eventual recovery of the mortgage capital markets.

Bill earned his undergraduate degree from Cornell University and MBA from Carnegie Mellon University.

Isaac Gradman is an attorney who was involved in some of the earliest litigation arising from the suprime mortgage crisis. He authors the law blog, *The Subprime Shakeout* and is the managing member of IMG Enterprises, an MBS consulting firm.

Isaac received his B.A. in Political and Social Thought with Highest Distinction from UVA, where he was a Jefferson Scholar, an Echols Scholar and a member of the Raven Honor Society, and received his J.D. *cum laude* from N.Y.U. School of Law, where he was a Dean's Scholar. Isaac also clerked for two years for the Hon. Joan Lenard in the United States District Court in the Southern District of Florida.

ENDNOTES

1   Ruth Simon, "Mortgage-Bond Holders Get Voice: Greenwich Financial's William Frey Challenges Loan Servicers Like Bank of America," *Wall Street Journal*, December 1, 2008, http://www.msfraud.org/Articles/FreyChallengesLoanServicersLikeBankofAmerica.pdf (accessed August 31, 2011).

2   Isaac Gradman, "Greenwich CEO William Frey Primed to Become the Lorax For Investors Without a Voice?," *The Subprime Shakeout*, February 11, 2009, http://www.subprimeshakeout.com/2009/02/greenwich-ceo-william-frey-primed-to-become-the-lorax-for-investors-without-a-voice.html (accessed August 31, 2011).

3   Edmund Conway, "WEF 2009: Global crisis 'has destroyed 40pc of world wealth,'" *Daily Telegraph*, March 21, 2011, http://www.telegraph.co.uk/finance/financetopics/davos/4374492/WEF-2009-Global-crisis-has-destroyed-40pc-of-world-wealth.html (accessed March 21, 2011).

4   Laurie Goodman, "Robosigners and Other Servicing Failures: Protecting the Rights of RMBS Investors" (presentation, Grais & Ellsworth, New York, NY, October 27, 2010), webcast available at http://video.remotecounsel.com/mediasite/Viewer/?peid=060f37b9b28a49ac8cbbea6716c46fed1d (accessed April 13, 2011).

5   Vikas Bajaj and Barry Meier, "Some Hedge Funds Argue against Proposals to Modify Mortgages," *New York Times*, October 23, 2008, http://www.nytimes.com/2008/10/24/business/24modify.html?scp=6&sq=%22Barry+Meier%22&st=nyt (accessed December 1, 2010).

6   Alex Ulam, "The Bank of America Mortgage Settlement Fiasco," *The Nation*, October 13, 2010, http://www.thenation.com/article/155380/bank-america-mortgage-settlement-fiasco?page=0,1 (accessed June 17, 2011).

7   James Hagerty and Ruth Simon, "Activist Financier 'Terrorizes' Bankers in Foreclosure Fight," *Wall Street Journal*, May 21, 2009, http://www.naca.com/press/wallStreet20090520.jsp (accessed December 1, 2010).

8   Danielle Reed, "Countrywide: Attorneys General voice support for lender's USD $8.4bn loan mod program settling predatory lending allegations in reaction to bondholder suit," *Debtwire.com*, December 3, 2008, http://www.graisellsworth.com/pdf/press/Attorneys_General_Support.pdf (accessed December 3, 2010).

9   Jody Shenn, "Mortgage Investors Form Battle Lines over Housing Aid," *Bloomberg*, April 23, 2009, http://www.bloomberg.com/apps/news?pid=newsarchive&sid=aJ6_vwmx_vlA (accessed June 17, 2011).

10 William Frey, "Vacuuming up first investors," *Washington Times*, May 18, 2009, http://www.washingtontimes.com/news/2009/may/18/vacuuming-up-first-investors (accessed June 17, 2011).

11 Maurna Desmond, "T. Rowe Price Calls For Halt To Obama Mortgage Bill," *Forbes*, May 1, 2009, http://www.forbes.com/2009/05/01/mortgage-modifications-congress-business-wall-street-mortgage-letter.html (accessed June 17, 2011).

12 See, e.g., Amended Complaint, *Ambac Assurance Corp., et al. v. EMC Mortgage Corp., et al.*, 08-CV-9464, ¶¶212-13 (S.D.N.Y. 2011).

13 Complaint, *Dexia Holdings Inc et al. v. Countrywide Financial Corp et al.*, 650185/2011 (N.Y. Sup. Ct. January 24, 2011)

14 Complaint, *Dexia SA/NV v. Deutsche Bank AG*, 651918/2011 (N.Y. Sup. Ct. July 13, 2011)

15 Complaint, *Federal Housing Finance Agency v. UBS Americas Inc., et al.*, No. 11-05201 (S.D.N.Y. July 27, 2011).

16 Complaint, *U.S. v. Deutsche Bank AG et al.*, No. 11-02976 (S.D.N.Y. May 3, 2011).

17 Nick Timiraos, "Fannie, Freddie Fix Is a Political Hot Potato," *Wall Street Journal*, May 24, 2010, http://online.wsj.com/article/SB10001424052748704167704575258503544541716.html (accessed December 4, 2010).

18 Timiraos, "Fannie, Freddie Fix," *Wall Street Journal* (accessed December 4, 2010).

19 Securities Industry and Financial Markets Association (SIFMA), "Outstanding U.S. Bond Market Debt—quarterly data to Q4 2010," March 17, 2011, http://www.sifma.org/uploadedFiles/Research/Statistics/StatisticsFiles/CM-US-Bond-Market-Outstanding-SIFMA.xls (accessed April 12, 2011).

20 FDIC, "Statistics on Depository Institutions Report," custom report, December 31, 2007, http://www2.fdic.gov/sdi/main.asp (accessed April 12, 2011) [Criteria = "Standard Peer Group", "All Institutions", "National"; Report Date = "December 31, 2007"; Report Selection = "Assets and Liabilities", "Dollars"].

21 SIFMA, "Outstanding U.S. Bond Market Debt."

22 Frank J. Fabozzi and Franco Modigliani, *Mortgage and Mortgage-Backed Securities Markets* (Boston: Harvard Business School Press, 1992), 19–20.

23 Fabozzi and Modigliani, *Mortgage and Mortgage-Backed Securities Markets*, 20.

24 Fabozzi and Modigliani, *Mortgage and Mortgage-Backed Securities Markets*, 20.

25 Fabozzi and Modigliani, *Mortgage and Mortgage-Backed Securities Markets*, 21.

26 Fabozzi and Modigliani, *Mortgage and Mortgage-Backed Securities Markets*, 21.

27 Fabozzi and Modigliani, *Mortgage and Mortgage-Backed Securities Markets*, 23.

28 Fabozzi and Modigliani, *Mortgage and Mortgage-Backed Securities Markets*, 25.

29 U.S. General Accounting Office, "Financial Audit: Resolution Trust Corporation's 1995 and 1994 Financial Statements," July 1996, 8, 13.

30 Securities Industry and Financial Markets Association, "U.S. Mortgage-Related Securities Outstanding–quarterly data to Q4 2010," January 31, 2011, http://www.sifma.org/uploadedFiles/Research/Statistics/StatisticsFiles/CM-US-Bond-Market-Outstanding-SIFMA.xls (accessed April 12, 2011).

31 Federal Deposit Insurance Corporation, *Bank Failures in Brief*, http://www.fdic.gov/bank/historical/bank/index.html (accessed April 12, 2011).

32 FDIC, "Bank Failures in Brief - 2008," January 4, 2011, http://www.fdic.gov/bank/historical/bank/2008/index.html (accessed April 12, 2011).

33 FDIC, "Bank Failures in Brief - 2009," January 4, 2011, http://www.fdic.gov/bank/historical/bank/2009/index.html (accessed April 12, 2011).

34 FDIC, "Bank Failures in Brief - 2010," January 4, 2011, http://www.fdic.gov/bank/historical/bank/2010/index.html (accessed April 12, 2011).

35 "Collateral Availability for Fixed Rate Agency MBS," Bloomberg L.P., index name = CAV <GO>, 2-3 (accessed March 31, 2011) [excludes MBS held in portfolio by GSEs].

36 "Collateral Availability for Fixed Rate Agency MBS," Bloomberg L.P., 2–3.

37 Jann Swanson, "FHFA Projects Continued GSE Losses. Surprise!" *Mortgage News Daily*, October 22, 2010, http://www.mortgagenewsdaily.com/10212010_fhfa_gses.asp (accessed April 12, 2011).

38 "Agency MBS Pool Issuance," Bloomberg L.P., index name = CAV <GO> , 3 (accessed March 31, 2011) [excludes MBS held in portfolio by GSEs]. Bloomberg screen name: IMBS <GO>, 3.

39 "CMO Issuance," Bloomberg L.P., index name = ICMO <GO>, 3 (accessed March 31, 2011) [listing only reissuance of existing issues for non-agency issuance].

40 Claude R. Marx, "NCUA Places U.S. Central and Wescorp into Conservatorship," *Credit Union Times*, March 20, 2009, http://www.cutimes.com/2009/03/20/ncua-places-us-central-and-wescorp-into-conservatorship (accessed May 25, 2011).

41 Sebastian Schich, "Financial Turbulence: Some Lessons Regarding Deposit Insurance," *Financial Market Trends*, 2008, 59, http://www.oecd.org/dataoecd/32/54/41420525.pdf (accessed April 12, 2011); Asli Demirgüç-Kunt and Enrica Detragiache, "The Determinants of Bank Crisis in Developing and Developed Countries," *IMF Staff Papers* 104 (Palgrave Macmillan, March 1998); Asli Demirgüç-Kunt and Edward J. Kane, "Deposit Insurance Around the World: Where Does It Work?" *World Bank Paper* No. 2679 (2001).

42 See generally Thomas Sowell, *The Housing Boom and Bust* (New York: Basic Books, 2009).

43 Chris Gamaitoni, Jason Stewart, and Mike Turner, "Mortgage Repurchases Part II: Private Label RMBS Investors Take Aim—Quantifying the Risks," Compass Point Research & Trading, August 17, 2010, 4, http://api.ning.com/files/fiCVZ-yzNTkoAzUdzhSWYNuHv33*Ur5ZYBh3S08zo*phyT79SFi0TOpPG7klHe3h8

RXKKyphNZqqytZrXQKbMxv4R3F6fN5dI/36431113MortgageFinanceRepur
chasesPrivateLabel08172010.pdf (accessed July 10, 2011).

44 Financial Crisis Inquiry Commission, Testimony of Richard Bowen, April 7, 2010
(transcript previously available at http://fcic.gov/hearings/pdfs/2010-0407-Bowen.
pdf).

45 Errol Arne and Anthony Guinyard, "Trends in U.S. Residential Mortgage
Products: Alt-A Sector Fourth-Quarter 2005," Standard & Poor's, March 8, 2006,
2, http://www2.standardandpoors.com/spf/pdf/fixedincome/ALTA405.pdf (accessed April 12, 2011).

46 See, e.g., Janet Morrissey, "Credit Default Swaps: The Next Crisis?" *Time*, March
17, 2008, http://www.time.com/time/business/article/0,8599,1723152,00.html
(accessed January 30, 2011); Matthew Philips, "The Monster that Ate Wall Street,"
Newsweek, September 27, 2008, http://www.newsweek.com/2008/09/26/the-
monster-that-ate-wall-street.html (accessed January 30, 2011).

47 Berkshire Hathaway, Inc., Annual Letter to Shareholders (2002), 15, http://www.
berkshirehathaway.com/letters/2002pdf.pdf (accessed August 1, 2011).

48 See, e.g., Amended Complaint, *Ambac Assurance Corp., et al. v. EMC Mortgage
Corp., et al.*, 08-CV-9464 (S.D.N.Y. 2011); Complaint, *Federal Home Loan Bank
of San Francisco v. Credit Suisse Securities, LLC, et al.*, 10-CGC-497840 (San
Francisco County Sup. Ct., 2010); Amended Complaint, *Federal Home Loan
Bank of Pittsburgh v. J.P. Morgan Securities, Inc., et al.*, GD-09-016892 (Allegheny
County Ct. of Common Pleas, 2010); Complaint, *Federal Home Loan Bank of
Seattle v. Credit Suisse Securities, LLC, et al.*, 09-2-46353-1 SEA (King County
Sup. Ct., 2009).

49 Valerie L. Smith, "Subordinated Debt Issuance by Fannie Mae and Freddie Mac,"
Office of Federal Housing Enterprise Oversight, Working Paper 07-3, June 2007,
27, http://www.fhfa.gov/webfiles/1274/workingpaper073.pdf (accessed August
15, 2011).

50 Associated Press, "Freddie Mac Settles Accounting-Fraud Charges," September
28, 2007, http://www.msnbc.msn.com/id/21027918/ns/business-us_business
(accessed April 13, 2011).

51   Mark Jickling, "Accounting and Management Problems at Freddie Mac," CRS Report, Order Code RS21567, November 15, 2005, 1, 3, http://www.policyarchive. org/handle/10207/bitstreams/18528.pdf (accessed April 13, 2011).

52   David Hilzenrath, "Report Slams Fannie Mae: U.S. Regulators Find Accounting Failures at Housing Financier," *Washington Post*, September 23, 2004, http:// www.washingtonpost.com/wp-dyn/articles/A41165-2004Sep22.html (accessed April 13, 2011).

53   "U.S. Office of Federal Housing Enterprise Oversight and the Federal National Mortgage Association Agreement," September 27, 2004, http://www.fanniemae. com/media/pdf/issues/092704.pdf (accessed April 13, 2011).

54   James Tyson, "Fannie Mae Plans to Bring Reports Up to Date by February," *Washington Post*, June 9, 2007, http://www.washingtonpost.com/wp-dyn/content/ article/2007/06/08/AR2007060802612.html (accessed April 13, 2011).

55   Tyson, "Fannie Mae Plans to Bring Reports Up to Date by February" (accessed April 13, 2011).

56   "Significant Declines in 90+ Day Delinquencies and Foreclosures in Latest MBA National Delinquency Survey" Mortgage Bankers Association press release, May 19, 2011, http://www.mortgagebankers.org/NewsandMedia/PressCenter/76676.htm.

57   Stan Liebowitz, "New Evidence on the Foreclosure Crisis: Zero Money Down, Not Subprime Loans Led to the Mortgage Meltdown," *Wall Street Journal*, July 3, 2009, http://online.wsj.com/article/SB124657539489189043.html (accessed February 16, 2011).

58   Liebowitz, "New Evidence on the Foreclosure Crisis" (accessed February 16, 2011).

59   CoreLogic, "New CoreLogic Data Shows 23 Percent of Borrowers Underwater with $750 Billion Dollars of Negative Equity," press release, March 8, 2011, http:// www.corelogic.com/About-Us/News/New-CoreLogic-Data-Shows-23-Percent- of-Borrowers-Underwater-with-$750-Billion-Dollars-of-Negative-Equity.aspx (accessed June 18, 2011).

60   Scott Lanman and Joshua Zumbrun, "Fed's Raskin Urges Mortgage Companies to Look Beyond Profits, Help Housing," *Bloomberg*, February 11, 2011, http://

www.bloomberg.com/news/2011-02-12/fed-s-raskin-urges-mortgage companies-to-help-housing-market.html (accessed February 16, 2011).

61   Experian/Oliver Wyman, "Market Intelligence Report: Understanding Strategic Default in Mortgages," June 28, 2010, 4, http://www.experian.com/newsletters/pdf/2010/strategicdefaultpartIIfinal.pdf (accessed April 13, 2011).

62   Mortgage Bankers Association, "Short-Term Delinquencies Fall to Pre-Recession Levels, Loans in Foreclosure Tie All-Time Record in Latest MBA National Delinquency Survey," February 11, 2011, http://www.mortgagebankers.org/NewsandMedia/PressCenter/75706.htm (accessed March 30, 2011).

63   Council of Mortgage Lenders, "Arrears and repossessions down, but vulnerability remains," May 13, 2010, http://www.cml.org.uk/cml/media/press/2612 (accessed February 17, 2011); "Changes in CML arrears and possession figures–press note," Council of Mortgage Lenders Research, December 5, 2010, 1, http://www.cml.org.uk/cml/filegrab/ChangesinCMLarrearsandpossessionfigures-pressnote.pdf?ref=7196 (February 17, 2011); Council of Mortgage Lenders, "24% fall in repossessions and 13% fall in mortgage arrears," February 10, 2011, http://www.cml.org.uk/cml/media/press/2836 (accessed February 17, 2011).

64   Council of Mortgage Lenders, "Arrears and repossessions down"; "Changes in CML arrears," 2; "24% fall in repossessions" (accessed February 17, 2011).

65   The Mortgage Forgiveness Debt Relief Act, Public Law 110–142, 121 Stat. 1803 (2007), 1-2.

66   See, e.g., Section 201, "Servicer Safe Harbor," Helping Families Save Their Homes Act, Public Law 111–22, 123 Stat. 163 (2009), 7-9; Isaac M. Gradman, "Constitutional Rights: Using Loss-Shifting to Reduce Foreclosures," *Daily Journal*, October 7, 2009, 7.

67   Board of Governors of the Federal Reserve System, "Mortgage Debt Outstanding," September 24, 2010, http://www.federalreserve.gov/econresdata/releases/mortoutstand/mortoutstand20100930.htm (accessed April 13, 2011).

68   U.S. Department of the Treasury, "OCC and OTS Mortgage Metrics Report: Disclosure of National Bank and Federal Thrift Mortgage Loan Data," December 2009, 25, http://www.occ.gov/publications/publications-by-type/

other-publications/mortgage-metrics-q3-2009/mortgage-metrics-q3-2009-pdf. pdf (accessed February 18, 2011).

69 Chris Mayer, Ed Morrison, Tomasz Piskorski, and Arpit Gupta, "Mortgage Modification and Strategic Behavior: Evidence from a Legal Settlement with Countrywide," National Bureau of Economic Research, Working Paper No. 17065, May 9, 2011, http://papers.ssrn.com/sol3/papers.cfm?abstract_id=1836451 (accessed May 25, 2011).

70 Laurie Goodman, "Robosigners" (accessed April 13, 2011).

71 See, e.g., Complaint, *Bear Stearns Mortgage Funding Trust 2007-AR2 by Wells Fargo Bank N.A. as Trustee v. EMC Mortgage Corp.*, CA6132 (Delaware Chancery Court 2011); Answer, *IndyMac Federal Bank FSB by the Federal Deposit Ins. Corp. as Conservator v. PMI Mortgage Ins. Co.*, 08-CV-04303 (N.D. Cal. 2008); Isaac Gradman, "Loan File Issue Brought to Forefront by FHFA Subpoena," The Subprime Shakeout, July 14, 2010, http://subprimeshakeout.blogspot.com/2010/07/ loan-file-issue-brought-to-forefront-by.html (accessed February 19, 2011).

72 Securities Industry and Financial Markets Association, "Outstanding U.S. Bond Market Debt—Quarterly Data to Q4 2010," March 17, 2011, http://www.sifma. org/uploadedFiles/Research/Statistics/StatisticsFiles/CM-US-Bond-Market-Outstanding-SIFMA.xls (March 30, 2011); Board of Governors of the Federal Reserve System, "Mortgage Debt Outstanding." September 24, 2010, http://www. federalreserve.gov/econresdata/releases/mortoutstand/mortoutstand20100930. htm (accessed March 30, 2011).

73 U.S. Department of the Treasury and U.S. Department of Housing and Urban Development, "Reforming America's Housing Finance Market: A Report to Congress," February 2011, http://www.treasury.gov/initiatives/Documents/ Reforming%20America's%20Housing%20Finance%20Market.pdf (accessed April 13, 2011).

74 Milton Friedman, *There's No Such Thing as a Free Lunch* (LeSalle, IL: Open Court Publishing Co., 1975).

75 Stipulated Judgment and Injunction, *The People of the State of California v. Countrywide Financial Corp., et al.*, LC-083076 (Los Angeles County Sup. Ct. 2008).

76 Legal Newsline, "AGs hail Countrywide settlement as model for future," October 7, 2008, http://www.legalnewsline.com/spotlight/216391-ags-hail-countrywide-settlement-as-model-for-future (accessed March 6, 2011).

77 See Stipulated Judgment and Injunction, *California v. Countrywide*, 18.

78 Connecticut Attorney General's Office, "Attorney General Announces Countrywide Settlement Saving Thousands of CT Homeowners from Losing Homes," press release, October 6, 2008, http://www.ct.gov/ag/cwp/view.asp?A=2795&Q=424350 (accessed March 6, 2011).

79 Connecticut Attorney General's Office, "Attorney General Announces," October 6, 2008 (accessed March 6, 2011).

80 Danielle Reed, "Countrywide: Attorneys General voice support for lender's USD 8.4bn loan mod program settling predatory lending allegations in reaction to bondholder suit," Debtwire.com, December 3, 2008, http://www.graisellsworth.com/Portals/0/images/pdfs/press/Attorneys_General_Support.pdf (accessed April 13, 2011).

81 Reed, "Countrywide: Attorneys General," December 3, 2008 (accessed April 13, 2011).

82 Christopher Mayer, Edward Morrison, Tomasz Piskorski, Arpit Gupta, "Mortgage Modification and Strategic Default: Evidence from a Legal Settlement with Countrywide," The Paul Milstein Center for Real Estate at Columbia Business School, January 6, 2011, 22, http://www.law.northwestern.edu/colloquium/law_economics/documents/Mayer-Morrison-Piskorski-Gupta_mortgage-modification-Northwestern.pdf (accessed March 6, 2011).

83 Section 201, "Servicer Safe Harbor for Mortgage Loan Modifications," Helping Families Save Their Homes Act of 2009, H.R. 1106, 111th Cong. (introduced February 3, 2009).

84 Section 201, "Servicer Safe Harbor for Mortgage Loan Modifications," Helping Families Save Their Homes Act, Public Law 111–22, 123 Stat. 163 (2009), http://www.gpo.gov/fdsys/pkg/PLAW-111publ22/content-detail.html (accessed April 22, 2011).

85 See Section 201, "Servicer Safe Harbor for Mortgage Loan Modifications," Public Law 111–22.

86 Memorandum Opinion and Order at 20–21, *Greenwich Financial Services, et al. v. Countrywide Financial Corp., et al.*, 08-CV-11343 (RJH) (S.D.N.Y. August 14, 2009).

87 Established by the Hope For Homeowners Act, Title IV of Division A of the Housing and Economic Recovery Act, Public Law 119–289, 122 Stat. 2654 (2008).

88 Brian Naylor, "Homeowners Rescue Program Shows Slim Benefits," *National Public Radio*, February 3, 2009, http://www.npr.org/templates/story/story. php?storyId=100163398 (accessed March 7, 2011).

89 Les Christie, "HOPE prevents 1 foreclosure," CNN Money, March 25, 2009, http://money.cnn.com/2009/03/25/real_estate/new_hope_plan/index.htm (accessed March 7, 2011).

90 Dina ElBoghdady, "HUD Chief Calls Aid on Mortgages a Failure," *Washington Post*, December 17, 2008, http://www.washingtonpost.com/wp-dyn/content/article/2008/12/16/AR2008121603177.html (accessed March 7, 2011).

91 Dawn Kopeki and Theo Francis, "U.S. May Retool Loan Program for Underwater Borrowers," *Bloomberg*, January 27, 2010, http://www.bloomberg.com/apps/news?pid=newsarchive&sid=aAJxmSnvsrwk (accessed March 7, 2011).

92 Established by the Helping Families Save Their Homes Act, Public Law 111–22, 123 Stat. 163 (2009).

93 U.S. Department of the Treasury and the Department of Housing and Urban Development, "Making Home Affordable Program: Servicer Performance Report Through January 2011," March 2, 2011, 3, http://www.treasury.gov/initiatives/financial-stability/results/MHA-Reports/Documents/Jan_2011_MHA_Report_FINAL.PDF (accessed March 30, 2011).

94 U.S. Department of the Treasury and the Department of Housing and Urban Development, "Servicer Performance Report Through January 2011," 3 n. 2.

95 Mortgage Forgiveness Debt Relief Act," Public Law 110–142, 121 Stat. 1803 (2007).

96 U.S. Department of the Treasury, "Obama Administration Announces New Details on Making Home Affordable Program; Parallel Second Lien Program to Help Homeowners Achieve Greater Affordability; Integration of Hope for Homeowners to Help Underwater Borrowers Regain Equity in their Homes," press release, April 28, 2009, http://www.treasury.gov/press-center/press-releases/Pages/tg108.aspx (accessed April 13, 2011).

97 U.S. Department of the Treasury, "Making Home Affordable: Summary of Guidelines," press release, March 4, 2009, http://www.treasury.gov/press-center/press-releases/Documents/guidelines_summary.pdf (accessed April 13, 2011).

98 U.S. Department of the Treasury and Department of Housing and Urban Development, "Housing Program Enhancements Offer Additional Refinements to Existing Administration Programs," press release, March 26, 2010, http://www.makinghomeaffordable.gov/news/latest/Pages/pr_03262010.aspx (accessed March 8, 2011).

99 David Stevens, "HUD Mortgagee Letter 2009-23, FHA Home Affordable Modification Program (FHA-HAMP)," Department of Housing and Urban Development, August 5, 2009, http://www.ncsha.org/resource/hud-mortgagee-letter-2009-23-fha-home-affordable-modification-program-fha-hamp (accessed March 8, 2011).

100 Moe Bedard, "Another Example of the Deplorable Conditions at Countrywide Home Loans," February 11, 2009, Comments, http://loanworkout.org/2009/02/countrywide-idiots (accessed June 17, 2011).

101 "Proposed Settlement Terms," released by state Attorneys General, March 3, 2011, http://cdn.americanbanker.com/media/pdfs/27_page_settlement2.pdf (accessed June 17, 2011).

102 See, e.g., Alex Ulam, "The Next Big Housing Crisis?" *Nation*, March 16, 2011, http://www.thenation.com/article/159281/next-big-housing-crisis (accessed April 13, 2011).

103 See Gradman, "Constitutional Rights," 7.

104 Edmund Conway, "WEF 2009: Global crisis 'has destroyed 40pc of world wealth,'" *Daily Telegraph*, March 21, 2011, http://www.telegraph.co.uk/finance/

financetopics/davos/4374492/WEF-2009-Global-crisis-has-destroyed-40pc-of-world-wealth.html (accessed March 21, 2011).

105 Jon Prior, "Mortgage delinquencies down 5% in August: LPS," *HousingWire*, September 17, 2010, http://www.housingwire.com/2010/09/17/mortgage-delinquencies-down-5-in-august-lps (accessed March 30, 2011).

106 Kerri Panchuk, "Bank of America completes sale of Balboa Insurance," *HousingWire*, June 2, 2011, http://www.housingwire.com/2011/06/02/bank-of-america-completes-sale-of-balboa-insurance (accessed August 1, 2011).

107 Jeff Horwitz, "Ties to Insurers Could Land Mortgage Servicers in More Trouble: Force-placed policies impose costs on both homeowner, investor," *American Banker*, November 10, 2010, http://www.americanbanker.com/issues/175_216/ties-to-insurers-servicers-in-trouble-1028474-1.html (accessed March 23, 2011).

108 Horwitz, "Ties to Insurers Could Land," November 10, 2010 (accessed March 23, 2011).

109 Horwitz, "Ties to Insurers Could Land," November 10, 2010 (accessed March 23, 2011).

110 "BofA Agrees to Sell Balboa Insurance Unit to QBE," ABC News, February 3, 2011, http://abcnews.go.com/Business/wireStory?id=12836474474 (accessed March 30, 2011).

111 Federal Trade Commission, "Countrywide Will Pay $108 Million for Overcharging Struggling Homeowners; Loan Servicer Inflated Fees, Mishandled Loans of Borrowers in Bankruptcy," press release, June 7, 2010, http://www.ftc.gov/opa/2010/06/countrywide.shtm (accessed May 18, 2011).

112 Federal Trade Commission, "Countrywide Will Pay," June 7, 2010 (accessed May 18, 2011).

113 Federal Trade Commission, "Countrywide Will Pay," June 7, 2010 (accessed May 18, 2011).

114 Laurie Goodman, "Robosigners" (accessed April 13, 2011).

115 Barry Ritholz, "Barrons: Putbacks to Banks Could Be $134 Billion," *The Big Picture Blog*, November 22, 2011, http://www.ritholtz.com/blog/2010/11/

barrons-putbacks-to-banks could be 134-billion (accessed June 18, 2011); Chris Gamaitoni, Jason Stewart, and Mike Turner, "Mortgage Repurchases Part II: Private Label RMBS Investors Take Aim - Quantifying the Risks," Compass Point Research & Trading, August 17, 2010, http://api.ning.com/files/fiCVZ-yzNTkoAzUdzhSWYNuHv33*Ur5ZYBh3S08zo*phyT79SFi0TOpPG7klHe3h8 RXKKyphNZqqytZrXQKbMxv4R3F6fN5dI/36431113MortgageFinanceRepur chasesPrivateLabel08172010.pdf (June 18, 2011).

116 Compass Point Research & Trading, "Mortgage Repurchases Part II," August 17, 2010, 6, 9.

117 Laurie Goodman, "Robosigners" (accessed April 13, 2011).

118 Seeking Alpha, "J.P. Morgan Chase & Co. CEO Discusses Q3 2010 Results — Earnings Call Transcript," October 13, 2010, http://seekingalpha.com/ article/229921-jp-morgan-chase-amp-co-ceo-discusses-q3-2010-results-earnings-call-transcript (accessed June 18, 2011).

119 Seeking Alpha, "J.P. Morgan Chase & Co. CEO" (accessed June 18, 2011).

120 Seeking Alpha, "Bank of America Corporation CEO" (accessed June 18, 2011).

121 Trustees have only begun to cooperate with investors and pursue loan files on their behalf. See Sophia Pearson, "J.P. Morgan's EMC Mortgage Sued Over Home Loan Documents," *Bloomberg*, January 18, 2011, http://www.bloomberg. com/news/2011-01-18/jpmorgan-s-emc-mortgage-sued-over-mortgage-loan-documents.html (accessed March 23, 2011).

122 David Grais, "Robosigners" (accessed April 13, 2011).

123 U.S. Department of the Treasury and U.S. Department of Housing and Urban Development, "Reforming America's Housing Finance Market: A Report to Congress," February 2011, http://www.treasury.gov/initiatives/Documents/ Reforming%20America's%20Housing%20Finance%20Market.pdf (accessed April 13, 2011).

124 Board of Governors of the Federal Reserve System, "Mortgage Debt Outstanding," September 24, 2010, http://www.federalreserve.gov/econresdata/releases/mor-toutstand/mortoutstand20100930.htm (accessed April 13, 2011).

125 See, e.g., Lew Sichelman, "Are we facing the end of the 30-year fixed-rate mortgage?" *Los Angeles Times*, May 15, 2011, http://www.latimes.com/business/realestate/la-fi-lew-20110515,0,7530882.story (accessed May 18, 2011).

126 Allen Frankel, Jacob Gyntelberg, Kristian Kjeldsen, and Mattias Persson, "The Danish Mortgage Market: As housing finance evolves, are there reasons to follow the Danish model?" *BIS Quarterly Review* (March 2004): 97, http://www.bis.org/publ/qtrpdf/r_qt0403h.pdf (accessed May 4, 2011).

127 U.S. Department of the Treasury and U.S. Department of Housing and Urban Development, "Reforming America's Housing Finance Market: A Report to Congress," February 2011 (accessed April 13, 2011).

128 Stan Liebowitz, "New Evidence on the Foreclosure Crisis" (accessed February 16, 2011).

129 The Dodd-Frank Wall Street Reform and Consumer Protection Act, Public Law 111–203, 124 Stat. 1376 (2010).

130 Council of Mortgage Lenders, "Arrears and repossessions down, but vulnerability remains" (accessed February 17, 2011).

131 See, e.g., Decision/Order on Motion to Dismiss at 6-7, *Greenwich Financial Services, et al. v. Countrywide Financial Corp., et al.*, No. 650474/08 (N.Y. Sup. Ct. October 7, 2010).

132 Carrie Bay, "GSEs Shooting for Decision on Servicing Fee Structure by Summer," *DSNews*, April 8, 2011, http://www.dsnews.com/articles/gses-shooting-for-decision-on-servicing-compensation-structure-by-summer-2011-04-08 (accessed May 19, 2011).

133 U.S. Department of the Treasury and Internal Revenue Service, "Canceled Debts, Foreclosures, Repossessions and Abandonments," Publication 4681, April 20, 2011, 8, http://www.irs.gov/pub/irs-pdf/p4681.pdf (accessed May 25, 2011).

134 Tax Reform Act of 1986, Public Law 99–514, 100 Stat. 2085 (1986).

135 Tax Policy Center, Urban Institute and Brookings Institution, "Tax Units with Zero or Negative Tax Liability, 2009-2019," July 1, 2009, www.taxpolicycenter.

org/numbers/displayatab.cfm?DocID=2408&topic2ID=150&topic3ID=168&DocTypeID=7 (accessed May 25, 2011).

136 Laurie Goodman, "Robosigners" (accessed April 13, 2011).

137 Jon Prior, "Rating agencies disregarded mortgage quality risks, former Clayton exec says," *HousingWire*, September 27, 2010, http://www.housingwire.com/2010/09/27/expert-testimony-with-boom-time-borrower-fraud-rife-rating-agencies-disregarded-risks (accessed June 18, 2011).

138 Joseph A. Grundfest and Evgenia Petrova, "Buyer Owned and Controlled Rating Agencies: A Summary Introduction," Rock Center for Corporate Governance at Stanford University Working Paper No. 66; Stanford Law and Economics Olin Working Paper No. 391, October 2009, http://www.sec.gov/comments/4-579/4579-10.pdf (accessed May 20, 2011).

139 Zainab Fattah, "Saudi Arabia's Mortgage Law Advances Amid Mideast Unrest," *Bloomberg Businessweek*, April 7, 2011, http://www.bloomberg.com/news/2011-04-06/saudi-arabia-pushes-ahead-with-mortgage-law-amid-public-unrest.html (accessed May 23, 2011).

140 Luisa Zanforlin and Marco Espinosa, "Housing Finance and Mortgage-Backed Securities in Mexico," International Monetary Fund, Working Paper No. 08/105, April 2008, http://papers.ssrn.com/sol3/papers.cfm?abstract_id=1153727 (accessed May 23, 2011).

141 Sebastian Boyd, "Chile Covered Bonds May Replace Mortgage Debt, De Gregorio Says," *Bloomberg Businessweek*, April 8, 2011, http://www.bloomberg.com/news/2011-04-08/chile-covered-bonds-may-replace-mortgage-debt-de-gregorio-says.html (accessed May 23, 2011).

142 Central Intelligence Agency, The World Factbook—Economy: Russia, 2011, https://www.cia.gov/library/publications/the-world-factbook/geos/rs.html (accessed May 23, 2011).

143 Interfax Center of Economic Analysis, "[Ranking] Interfax-100: Russian banks," 2010, http://www.finmarket.ru/z/bw/rankings.asp?rt=20&region=0&per=43&orgname=&page=1&s=5&d=0&p=1 (accessed May 26, 2011) [translated using http://babelfish.yahoo.com].

144 Interfax Center of Economic Analysis, "[Ranking] Interfax-100: Russian banks," 2010 (accessed May 26, 2011).

145 Joshua D. Rauh, "Are State Public Pensions Sustainable? Why the Federal Government Should Worry About State Pension Liabilities," Kellogg School of Management and National Bureau of Economic Research, 26, May 15, 2010, http://papers.ssrn.com/sol3/papers.cfm?abstract_id=1596679 (accessed August 4, 2011).

146 See, e.g., Jon Prior, "Sen. Shumer to introduce covered bond legislation," HousingWire, March 15, 2011, http://www.housingwire.com/2011/03/15/sen-schumer-to-introduce-covered-bond-legislation (accessed June 14, 2011).

147 Nora Colomer, "PIMCO Plans New REIT," *Asset Securitization Report*, April 6, 2011, http://www.structuredfinancenews.com/news/-218206-1.html (accessed August 10, 2011); Al Yoon, "BlackRock, Two Harbors Eye Alternative To AAA Mortgage Bonds," *Wall Street Journal*, July 14, 2011 http://online.wsj.com/article/BT-CO-20110714-707449.html (accessed August 10, 2011).